Does Your Marketing Sell?

Does Your Marketing Sell?

The secret of effective marketing communications

Ian Moore

NICHOLAS BREALEY
PUBLISHING

LONDON   BOSTON

I fy rhieni

First published by
Nicholas Brealey Publishing in 2005

3–5 Spafield Street	100 City Hall Plaza, Suite 501
Clerkenwell, London	Boston
EC1R 4QB, UK	MA 02108, USA
Tel: +44 (0)20 7239 0360	Tel: (888) BREALEY
Fax: +44 (0)20 7239 0370	*Fax: (617) 523 3708*

http://www.nbrealey-books.com
http://www.newaida.com

© Ian Moore 2005
The right of Ian Moore to be identified as the author of this work has
been asserted in accordance with the Copyright, Designs and Patents Act
1988.

ISBN 1-85788-350-0

British Library Cataloguing in Publication Data
A catalogue record for this book is available from the
British Library.

Printed in Finland by WS Bookwell.

CONTENTS

Introduction   1

Step 1 Nᴀᴠɪɢᴀᴛɪᴏɴ – understanding   9

Step 2 Eᴀsᴇ – convenience   36

Step 3 Wᴏʀᴅɪɴɢ – conversation   73

Step 4 Aᴛᴛᴇɴᴛɪᴏɴ – serendipity   113

Step 5 Iɴᴛᴇʀᴇsᴛ – persuadability   157

Step 6 Dᴇsɪʀᴇ – knowledge   189

Step 7 Aᴄᴛɪᴏɴ – permission   225

          Summary   252
          Appendix   253
          Notes   261
          Index   271
          Acknowledgments   279

INTRODUCTION

Putting the salesmanship back into marketing

Whether you run a small business or a big corporation (or work somewhere in between), you probably get involved with marketing communications. This could mean ads, brochures, display cards, leaflets, mailings, on-pack offers, posters, sales presenters, websites... or simply "marketing" for short.

And like most people, you probably wonder if your marketing sells. I expect you're not 100 percent sure, even if you employ a specialist advertising, design, or promotional agency to help you. In fact, I bet you're not even 50 percent sure.

Don't worry, you're in good company. Lord Leverhulme, founder of Lever Bros, famously said:

> **"Half the money I spend on advertising is wasted, and the trouble is I don't know which half."**[1]

In fact it can be more serious than that. John Caples, one of the pioneers of "scientific advertising" in the US, cited a campaign in which one headline created *19½ times* more response than an otherwise identical ad.[2]

The missing ingredient

So why does one piece of marketing succeed where another fails? What is it that causes almost 20 times as many people to respond to one message than to another? Just how *do* you make your marketing sell?

In my experience, there's a paradox. What well-intentioned marketers *think* they should do to make their marketing sell often doesn't work. And that's because they get salesmanship confused with showmanship.

Salesmanship is the missing ingredient in making your marketing sell.

What I mean by salesmanship — and you may be relieved to hear this — are the quiet skills of empathy and perception. These are skills that are so often abandoned in modern marketing communications. This book is all about how to put them back.

But what do I know?

I was immediately struck by the lack of salesmanship in marketing communications when I started my first classical marketing job. (I became a product manager launching a new brand of bathroom tissue.) Having spent the previous six years working in sales and sales training, I suppose I was well placed to note the contrast. I've since been reassured to discover that many of history's most feted and successful advertising copywriters, including greats such as Claude Hopkins and David Ogilvy, started out life treading the streets as lowly salesmen. Perhaps this is no coincidence?

For my own rather more modest part, I was astonished by the general lack of urgency, or even interest, shown by the professional marketing community toward selling. By this I mean that nobody seemed able to tell me, then a relative novice in the art of ad making, how the ads actually worked. Even people in my advertising agency — one of the grandest in London at the time — were puzzled that I should pose the question.

I was determined not to accept this state of affairs. But despite working for some of the world's biggest companies and best-known brands, and studying in my spare time for an MBA specializing in marketing communications, I never found an easy helping hand. At work there was lots of "what we did" (but not "why we did it") and at college there was lots of theory (but not how to apply it). It seemed that practitioners were too busy and academics too detached. The result: Marketing does not sell like it could.

So my quest has been for a simple understanding. For 25 years now I've collected marketing tips, scoured textbooks, attended courses and seminars, and picked the brains of anyone who appeared to understand what makes for good communication. I gained invaluable practical experience working in marketing for firms such as Kimberly-Clark and Cadbury Schweppes, where I did my share of television advertising, and for Lloyds bank (now Lloyds TSB), where I ran a direct marketing operation. I also spent a couple of years as a director of the sales promotion agency Clarke-

Hooper, working on a wide range of clients' businesses, ranging from Bell's whisky to Pyrex dishes. (I've now worked on over 100 major brands.[3])

By 1990 I felt ready to take the plunge and formed my own marketing agency.[4] My learning curve steepened dramatically. But right from the start I was able to put into practice a mixture of knowledge and intuition, and we began to achieve exceptional results for our clients. We regularly doubled and trebled the accepted "industry norm" response rates — often it was 10 or more times.[5] And it didn't seem to matter whether it was an ad, a mailing, or a promotional offer. For instance:

☆ An ad for Royal & SunAlliance[6] achieved a response of 27.9 percent.

☆ An on-pack offer for Newcastle Brown Ale[7] achieved a response of 43.2 percent.

☆ And a direct marketing program for Reebok[8] achieved a response of 91 percent.

Campaign after campaign, results exceeded expectations. Our case studies began to be featured in respected marketing textbooks and journals.[9] And we won over 50 effectiveness-based awards for our work.[10]

In our first year I came up with the idea of a Hay Fever Survival Kit for Kleenex tissues.[11] This won the Institute of Sales Promotion Grand Prix[12] for the best campaign of 1991, beating British Airways into second place (there were over 800 other entries), and was also voted the best European consumer activity.[13] It has been credited with a major contribution to the growth of the brand[14] and it is still alive and kicking — possibly the longest-running and most effective campaign of its kind.[15]

Evidently we were doing something right. And perhaps something different. I was flattered by the attention we received, but as far as I was concerned, there was no secret.

Sure, we had some good creative ideas, but neither we nor our clients had a monopoly in that department. If we excelled anywhere, it was in our obsession with selling. By this I mean not selling *to* our clients, but *for* our clients.

I've always made it a golden rule never to propose anything — ranging from a rough idea for a single ad to a complex multifaceted campaign — unless we could justify why we believed it would sell. If we couldn't explain how it would engage the customer to achieve the desired outcome, it didn't get presented. When you apply this discipline to your proposals, you find — magically — that the words of explanation come out in the simple language of salesmanship.

Meet AIDA

But what do the experts say about making your marketing sell? The single most widely taught method is of course AIDA.[16] This stands for **Attention–Interest–Desire–Action**.

We in marketing are encouraged to design our ads, mailings, and sales pitches in a way that mirrors consumer behavior. You start by getting attention. Then you create interest. Next you build desire. And finally you stimulate action.

I first met AIDA in the late 1970s when I was being trained as a salesman. Subsequently, as a sales trainer, I used it (rather clumsily) as a teaching aid. After that, I noticed it popping up at conferences and seminars, in articles and presentations, and prolifically in the marketing courses I studied at various institutions. During a recent visit to bookshop Waterstones, I managed to find mentions of AIDA in books on sales and marketing at a rate of about one a minute.

Academic marketing texts attribute the concept of AIDA to US advertising giant E K Strong.[17] Marketing folklore, however, has it that AIDA was invented in the US by traveling salesmen at the beginning of the twentieth century. (In fact neither of these is correct; for the true story read the Appendix at the end of this book.) Regardless, AIDA is certainly not a modern innovation and was followed by a procession of supposedly improved models throughout the twentieth century.

Today, despite some minor dissent, there's little doubt that AIDA remains the definitive model. (Even those who seem to eschew AIDA, or claim to subscribe to another philosophy entirely, find themselves measuring impact or awareness, which are synonymous with the AIDA approach.)

As my former marketing professor — one of the world's leading academic marketers — puts it:

> "It is necessary to recognise that AIDA and its kin will remain the implicit conceptual underpinnings of present-day practice until marketing academics are able to produce a better model which practitioners can understand and are willing to use."[18]

I couldn't agree more... but does it work? In my experience — and here's the strange thing — not really. Leastways, it's not how you smash the industry norm.

The trouble with AIDA

While this book is about *all* types of marketing communications, about a fifth of the case studies concern examples of direct marketing. (That happens to be roughly in line with its share of overall marketing expenditure.) Direct marketing is a growing discipline and a valuable tool for marketers wishing to understand their work: in less than a week you usually know if your mailing has been a success. Indeed, for an office-based marketer it's a heaven-sent opportunity, because it can teach you to think like a salesman.

Direct marketing is renowned for its formulas — things you should always do to maximize response, like putting a PS at the end of the letter. In the mid-1980s I went on a course for copywriters.[19] It was run by two of the leading direct marketing practitioners of the time. I still have the handouts and notes, and here's an extract:

> "The letter is the most important part of your mailing. This is where you should spend most of your creative time. You'll spend it profitably by using the magic formula AIDA."

A decade later I sat down to write a direct marketing module for our own graduate training program. Its purpose was to teach our trainees how to create an effective basic mailing, or how to evaluate one already produced. By then, I'd worked on hundreds of mailings and felt pretty confident that I had some useful ideas of my own to impart, even though I'd never committed them to paper. Nevertheless, I turned first to AIDA to provide a structure.

OK, I thought, let's start with A for "attention." I got my layout pad and pens ready, and after a few minutes of scribbling and sketching... well, despite my best intentions, "attention" was not putting in an appearance. And no matter how hard I tried, I could not get AIDA to fit with the point at which I wanted to begin. AIDA did not match practical selling reality.

When customer meets marketing

As I struggled to find the right words to start the training module, I had of course revisited my own golden rule: Explain why it will work, or else. *Why?* Why will it influence my customer to respond or to buy? Unless I could answer why, my training sessions would be of little value.

Look at it the other way for a moment and ask: Why do so many marketing communications fail? The most frequent answer in my experience is quite simply because the recipient — your customer — can't work out what's going on. For some reason, marketers forget to explain who they are, and what they are asking for, in an intelligible manner.

This basic, common courtesy has little to do with attention, or interest, or desire, or action. It's a simple acknowledgment that a customer's mind won't shift out of first gear until it knows where it's going and how to get there. All too often, when customer meets marketing, the marketer's gone missing.

I believe that every successful marketing communication needs a kind of "guardian salesman." (I don't mean somebody hawking the eponymous newspaper, but someone more like the invisible characters in *City of Angels*.) Of course, if you're the marketer, it's your job to act the angel.

This involves some simple mental projection. Picture the moment when your customer meets your marketing. Then watch and listen as the imaginary interaction takes place.

The first thing you should notice is that AIDA isn't what happens. Indeed, when I finally completed the first draft of my training module, I realized I had come up with the sequence S–W–E–A–R,[20] so for a while we had a subject called SWEARing on the graduate training schedule! This caused some amusement in the agency, but I couldn't see it catching on. So I revisited AIDA.

NEW AIDA™

AIDA shares with its fellow models of buying behavior a common goal: to represent the process when a customer receives a marketing message and reacts to it. AIDA is simple to grasp and worthy in its intentions. And for many people it's a familiar and user-friendly framework.

The best thing about applying AIDA to your marketing is that it makes you think about selling. The worst thing is that it isn't how to sell. My approach, therefore, is a compromise, which I call NEW AIDA — you could say it's the guardian salesman's version. It's based on the century-old formula, but subtly adjusted in a way that releases its extraordinary selling potential. It puts the salesmanship back into marketing.

Size doesn't matter

As I've indicated, much of my experience has been with major multi- . nationals, both as an employee and as a provider of creative services. My own marketing communications firm was named The Blue-Chip Marketing Consultancy to indicate the type of blue-chip client it was created to serve. In consequence, much of our work was played out on a national and indeed international stage, for some of the world's best-known brands and companies. Literally millions of consumers responded to our campaigns, across some 15 countries.[21]

However, my agency was never large (we grew to three offices and about fifty staff), nor are its present-day incarnations. This meant that we were able to try out theories and ideas on a small scale, as part of our own marketing communications program. For instance, for about a decade we sent out a bi-monthly mailing to our client and contacts database (between 250 and 1,000 letters or packages at a time), testing different types of propositions, offers, writing styles, and response mechanisms. The enduring lesson for me was that things that worked on a modest scale subsequently worked on a grand scale — it's no surprise really, but something that helps you keep your feet on the ground.

So if you're reading this book from the perspective of a smaller organization — perhaps even your own one-person business — you can be reassured on two fronts. First, the principles have what you might call blue-chip credentials (it's the way big blue-chip firms do their marketing). Second, they should work for you, however small your operation.

For instance, not long ago my uncle Bill asked me to look at a mailing on behalf of one of his friends who was trying to start up an online racing tips service.[22] It was just a cottage enterprise, although the chap in question was a highly successful professional tipster. His problem was recruiting punters to subscribe in the first instance. The initial mailing of 750 had generated only a handful of replies (under 1 percent), even though the list was up to date and comprised serious gamblers. I thought that the copy was well written and contained a strong no-obligation offer, but it was immediately apparent to me why it wasn't working.

With just a few tweaks, the second mailing produced a 7.5 percent response — more than enough to take the business past its breakeven target. How come? Basically I changed what the customer saw *first* and thought about *first*, without really changing any of the content. This is the starting point for NEW AIDA: N for *Navigation*.

STEP 1 — NAVIGATION

Help your customer see what to do or think about

W hen I was younger and shyer than I am now, I went on a trip to New York. While I was there, I intended to buy a pair of Leica binoculars, as I'd heard they were much cheaper than in the UK. I walked into an optical equipment store on Fifth Avenue, but the staff were surly and seemed too busy to speak to me. This was a surprise, as I'd heard all about excellent American service. After five minutes hanging around being ignored, I left. In the next shop, the same thing happened. And the next. I gave up and never did get my Leicas.

A few years later I recounted the tale to a colleague, a seasoned New York shopper. He just laughed at me and said, no wonder — you need to grab a shop assistant, put your face in theirs and say forcefully: "Hey buddy, I wanna buy a pair of Leicas — what's the deal?" I hadn't known what to do, so I'd gone away.

The tear-off reply card

In 1989, while I worked for the agency Clarke-Hooper, I developed a mailing for a division of the utility company that is now known as ScottishPower.[1] My idea was to make this look like a Christmas card and it was intended to get small, independent retailers to contact the organization with a view to buying heating equipment for their shops. Not an easy task (confessed our client).

I figured out how I wanted the message to fit together and "scamped" a draft for my designer, Colin, so he could make me a mock-up to show to the client. Colin wasn't at his desk that day, and I was due to be away the next, so I had to leave my scrawls for him to interpret as best he could. But to make sure he understood that I wanted a tear-off reply card attached to the side of the main Christmas card, I wrote "tear-off reply card" with a red marker and circled it with an arrow. (The finished version is shown in Figure 1.)

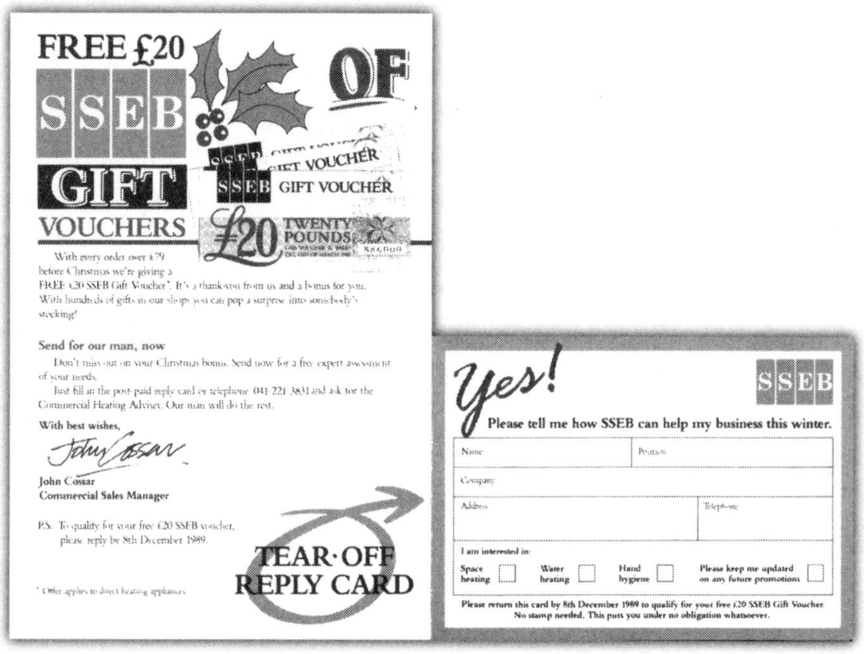

Figure 1   *A section of the ScottishPower mailing showing the prominent "tear-off reply card" message — a quick and clear indication to your customer of what is expected of them. Reproduced by kind permission of ScottishPower plc.*

As you can see, when I returned I found that Colin had taken me rather literally. There on the mock-up were emblazoned the words "tear-off reply card" surrounded by a big red arrow! It wasn't particularly pretty... but actually I liked it.

So did the client. And so did the recipients. Against a breakeven sales target we achieved a 300 percent response — pleasing for us, as we were being paid in part by results.

And the lesson? I wasn't sure at the time, but I had a feeling about it and kept a copy of the mailing safe in my archive. Some years later, when it came to writing the Blue-Chip training module, it was this mailing that helped me to realize just what was wrong with the old AIDA.

The main reason the ScottishPower Christmas card mailing worked so well was because you could see *instantly* what to do.

What happens when you know what to do? Answer: You relax. What happens when you *can't* work out what to do? Answer: You panic (or at least become frustrated and impatient). If you can, you flee (like I did in New York). If it's a mailing, you probably bin it. If it's an ad, you turn the page or switch the channel.

So while AIDA might be the process your customer theoretically has to go through in order to respond to your communication, it isn't how their mind works in practice. As a marketer, you must first show them what to do — help them to *navigate*. If your customer is remotely interested in your product, they'll want to know *first* what's expected of them.

Your customer is busy

The single most important reason you should think navigation is because your customer has *already* got enough to do. You're unlikely to find them loitering by their front door waiting for so-called junk mail to drop through the letterbox. Nor doubling their concentration when the commercials are screened during their favorite television program. Nor at their desk meticulously perusing the ads in trade journals (unless they're looking for a new job, perhaps).

There's one monthly magazine I subscribe to that regularly contains 60 full-page ads for financial products.[2] I reckon the average ad takes two minutes to read. Yet I rarely seem to have a couple of minutes spare to read the editorial, let alone the couple of hours it would require to digest all the ads.

Just how long is the typical customer going to hang around trying to work out what's going on in an ad? Answer: not long. If you're lucky, the time it takes them to turn the page. You'd think that this point would be obvious, but — as you can see in Figure 2 — while some advertisers make this their first priority, others barely give it a second thought.

Invariably, when your customer meets your marketing, they're busy and distracted. So it's vital to show them what you expect of them. Until they know that, they can't relax and concentrate on the benefits of your product, service, or offer. The bare minimum for this is at least to announce your subject, as Scottish Widows sensibly does in the example I have shown.

Figure 2 *Two of over 60 ads placed in a single edition of a consumer money magazine. (The ad with the chameleon is a mock-up based on a real example.) Compare their speed of navigation against the time it takes a busy customer to turn the page. Pensions ad reproduced by kind permission of Scottish Widows.*

In Blue-Chip we used what we called the "two-second test" to make sure we dealt with this issue. (Will the customer understand within two seconds?) In fact "one-mississippi, two-mississippi" is probably a little generous, going by the rate I've watched many people browse magazines (and supermarket shelves), but it's a good stock principle on which to judge effective navigation.

Good manners

One of the first things a salesman is taught to do when he goes in to make a presentation to a panel of customers is to ask the audience how long they've got. Then he tells them what he's going to tell them. (He doesn't give away his exciting "reveal," but he orientates them within a framework so that they know what to think about and what is expected of them.) It's exactly the same principle in printed marketing communication.

> **The pivotal question your customer asks is not "What's in it for me?" but actually "What's this about?" They also want to know "How much time and effort do I have to invest here? And where am I going?"**

NEW AIDA thinking is a simple piece of good salesmanship. By forcing yourself to think this way you will get a better result than if you *start* by asking "How will I get their attention?" or "What will I say to make them want my product?" (These are perfectly valid questions, but not the ones you should ask yourself *first* as you sit down to design your ad or mailing.)

For direct marketing in particular, this point cannot be overstated. It's make or break. If your customer has to spend more than a few seconds trying to work out what to do and what they're supposed to be sending off for, your response rate will suffer badly.

In Figure 3 overleaf is an example from the consumer magazine *Which?*. With no prevarication, the navigation task is tackled head on. Right away, your customer can see and understand what is expected of them. They know that this is *Which?* talking, what the magazine wants from them (to subscribe), what it's all about (cars), and what they'll get in return (the chance to win a valuable prize).

An important characteristic of many successful mailings is that this approach is then carried across all of the separate components. So whichever piece the recipient chooses to study first — the letter, the brochure, the order form, even the reply envelope — there is a potted navigation message ready and waiting.

Figure 3　*A recruitment flyer. It comes straight to the point in telling customers what to do and what to think about. Reproduced by kind permission of* Which?.

Navigation before attention

Twelve years after accidentally using the prominent "tear-off reply card" message for ScottishPower, I intentionally employed the same technique in a mailing for Warburtons (Figure 4), a brand that has made a dramatic impact on the UK bread market.[3] This mailing was aimed at independent grocers, an audience notoriously difficult to get a good response from. If you've ever done one-to-one sales calls to these guys, you'll know what I mean — they're either serving customers or stacking shelves (and when they're not in their shops they're down at the cash and carry).

Yet we got a 28 percent response (almost four times the target figure of 7.5 percent). Again, I put this down to the simple fact that busy store managers could see at a glance what was required of them.

Playing devil's advocate, you could say: "But surely you had to get their attention first, otherwise they would never have opened the mailing?"

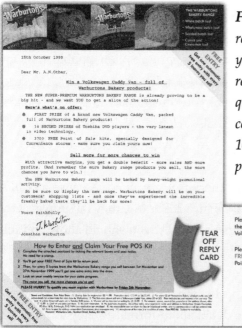

Figure 4 The prominent "tear-off reply card" message reemerges 12 years later. A mailing to Warburtons' retail customers that, at 28 percent, quadrupled its response target and coincided with a sales increase of over 10 percent. © Reproduced by kind permission of Warburtons Ltd.

True — technically we did command their attention (unless they opened the mailing while distracted or daydreaming). But think about this: If you can target with 100 percent certainty customers who buy a lot of your product already (and it's one of the most important items they sell to *their* customers), how hard is it going to be to get their attention?

Not difficult, I'd say. Warburtons' "vanmen" call on their customers every day of the week. Their address list is enviably up to date. Reaching the right hands is not the issue.

What *is* the issue (and I repeat) is this: When you're designing your communication, just for a short while suspend all thought of attention. Start with what you want your customer to do. Confirmed time and again by results is my experience that marketing sells better if you make it your priority to orientate your customer. First think navigation.

Navigation in advertising

It's tempting to think of "advertising" as a big-budget television campaign. In fact, television is the province of only a tiny minority of advertisers. The vast majority of ads are made for the print medium. It has been estimated that at least 1,000 press ads are produced for every television commercial filmed.[4] And media expenditure for press is more than double that for television.[5]

So whatever your job or the scale of your business, you probably place print ads of some sort — in trade journals, *Yellow Pages*, or perhaps in your local newspaper. And navigation can play a key role in effective advertising.

Of course, many ads (print or otherwise) are *direct-response* ads like those for financial services shown in Figure 2. For me, they fall into exactly the same category as direct mail. Unequivocally, you should show and tell the reader what to do. Indeed, I'd argue that it is *even more* critical for a direct-response advertisement: Compared to a mailing there's far less scope to use the format — the physical components — to help you communicate what to do. (I'll talk in more detail about format in Step 2, Ease.)

Conventional advertising

It's relatively easy to see the importance of navigation in relation to direct marketing. Direct marketing very obviously traverses the whole of old AIDA. By its very definition, it expects the customer to do something.

In ordinary advertising, however, the role of navigation might at first seem more obscure. If your customer doesn't actually have to do anything other than register your message, where's the need for navigation? Surely the job of these ads is merely to get attention, create interest, and perhaps build desire. When it's time to shop in your category, your customer already wants your brand. Simple.

Or not. How often have you discussed "great" ads with friends and yet been *unable* to recall what they were for? During 2003 a television campaign for a car manufacturer attracted much publicity. The ad featured components from the car gently knocking together in a domino effect, an idea reportedly inspired by the "Mousetrap" game. The brand of car, and the point of the ad, were revealed at the end of an absorbing two minutes' watching.

But today can you remember the brand? Can you remember what the ad wanted you to know about the car? (Like why you should buy one?)

"Ah, but it doesn't work like that... it's subliminal... subconscious... much more subtle" (say the experts).

The king is in the altogether (I say).

Where it isn't appropriate to tell your customer what to do, begin instead by telling them what to *think about*. It really amounts to the same thing.

Even if an ad is just one small part of the longest-term, slowest-burning campaign ever conceived, written, and produced, surely there is a point in conditioning your customer's mind to the message that's coming their way? Yet in ads like the one I have described, it seems to me that navigation never even got started. And I reckon that one of the world's most successful communication organizations would agree with me.

Problem hair?

Some members of the creative fraternity deride what might be called the rational Procter & Gamble approach to advertising. But at least P&G begins its ads by telling you what to think about. And why leave it to chance?

I don't imagine P&G would ever expect you to sit through two minutes' showmanship to find out why you're paying attention. Why would you listen to someone trying to sell you something you might not want, when you could be making a cup of tea or having a much-needed comfort break? Most P&G ads inform you of your problem and the solution the company offers within 8 seconds.[6]

I repeat: Why leave it to chance? In Step 5 I'll talk about the importance of selling to customers who are *already interested* in buying from us. Isn't it common sense to give them a clue about whom and what we represent? Showmanship is but a poor shadow of salesmanship.

Think tabloid

Do people drive you mad when they won't come to the point? They have some news but they won't tell you upfront. While they hold stage as story-teller, you're screaming inside your head" "Just tell me where we're going!" (If they were an ad, you would have turned the page long ago.)

As someone who has trained myself to be impatient with communications, I love tabloid newspapers. They tell you what to think.

By this I don't mean what *opinion* to have (though they may do that too), but that they tell you what you're going to get. Right upfront. Take a look at Figure 5. There's no procrastination, no "once upon a time" pantomime.

Figure 5 *The tabloid approach. A typical front page telling customers in less than a second what they are being asked to think about. Stars (who) flee (what they did) palace (where) fire (what happened). Reproduced by kind permission of News International.*

With the tabloids it's straight to the punchline every time. If *The Sun* had been around the day the Cinderella story broke, it would have been: "SHOE FITS: CINDERS QUEEN." Boom.

Shoe fits: Cinders Queen. It's all you need to know. And it's not the language that matters here (though short words do work better[7]), it's the reverse storytelling technique that is so effective. You get the last line of the romance in the headline. That's the key information you need so you can decide in seconds whether this article is something you want to devote precious minutes to.

I remember having a conversation about headlines with an editor in the Mirror Group. He said:

"When it comes to off-the-shelf sales, I effectively have to launch a new product every single day. If the customer can't see at a glance what he's getting, he'll pick up my competitor."

The corollary for advertisers? Identify yourself to your customer. Tell them what you want them to think about. They're almost certainly interested — so help them with the navigation.

Crazytivity

Edward de Bono invented the word "crazytivity" to describe the act of being different just for the sake of being different (and believing that it equals "creativity").

It's not difficult to find ads like this. They make me think of a salesman in fancy dress, who says to his customer: "OK, guess what I'm trying to sell you today?" Give me a break.

In Figure 6 overleaf is an ad (disguised) that I found in a recent edition of *Stuff* magazine. Try to guess what it's for. I've made this more difficult by removing all references to the product.

"Impossible!" you cry. I agree. Upfront, there are few clues to be found. (But it was the same with the real ad.)

At a glance, the main image is actually not that inherently interesting or impactful, and is certainly not informative. The headline is set in a typeface that is rather difficult to read. Added to that, it's written as a riddle that is quite hard to understand, never mind begin to solve.

Even taken together, the headline and the image don't exactly explain one another. You'd be excused for thinking that it's something to do with computer games. At a glance, the body copy is too small to read (so no quick clues available there) and is made more awkward by being set in reverse (white on black), which the eye finds uncomfortable.[8]

If choices have no limits,

your imagination can know no bounds.

Explore to infinity and beyond.

Another example of an ad (now disguised) which pays less-than-lip-service to navigation. The main image is fairly mundane and gives no indication of the subject matter. The headline is hard to read, and does not make a great deal of sense. Even taken together, the headline and the image don't reveal what's going on.

Computer games, perhaps? The 8-point body copy is too small to read comfortably, and is made more awkward by being set in reverse. Tucked away in the corner was a tiny and well-camouflaged image of the product, and the brand name - also set in 8-point type. Not an ad for the busy reader.

BRAND X

Figure 6   *The risk of not telling the customer what to think about. This is a disguised ad, with the same characteristics as its real counterpart. At a glance this ad provides almost no navigation clues.*

The only direct reference to the subject of the original ad — *what the advertiser wants you to think about* — is a well-camouflaged image, a dark object on a black background about 3cm x 3cm in real size, placed down in a corner where the eye won't naturally go at a glance. Even the brand name — one of the best in the business and sure to have given the reader a helping hand — took some finding.

I have used the expression "at a glance" several times. This is to emphasize what for me is the key navigation issue. The averagely busy reader of *Stuff* magazine has to deal with some 50 ads and 100-odd pages packed with endless new gadgets. If you're placing an ad, "at a glance" is about the most you should plan for.

Your customer is whizzing past. Sure, they're actively searching for information in your product category (else *I* wouldn't be calling them your customer and *you'd* be wasting your time trying to speak with them) — but if they can't tell at a glance that this *is* your product category, why would they stop to read your ad?

Perhaps viewed in the splendid isolation and time-rich environment of the boardroom, the ad was considered to be imaginative, intriguing, and distinctive. That's fine. But if the boardroom isn't the same as when customer meets marketing, it's a dangerous place to take your artwork.

In a simple browsing test that I use to check out points like this, the real version of this ad got a score of under 20 percent versus an ad for a similar product placed nearby in the same magazine.[9] I won't pretend that this method is scientific or comprehensive, but when five people understand your competitor's ad for every one that notices and understands your own, I think alarm bells should begin to ring.

The lesson? If you decide on an obtuse approach to your customer, you need to be extremely confident that your graphics and headline will stop them in their tracks — and engage their minds.

If they don't know what you want them to do (in this case, what to think about), are they really going to expend valuable time trying to find out? More likely they'll pass you by.

Straight talk

Now compare the ad shown in Figure 7 with that discussed above. This was also placed in *Stuff* magazine.

Does it tell you — at a glance — what to think about? Of course. Does it tell you — at a glance — whom it represents? Certainly. (Look at the size of the logo.)

In fact, from the simple feature/benefit headline to the exploded-diagram technique linking the visual and the copy, in my book this ad does a number of things well — and simply. It starts with navigation in mind and sticks to its course.

It's hardly a new or "creative" idea, but does that really have any relevance as an argument? (Think *crazytivity*.) Francis Ogilvy described gratuitous creativity as "skidding about on the slippery surface of irrelevant brilliance."[10] Edward de Bono, meanwhile, insists that any definition of the creative process should include the requirement that it must end with a value.[11]

I come back to the words showmanship and salesmanship. While the former attracts blank looks, the latter attracts blank checkbooks.

Websites

Navigation is a word often used in relation to websites. In such a context it concerns finding your way around, but there's a much broader issue at stake.

Recently I read a statistic in a respected business journal suggesting that the typical surfer takes about seven seconds to make up their mind whether your website is for them.[12] It may not sound much, but for the marketer seven seconds is a rare luxury.

Your customer can read about 50 words in seven seconds. And, given that a website is a form of marketing communication that they've *chosen* to look at, that's 50 words that by rights should be swallowed and digested. The customer is in ad-seeking mode.

I have worked on the development of a variety of websites, ranging from the very basic small-firm site to one of the first offering downloadable

Figure 7 In contrast to the ad shown in Figure 6, this one promptly tells the reader what to think about. In my test five times as many people noticed it and could remember what it was for. Reproduced by kind permission of Nikon UK.

music in MP3 format (which we invented for the beer brand Miller Genuine Draft as a platform for its music promotions). In my experience — and from my personal observations as a critical website inspector — website visitors might be there on purpose, but they still need to be told what to do and think about.

> **Many people connected with websites are obsessed with how good they look (I mean the websites, although it's sometimes both).** *This should not be your first priority.* **Instead, be obsessed with those seven seconds: tell your customer what you offer them and how to access it.**

It's easy to fall into the trap of thinking that the surfers who visit your site will know what it's about. After all, they're clued up. They're internet literate. (Aren't they?)

Maybe. But who says there's a connection between being clued up and understanding a marketing message?

I'll give you a conventional example that you can try out. Pick a country about which you feel quite clued up, but whose language you don't speak. Now go to the travel section of a bookshop and locate the corresponding Michelin Red Guide. (Try Spain, for instance, *La Guia Roja*.) Find yourself a hotel that accepts pets in the center of Barcelona for under 100 euros a night. Not so easy (since, comprehensive though the guide is, it's in Spanish).

I think it's no coincidence that the business end of the Amazon.co.uk homepage sports just 56 words.

Navigation equals *understanding*

Your customer is busy and distracted. If you confront them with the advertising equivalent of a lateral thinking quiz or a foreign-language paper, you know what to expect. Their reaction will range somewhere on the scale between confusion and rejection.

If, on the other hand, you begin by helping your customer understand what you want them to do — what you want them to think about — you should be pleasantly surprised by their response. It's common sense, basic salesmanship — though not always the way things are taught.

Indeed, I have a certain well-regarded marketing handbook that espouses AIDA in the usual enthusiastic terms. Then it lists a series of eight stages you should go through to ensure you create an effective communication. Like to guess what stage 8 says? Correct: "Finally, what is the customer supposed to do?" Aargh!

The next few sections outline precautions to help you make navigation a first thought, rather than an afterthought.

Steps you can take

Write down your desired customer reaction

Desired customer reaction. I'll call it DCR for short. Whether you're beginning with a blank page to design something yourself, or looking at an ad, brochure, or mailing prepared by your agency, the most useful thing you can do is write about your DCR.

Fact: The simpler your DCR, the more likely it is that you can create an effective piece of communication. But don't worry if your draft DCR starts out as a whole page of scribbles or a long list of bullet points. You can soon put them into a common-sense priority order.

Consider the press insert (also used as a door-drop) shown in Figure 8 overleaf. For me, this is an outstanding piece of marketing, not least because it carries such an elegant co-promotion between Cancer Research UK and a coalition of solicitors.

The idea is that you can — if you're aged over 55 — have your will made (or updated) *at no cost* by a local solicitor. Cancer Research UK gains because you might leave it a legacy. Participating solicitors gain by acquiring you as a customer who might buy other services in future.

Figure 8 A press insert produced by Cancer Research UK, co-promoting with a coalition of solicitors. This illustration shows the outside cover as the recipient would first see it. Reproduced by kind permission of Cancer Research UK.

OK, what would you include in your DCR? Having had the benefit of examining the insert, here's my list of suggestions (in no particular order):

1 I need to make a will.
2 I need to update my will.

3 I've heard of Cancer Research UK and trust it.

4 Cancer Research UK is a very good cause.

5 I'd like to leave a legacy to Cancer Research UK.

6 This seems like an excellent offer.

7 There isn't any catch.

8 This looks like it's for someone like me.

9 The form seems easy to complete.

10 The solicitor will handle any complex paperwork.

11 I need to phone a local solicitor.

12 My solicitor is already on the list.

13 Any solicitor on the list can do this for me.

14 I'd better do something before the offer closes.

That's 14 points, and you can probably think up a few more. As an aside, it's quite common for agencies to be given what we call "kitchen sink" briefs like this. My advice: Don't be tempted to try to get too much for your money. (And don't be offended if your agency comes back to ask what's the main point — be happy they've noticed.)

Find the navigation point

So if leading with all 14 points is out of the question, where do you start? My answer is that this is when you have to steel yourself and *not think* about gaining attention. Likewise, you must avoid the temptation to focus — for the time being — on the offer.

Instead, engage NEW AIDA thinking. Good salesmanship recognizes that the communication is most likely to fail over a navigation issue. So to set off on the right track to enable this insert to generate an above-average response, I'd be looking for a navigation point.

At such a juncture I always find it salutary to picture a friend of mine who moved to Britain from Texas a while ago. His name's Hal. I think Americans are generally used to a higher standard of customer navigation than us Brits. In an unfamiliar sales environment (it can be as simple as a café where it's not clear whether you go to the counter or take a seat and wait to be served) Hal's got a great turn of phrase: "Okay, but... waddawa do here?"

When marketing provides no answer, he walks. I can just hear him muttering the same thing at home, moments before he bins his mail, or at his desk, as he wrestles with and then exits yet another uncooperative website — when all he wanted was the navigation point.

Waddawa do here? In order for the Cancer Research UK insert to sell, what the customer needs to do is phone a local solicitor. They must cross a bridge from thought to action. It's the communication crux.

And there it is, number 11 in my list: "I need to phone a local solicitor." This should be the starting point for thinking about the design of the message.

Let navigation lead design

So how does the Cancer Research UK insert shape up?

Take a look at Figure 9. This is what the customer sees on opening the first fold of the insert. Not a repeat of the offer. Not a claim about how much they will save. Not a list of the supporting benefits.

Instead, what the customer sees first is what to do. Bingo! An entire double-page spread is given over to listing all the local participating law firms, with a simple call to action: Choose a solicitor, phone for an appointment.

I wouldn't expect a customer to read this spread in any great detail. But at a glance they'll get the idea, knowing that they can come back to it later. (I think, if anything, they are most likely to check if their present solicitor is on the list.)

Uncertainty minimized, the way is clear. The customer can relax and read more about the offer. The next fold opens out the insert in its entirety — Figure 10 — and what I like about this is the continued emphasis on navigation. Through a mix of position and typography, the eye is led to a further explanation of what to do.

The layout of this Cancer Research UK insert is not "natural." Nine times out of ten in a leaflet such as this you would find the navigation point on the back, or at the end in minuscule type (or missing completely). Happily, navigation has been allowed to lead the design. Great.

Local solicitors taking part in our FreeWill Service

CANCER RESEARCH UK

Bo'ness
Liddie & Anderson
Mr W MaCrae 01506 822727

P H Young & Co
Ms A Laing 01506 826166

Stephens
Mrs P Stephens 01506 828801

Bonnyrigg
Macbeth Currie & Co
Mrs S Brydon 0131 654 9995

Edinburgh
A & W M Urquhart
Mr C Lucas 0131 556 2896

Aitken Nairn
Mr A Stevenson 0131 5566644

Allingham & Co
Mr B Allingham 0131 447 9341

Bennett & Robertson
Mrs E M Paget 0131 2262011

Bonar Mackenzie
Mr A Bowman 0131 225 8371

Connell & Connell
Ms A Mackenzie 0131 556 2993

Davidsons
Mr I Haigh 0131 5589999

Dickson McNiven & Dunn
Mrs A M Bradley 0131 316 4666

Drummond Miller
Miss C Hope 0131 2265151

Erskine Macaskill & Co
Mr G Scott 0131 622 6062

Fyfe Ireland
Mrs C Miller 0131 343 2500

Gillespie McAndrew
Mr J McArthur 0131 225 1677

Henderson & Co
Mr N Henderson 0131 4773511

Lindsay Duncan & Black
Mr J Davidson 0131 225 2354

MacBeth Currie & Co
Mr K Brydon 0131 226 5066

MacLachlan & MacKenzie
Mr A Crocker 0131 220 2226

McKay & Norwell
Ms S Mendelssohn 0131 2292212

Morison Bishop
Mr E Dyce 0131 226 6541

Morton Fraser
Mr R Girdwood 0131 2471000

Murray Beith Murray
Miss M Main 0131 225 1200

Peddie Smith Maloco
Mr K Peddie 0131 446 0662

Purdie & Co
Mr A S Douglas 0131 225 8088

Rae Reid & Stephen
Mr P Stephen 0131 337 5577

Shepherd & Wedderburn
Mr M Rust 0131 2289900

Snell & Co
Ms P Snell 0131 2263600

Stuart & Stuart
Mr J Colquhoun 0131 228 6449

Sturrock & Armstrong
Mr N Patrick 0131 225 7524

Thomas H G Stewart
Mr T Stewart 0131 229 4939

Ward & Co
Mr J A Ward 0131 539 7200

Warners
Mr B Warner 0131 6624747

Wright Johnston & Mackenzie
Mr K Fitzpatrick 0131 225 4181

Leith
Beveridge & Kellas
Mr J Campbell 0131 554 6321

Beveridge Philp & Ross
Mr M E Watson 0131 554 6244

G W Tait & Sons
Miss E Brownlie 0131 554 3441

Mowat Dean
Mrs E A Williamson 0131 555 0616

Linlithgow
Peterkin & Kidd
Mrs M Bagust 01506 845191

North Berwick
Wallace & Menzies
Mr A Anderson 01620 892307

Peebles
Blackwood & Smith
Mr Fyfe 01721 720131

Penicuik
Stuart & Stuart
Mr D McKenzie 01968 677294

Prestonpans
McKinnon Forbes
Ms S Forbes 01875 813219

Tranent
Garden Stirling & Burnet
Mrs S Lynn 01875 611616

McKinnon Forbes
Ms S Forbes 01875 611211

Once you have chosen a solicitor from the list above, please call them to arrange an appointment.

Figure 9 *The answer to "waddawa do?" The first fold of the Cancer Research UK insert opens to deal immediately with navigation. This layout achieved twice the response of the control against which it was tested. Reproduced by kind permission of Cancer Research UK.*

Figure 10 *The inside spread of the Cancer Research UK insert, with a strong continued emphasis on navigation. Reproduced by kind permission of Cancer Research UK.*

And navigation *leading* the design doesn't mean navigation *dominating* the design. (The offer is on the outside, front and reverse — exactly where it should be.) It is just that the communication sequence has been constructed to act in harmony with the recipient's thought process.

When I spoke to the marketing team at Cancer Research UK, initially to ask permission to use their insert for a magazine article, I wasn't surprised to hear the response rate: It was *double* that of the control against which it was tested.

Check if your customer already knows what to do

You've probably noticed Figure 11. It relates to the consumption of services of a sort. For a customer involved in this particular buying process, navigation information can be kept to a minimum. It also highlights the role that a visual can play in achieving speedy navigation.

Figure 11 Little explanation required! Navigating the "forearmed" customer can be quite straightforward.

However, the point I want to emphasize here is that you will often be communicating with a customer who *already* has a pretty good idea of what to do (or what to think about).

Take the fundraising mailing shown in Figure 12: "Save the capercaillie." This was sent to me by the RSPB, of which I have been a member for many years. During this time I have received scores of similar appeal mailings, and occasionally I have responded.

My experience profile (as a recipient) is probably quite similar to that of other potential donors. This means that initial navigation can be dealt with in a taken-as-read fashion. You could say *implied*, rather than *express*.

I already know why the RSPB exists and about the phenomenal con-

Figure 12 Navigation *"implied" rather than "express." RSPB members are familiar with regular fundraising mailings, so emphasis can shift to making the communication of the central concept as powerful and emotive as possible. Reproduced by kind permission of the RSPB.*

servation work it does. Like a million other members, I pay an annual subscription, which I think of as a general donation. And — as I said — I'm familiar with the society's frequent one-off appeals.

So I don't really need any upfront help with navigation in the "waddawa do" sense. I know what the organization wants me to think about. I know what it wants me to do.

In turn, the RSPB knows it can concentrate on making the communication of the central concept ("magnificent capercaillie nearing extinction") as powerful and emotive as possible. It can cut to the chase and lead with the crisis. Since I know it's an appeal, I don't feel conned into reading it.

Obviously, if the mailing were targeted at new members or first-time recipients, a bit more emphasis on navigation would almost certainly be beneficial.

Don't assume that ad seekers know what to do

Hold up a typical copy of *Yellow Pages* (if you can) and you've probably got 15,000 display ads in the palm of your hand. I doubt your customers read *Yellow Pages* for entertainment purposes. Almost certainly they're ad seekers.

What does NEW AIDA thinking prescribe? Surely your customer knows what to do? Surely you can forget about navigation altogether?

My answer to this is no. Definitely not. Your customers might be ad seekers, but that *doesn't* mean they know what to do.

Consider this: As a teenager, for several years I worked part-time in a local DIY store, where I learned among other things to cut large sheets of glass to size. Bizarrely, it seemed, customers would see our ad and then turn up expecting to buy glass.

We Saturday lads used to joke among ourselves about this. You wouldn't believe the number of times a customer couldn't even tell you the dimensions of the window his son had broken that morning.[13] And if he knew the size, he often forgot the thickness (which can be just as important). Then had he checked his shed to see if he needed nails, and putty, and undercoat, and exterior gloss? (Customer: "I need *nails*?") This predicament led to many lost sales. Customers often couldn't be bothered to come back into town equipped with the right information.

I've made it sound like it was the customer's fault for not being able to buy glass. But you know that's an attitude stemming from poor salesmanship. The lesson is that even an active ad seeker benefits from a few words of direction: The instructions should have been in the ad.

I've taken two examples from the Mortgage Brokers' section of a recent edition of *Yellow Pages*. They provide an interesting contrast and might help you to assess your own communications.

In Figure 13 is an ad for a firm called Financial Tactics Ltd. I like this. It leads with a dominant image and a headline that unravels the visual message. (More about this in Step 4, Attention.) The web address reinforces the accessible tone: Why call it financialtactics.co.uk when you can say askforamortgage.co.uk? For the confident ad seeker, it's a clear and engaging piece of communication.

Figure 13 For the confident ad seeker, Financial Tactics Ltd provides a simple navigation message. © Reproduced by kind permission of Yell Ltd and Financial Tactics Ltd. ® YELLOW PAGES is a registered trademark of Yell Ltd.

Now look at the ad shown in Figure 14 overleaf. At first sight this is heavy with words. But what immediately struck me is its emphasis on navigation.

Put yourself in the shoes of a first-time customer and read the subheads. It reminds you that this stuff should have been on the curriculum at school. The novice homebuyer faces a maze of uncertainty – and here's an ad that guides them through it.

All credit to the Mortgage Advice Network. You could say it's done a navigation job for the whole category. But while it might be inadvertently helping its competitors, I'm sure the bulk of extra leads that this perceptive ad generates will flow its way.

Figure 14 This ad tackles head-on the navigation hurdles experienced by the first-time customer. © Reproduced by kind permission of Yell Ltd and Mortgage Advice Network. ® YELLOW PAGES is a registered trademark of Yell Ltd.

NAVIGATION — SEVEN TOP TIPS

1 Think navigation before attention.

2 Write down your desired customer reaction.

3 Find the navigation point.

4 Let navigation lead design.

5 Identify yourself.

6 Identify your subject.

7 Check, using the two-second test.

KEY QUESTION
"Does my customer know what to do or think about?"

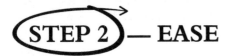

STEP 2 — EASE

Make it easy and show your customer

A s I mentioned earlier, at Blue-Chip we regularly sent out promotional mailings to our customer database. It was our long-term advertising campaign. Typically, there was a reply element (and a potential reward), designed to get the recipient to think about our message. Figure 15 shows an example. With mailings like this, we usually got a response ranging between 25 and 50 percent.

For our mailing way back in June 1994, following a heated debate, we decided to split the database into two equal test cells. I'll call these mailback and faxback. In the mailback cell, the recipient could enter by the normal method: a prepaid envelope. In the faxback cell, the recipient could *only* respond by faxing the form back to one of our offices.

The mailing was aimed at somebody probably quite like you: working in a modern environment, at a desk, in marketing, or sales, or business. The argument went that it would be easier to reply by fax than to fiddle about with an envelope. I wasn't convinced.

You know what I'm going to tell you. Mailback response 30 percent. Faxback response 6 percent. The mailback cell outperformed the otherwise identical faxback cell by a factor of five — 500 percent better.

How come?

As I had suspected, actually we had made it *harder* for our customer to reply. When you think about it, this is common sense. Few people have a fax machine right next to their desk. Indeed, for staff in larger companies, the departmental fax could be some distance away. Sometimes (and more so in those days) there were even rules about who was allowed to use it.

But every firm has a system that conveys mail to and from in- and out-trays. So asking our customer to reply by mail was simply going with the established flow — and almost zero calories required. Expecting them to

Mr T.A. Ablett
Divisional Director
Sun Alliance Insurance
Werneth House
Oldham OL8 4TZ

blue-chip
marketing

Dear Tim

"43% RESPONSE!
YOU MUST BE JOKING?"

NO IT'S TRUE! Offering a humble pack of playing cards, and the chance to win a trip to the Montreal Comedy Festival, 'Joker in the Pack' has broken all records for Newcastle Brown Ale.

With two ISP Award nominations (Best FMCG Promotion and Best Promotional Merchandise) and stocks selling through in half the scheduled in-store period, consumer response reached an unbelievable 43%.

How come? Well, we'd like your opinion! Examine the samples enclosed and use your marketing skill and judgement to match the views of our expert panel. You could win a mouth-watering prize!

WIN A CRATE OF *BROON!*
Rank in order of importance (1-4) the key factors which made 'Joker in the Pack' so successful:

☐ **COMEDY THEME**
to appeal to target audience

☐ **STRONG BRANDING**
to reinforce produce heritage

☐ **GUARANTEED REWARD**
to gain attention

☐ **IN-PACK POSTCARD**
for ease of response

FIVE CRATES MUST BE CLAIMED BY 1ST APRIL 1997

To enter simply fax or post this completed sheet to Blue-Chip's Edinburgh office. The first 5 out of the hat on 1st April which agree with our judges will win the beer!

Good luck!

Yours sincerely

Ian Moore.

LONDON
88 LONG ACRE
COVENT GARDEN
LONDON WC2E 9J8
Tel: 0171 312 5050
Fax: 0171 312 5060

EDINBURGH
45 FREDERICK ST.
EDINBURGH EH2 1EP
Tel: 0131 225 5050
Fax: 0131 220 5060

MANCHESTER
8 TRUMPET ST.
MANCHESTER M1 5LW
Tel: 0161 237 5050
Fax: 0161 237 5060

THE BLUE-CHIP
MARKETING
CONSULTANCY LTD
COMPANY N° 121186

directors
Ian Moore MBA MCIM

Figure 15 *Example of an "advertising" mailing sent out by Blue-Chip Marketing to its customers and contacts. Where practical, this would also include a sample of the actual campaign materials. A response level of 50 percent was not unusual. This program was an important testbed for developing effective techniques.*

toddle off to the fax machine proved to be a greater barrier than might have been imagined.

Thereafter, we never depended on a solely faxback reply mechanism. Sometimes we kept it in as an option, but the faxed-back component rarely accounted for more than a tenth of the total number of replies we received.

Navigation, ease, and action

There are times when navigation and ease become hard to tell apart. If you think back to the tear-off reply card in the last chapter, you could argue that it deals with navigation and ease simultaneously. At a glance, it tells the customer what to do and makes it easy to do it.

When you create a piece of marketing communication, you may not even separate navigation and ease in your thinking. However, when it comes to *evaluating* an ad or a mailing or a brochure, you can certainly treat the two steps independently. And there is a clear distinction.

While navigation focuses on the customer's thought process, ease emphasizes the physical aspects of the communication piece (or the sales environment) and the customer's practical interaction with it. Navigation concerns the *what*, ease the *how*.

If the race to the sale were a steeplechase, navigation would be the plan of the course and the orders to the jockeys; ease would be the hurdles, ditches, and protesters en route.

I'm pretty certain that our customers in the faxback cell gained just as good an understanding as those in the mailback cell. The core messages and enclosed materials were the same. I think we made quite a good job of navigation. Recipients knew what to think about and what to do. The directions were clear. But when it came to action, the hurdles proved to be a significant deterrent.

Looking at that last sentence, you might wonder if ease is interchangeable with the traditional *action* of old AIDA. Aren't they just the same thing in a different order?

In fact, there is no paradox (but you'd be right to raise the question). To continue with the steeplechase metaphor, ease is all about smoothing the course that lies ahead of your customer. In particular, it focuses on those first few moments when they set off and interact with your marketing.

However, ease doesn't necessarily get them across the finishing line. And that's where the distinction lies in my mind. As you can read in Step 7, action concerns the psychological matter of closing the sale. Meanwhile, in this chapter I'd like to highlight the wide-ranging practical obstacles that cause many customers to fall by the wayside.

The tipping point

As the faxback "calamity" demonstrated, there can be a fine line between an ordinary (6 percent) and an extraordinary (30 percent) response. The difference was a modest prepaid envelope. There are great gains to be made by finding such tipping points. Deal with ease upfront, and you may save a fortune later when the time comes for action.

In effect, we were able to increase the response of faxbackers simply by giving them an envelope and the option to reply by post. But say we'd persevered with faxback only: I wonder what value of reward it would have taken to achieve the same fivefold uplift?

Free trial offers

Here's another startling contrast provided by some equally unobtrusive hurdles. Take a close look at the shelves in your local supermarket (or, to save time, Figure 16 overleaf) and it shouldn't be long before you find products advertising the following offers, or "mechanics" as they are called in sales promotion parlance:

1 "Try me free," or
2 "Money-back guarantee"

To all intents and purposes, these two offers are identical. With the try-me-free mechanic, customers mail in a proof of purchase and get their purchase price refunded. With the money-back-guarantee mechanic... spot

Figure 16 *For every 300 customers who apply for a try-me-free offer, only 1 responds to a money-back-guarantee offer. Indeed, the ratio can be greater than 1,300 to 1. Reproduced by kind permission of Lever Fabergé Ltd and Bendicks (Mayfair) Ltd.*

the difference! Customers mail in a proof of purchase and get their purchase price refunded.

Despite this similarity, for every 300 customers who apply for a try-me-free offer, only 1 applies for a money-back guarantee.

It's strange, but true. "Try me free" will typically get a 30 percent response, while a money-back guarantee struggles to a barely measurable 0.1 percent. (I know of a try-me-free offer from the Netherlands that reached 40 percent[1] and a money-back guarantee in the UK that came in at a microscopic 0.03 percent[2] — that's a ratio of over 1,300 to 1.)

The explanation lies in a series of hurdles that are not immediately apparent. When customers pick up the money-back-guarantee offer they see the proposition: "100 percent satisfaction or your money back." That makes it a no-risk purchase, just like a try-me-free offer.

But what they don't see is the small print: "To claim your refund return your till receipt with your purchase of Bloggo circled, along with the barcode cut from the bottom of the pack, plus a letter stating in not less than 30 words the reason for your dissatisfaction."

It's the high hurdles.

I don't know about you, but my till receipt rarely seems to make it back to the house. Then there's the barcode conundrum — how do you cut it out until you've finished using the product? (And how do you remember until then?) Finally there's the minor essay, when you have to eke out your very flimsy (though legitimate) excuse for not quite experiencing 100 percent satisfaction. No wonder hardly anyone bothers.

OK, that's not entirely true. When we ran the money-back-guarantee mechanic for the 1996 launch of a new tissue brand, 8,812 customers did bother. However, although this was one of the highest such responses I've seen, at 0.3 percent, it was still 100 times less than we'd have expected for a try-me-free offer.

In my experience, in most cases — and I'm talking leading brands of bread and beer, soap and soup, and tissues and loo rolls — money-back guarantees consistently come in below 0.1 percent response.

Despite its low response, the money-back-guarantee mechanic has its place in the marketer's toolkit. It's a low-cost way of making a bold claim to the customer. It proclaims product confidence and customer care in one fell swoop.

It's really on-pack *advertising* masquerading as a sales promotion offer. In 2003 Lever Fabergé built an impressive through-the-line campaign around the Surf Promise (see Figure 16). By naming 99 top stains, its customers were invited to think beyond the bland standard "gets your clothes cleaner."

But left to their own devices, money-back guarantees aren't a behavior-shifting promotional technique. If it's in-store brand switching or trial you're after, you need to remove the hurdles. That means try-me-free offers. Don't ask for a till receipt — just refund the maximum retail price. Let your customer reply on an easily removable (and writable-on) piece of the packaging. Make the claim address freepost, and short and simple. And refund the postage as well as the purchase price.

Tear-strips

In 1985 I joined Cadbury's, as a product group manager in charge of assortments. The company let me loose on huge and famous brands, including Milk Tray and Roses. I got rid of those horrible cracknel things from Milk Tray and fought a rearguard action to keep the marzipan in Roses. (It was the most expensive choc, so the accountants wanted to ditch it, but in research 17 percent of customers said they bought Roses because of the marzipan. I noticed that it quietly disappeared a few years later.)

At the time I was recruited, the company was about to launch an exciting new product, designed to replace the aging Bournville Selection and rejuvenate Cadbury's sales in the dark chocolate assortment sector. The new brand was named Biarritz and — as you may recall — it had a striking metallic blue triangular box.

The launch became one of my projects. Biarritz gained a 21 percent market share within four months and grew the sector by 16 percent in its first year. In the *Super Marketing* Awards it was voted the best new confectionery product of 1986 (see Figure 17).[3]

Biarritz, however, was not a long-term survivor and was withdrawn a few years later. While I believe that its ultimate failure was largely due to positioning,[4] there was one practical issue that emerged at the outset.

Just a few days after joining the company, I remember a production sample appearing on my desk, hot off the new wrapping machine. It looked great. Since I had a marketing pass, I was allowed to take products off company premises. That evening (for research purposes) I gave the pack to a girlfriend.

Opening a box of chocolates is supposed to be a romantic moment. But despite my friend's impressive talons, we eventually had to resort to a kitchen knife to get through the polythene shrinkwrap.

The next morning I went to see my boss. As the new boy I was a bit nervous and didn't want to appear critical. I explained about my ruined date and asked if we'd thought about including a tear-strip.

To my surprise he said of course, but I should know that the factory already wanted to kill us (for making it manufacture and wrap a stupid

"TOP NEW CONFECTIONERY PRODUCT OF 1986"

Super Marketing Awards, 12 March 1987.

Figure 17 Cadbury's Biarritz – *great once you could get into the box. Reproduced by kind permission of Cadbury Schweppes plc.*

impractical triangular box) and I could imagine what would happen if I dared raise it at the next production meeting. I got the message.

At the said meeting I opened by apologizing for taking a career in marketing, and explained that I had always wanted to be an engineer. Seriously though, the production team were a great bunch and had sweated night and day to get the complex high-speed wrapping machine installed and commissioned to schedule. The oversight was a classic marketing Catch 22 – none of our other lines had tear-strips, so no one guessed that Biarritz would need one.

Eventually a tear-strip was introduced, but in vain. The majority of boxed chocolates are sold between Christmas and Easter, and all of the stock produced during the launch year was of the non-tear-strip variety. Most customers only buy one or two packs of assortments in a 12-month period, and a large proportion of these are given as gifts *by* elderly women *to* elderly women.

Even if these customers *didn't* suffer from arthritis, getting into the box was no picnic, as my girlfriend had demonstrated. With scores of alternative brands and products to choose from, when next time to buy came around, the first impression left by the previous year's Biarritz was probably already starting to tell.

The trouble with packaging

Plainly, my chocolate-box tale is about packaging — manufacturing, even — on the face of it, perhaps a bit of a diversion from the main theme of marketing communications. However, this book is really about *sales*. After all, that's why we use marketing communications in the first place.

What is more, packaging often carries marketing communications and certainly can play a role in encouraging (or discouraging) customers to buy a product again.

We all have our pet hates when it comes to packaging. For me it's Imperial Leather — a product I like, but just try getting the soap out of the wrapper when you've got wet hands. (Or even when you haven't.) Perhaps it's because it's another tear-strip issue that it bugs me so much. Extracting toothbrushes from their blister-packs can require tools. For years, my older relations have fumed about milk packaging — a positive triumph of the producer over the consumer. And I remember Paul Merton consigning videotapes into Room 101 to tumultuous applause. (Tear-strip again, you see.)

Of course, there are many more examples of brilliant packaging that we don't even notice because they're so convenient. How about Twining's tea bags with their immaculately perforated caddies? P&G's detergent tabs are pretty nifty, too. And I like egg boxes. (But why don't they tell kitchen duffers like me how to make scrambled eggs, or even how long to boil for that perfect soft center? I'm sure I'd buy far more if I knew what to do with them.)

For Warburtons, to coincide with a campaign entitled "Respect the Bread," we invented expanding cartons rather like wine carriers, so that customers could get extra loaves from shelf to home without crushing them under a bootful of groceries.

A plea to design engineers

Last year I made a presentation at the request of the managing director of a market-leading British food producer. His question was how sales promotion could become a more potent weapon in the company's armory (think of free gizmos in breakfast cereals and cash prizes in crisp packets).

I'd got lots of ideas, but unfortunately there were stumbling blocks:

1 Insertion of free gifts or gamecards: not possible.
2 Random printing of winning numbers or prizes inside the packaging: not possible.
3 Online labeling or banding of free gifts: not possible.

Sadly — although understandably — few companies approach production with a "marketing-engineering" hat on. Yet they spend millions downstream on sales promotions. If I were launching a product and buying new equipment on which to make it, I would insist that maximum scope for marketing communication was designed in to the manufacturing operation.

As it is, people in the sales promotion business have to invent ever more ingenious ways of turning existing products and packaging into Heath Robinson-type communication devices. Codes hidden beneath ringpulls on beer and soft drinks. Winning cans that sing when you open them. Labels that reveal your prize when you chill the bottle. Foam bath that changes colour on contact with water.

During the time we worked on Kleenex tissues, we had the idea of using the tear-out oval as a reply postcard. This is the bit you remove from the top of the pack to get at the tissues and throw away. On the mansize packs the oval was large and thick enough to satisfy the Post Office's mailing requirements. All it needed was for the packaging supplier to be able to print one color on the inside of the box.

After a few years this went ahead. We tested a free-prize-draw mechanic for the annual hay fever promotion. The result? A record response, with applications for our promotion peaking at a staggering 112,000 per week. (And see Figure 18 overleaf for a similar example.)

Figure 18 *Reply made easy. A "postcard" printed on the inside of Newcastle Brown Ale packaging. This device undoubtedly contributed toward the extraordinary (43.2 percent) response that this campaign generated. Reproduced by kind permission of Scottish & Newcastle plc.*

We shouldn't have been surprised. All of a sudden it was so easy for the customer. Hurdles were minimized.

And even if your customer ignores the promotional message in the store, there's a second chance to gain their involvement as they open the pack. Indeed, many on-pack offers are created with this in mind. We used to design Kellogg promotions for reading at the breakfast table rather than beside the supermarket shelf.

If you can make participation in your sales promotions easy, they will be much more effective. If you can't, and the limitations of your product and packaging mean hurdles and hassle for your customer, perhaps you should think again. You might only serve to irritate them. A few days ago I opened a new tub of margarine to find that the slip of greaseproof paper beneath the lid was in fact a 50p coupon. Nice offer... except that the underside was covered in low-fat spread.

The lottery

The UK National Lottery has come in for a deal of unjustified criticism, mainly from people with little understanding of brands and marketing. As a product launch – in most other categories – it would be viewed in many respects as a considerable success. However, in terms of ease, it's an illuminating case study.

A few pages earlier I used the expression "triumph of the producer over the consumer" to describe milk packaging. The lottery is another cracking example of this. I'm looking now at an entry form (a "play slip," they euphemistically call it) and it rather reminds me of a multiple-choice exam paper.

I'm a non-player of the lottery, so it's people like me they want. A while back, for the launch of the rebranded Lotto, I received a door-drop communication, apparently one of 14 million sent out.

The navigation step I got (at least I thought I did): "They've sent me a free entry, already made out with random numbers, to take down to my local retailer."

From a marketing point of view it seemed like a sensible exercise in free sampling. Studies have shown that free samples can create 40 percent more trial. And free-sample users tend to exhibit greater levels of repeat purchase (+12 percent), leading to almost 60 percent higher long-term penetration.[5]

However, when I read the body copy on the leaflet, I realized that it wasn't a free entry – I still had to pay the £1. I'd just assumed that they'd made it that bit easier and had offered me a carrot to get me over the remaining hurdles.

Of course, if you send out 14 million free entries (that's more than every other home receiving one) for an established product, you'll get a massive take-up by existing customers. Not very good use of lottery funds. So I can appreciate why they didn't do it.

But that doesn't help me as a non-user. I need to understand and experience just how easy it is and I need a bit of a shove to do so. Perhaps the budget would have been better spent paying a polite salesperson to single me out in the foyer of my local supermarket?

Why do I need help? Have a look at a play slip through the eyes of a first-time customer. It's been designed not for the human that plays it, but for the robot that processes it.

For a start, I wonder why it looks like an official form. It's not exactly the most inviting first impression. Then why do you have to mark six numbers when they are arranged in four rows and twelve columns? (It doesn't tell you how many to select.) Next you have to draw an unfamiliar horizontal line (when you usually choose things by ticking them). A tick is much easier. And why all the small print on the back?

Oh! It's the instructions. What to do is set in the 5-point type that marketers normally reserve for the stuff they don't want their customer to read (eventually I found the bit about six numbers), plus a plethora of options I could never have guessed at. It seems I don't have to mark any horizontal lines at all if I don't want to (I just mark the Lucky Dip box). I can enter draws on different days and in different weeks. Further down are even more instructions about another game entirely, called Lotto Extra — but by now my eyesight's starting to give up.

There are almost 1,000 words printed on the back of the play slip. That's about three pages of the average novel crammed into a quarter of the space. Over the years I've devised scores of gamecards and I worry if the wordcount gets past 50. (See Figure 19 for an example.)

If the lottery play slip were designed with ease in mind (with the *customer* in mind, instead of that darned robot), it would look decidedly different. Maybe there wouldn't even be a game piece. Since the entry has to go into a computer, why can't you play directly at a terminal?

It could be really fun, with great graphics. Your confirmation slip could include your horoscope or tell your fortune. We all use technology these days. Young people are experts. If our banks trust us to take money out, surely the lottery could trust us to pay money in? Perhaps you could even enter via ATMs — places you already go to, with cash on tap! Then you could play 24 hours a day, when it suited you.[6]

This sort of thing would help to overcome another of the lottery's hurdles — the queue. The times I've had my car sitting on a yellow line while I'm buying milk from a convenience store and had to wait in the same

Figure 19 An in-bar gamecard designed by Blue-Chip Marketing for Morgan's Spiced. Note how it sticks to the bare necessities. Reproduced by kind permission of Diageo.

queue as customers getting their lottery slips processed. That puts me right off. Especially when I'd be worried about having made a mistake and people grumbling behind me. In my local Sainsbury's there's one lottery terminal at the cigarettes counter — and nearly always a queue — and in the foyer a bank of six loyalty-card terminals usually standing idle.

Ease in the service sector

Think about this: A study of customer-service programs by General Motors led to the conclusion that while a satisfied customer will positively influence eight others (and spur at least one more sale), a soured customer will negatively affect 25 people.[7]

In the retail environment, one of the challenges you face if you wish to improve your marketing communications is actually defining what they are. Sometimes it's hard to draw any clear distinction between communications, customer service, and selling. My local bar is a good example of this and always reminds me of the power of ease in the buying process.

I've known the head barman for a number of years — but only in the pub. (Just once I met him in the street, the worse for wear, on his way back from a wake. He was muttering "Wrath of God" and I don't think he remembers the incident.)

The pub itself is a large, traditional city watering-hole, and often there are 50 or 60 drinkers there, even on a quiet weeknight. Nevertheless, once we've got our first round and found some seats, that's it — job done. By this I mean we don't have to — how can I put it? — bother our butts for the rest of the evening.

The barman keeps a regular watch on our beer and when it's nearing its last inch, conveys an inquiring look across the room. My friend Ken and I are in competition to see who can summon a round with the tiniest possible movement in response. At the time of writing Ken is leading with a minor twitch of an eyebrow (an order he claims not to know he'd placed). Within a minute or two, fresh beer arrives.

A couple of months ago I got talking with a guy on a plane. He said that he was in the licensed trade, on his way to spy out some new retail concepts on the continent. That took us on to the subject of table service and I mentioned my local. I said I was amazed that more British pubs didn't do the same thing. I asked him if perhaps it was against some regulations. He said no. I asked if he did it in his pubs. He said no. So I asked if there was a particular reason why not. After quite a few moments deep in thought, he said no.

From a sales point of view, my local clearly scores. With no time wasted queuing at the bar with empty glasses, we reckon we spend 20–25 percent more per visit than on an equivalent night in another pub. What is more, we keep coming back.

The barman scores because we always buy him a couple of drinks — which he takes as tips and supplements his wages. He gets to chat with the customers. We get to chat with him. It's just like in *Cheers*.

I'm not saying that if a bunch of strangers walked in the same level of service would be available. In fact, in this respect the place really fails in its marketing communication. Passing on foot recently, I watched a group of three American couples loitering on the sidewalk, peering through the frosted glass windows and the crack in the big swing doors, trying to work the place out. ("Waddawa do here?") After a minute or so they gave up and wandered away. Yet I'm sure all it needed was a simple door sign: "Visitors welcome. Please order at the bar. Try a free taste of our traditional local beer. Hot pies available too."

The communication of basic navigation and ease represents a huge opportunity in the service sector. Yet the impatient Anglo-Saxon psyche is so often ignored from the selling side of the counter. There are few things more frustrating than waiting anxiously to get *acknowledged* (never mind served) when you're hungry or thirsty or the kids are playing up. No wonder so many people use the fast-food drive-through: you get priority service, in the order that you arrived (paradoxically quite the opposite of the in-store experience).

Direct-response ads

I'm endlessly amazed by television ads where a phone number or web address flashes up briefly at the end. What are the advertisers thinking of? Never mind that you don't have a phone, online laptop, or even a pencil and pad sitting beside you — how do they expect you to remember the details long enough to record them in some way?

Spend a few minutes watching daytime television and see how the DRTV (direct-response television) experts operate. These are companies that actually measure their advertising effectiveness by the sales they make. You'll notice how long their (memorable) phone numbers are displayed, often for the full 40 seconds of the ad, and verbally repeated at least two or three times.

Also notice that in 9 out of 10 ads they won't try to confuse you with a web address as well (or even pretend you'll take the trouble to visit one).

Conversely, the presenter in a current elephant.co.uk television ad announces the website address *five times* in 20 seconds (and no competing phone number). It's equally single-minded, and no doubt equally effective.

I'm also bemused by much of the "off-the-page" advertising that I see. (An apt name, because that's where a lot of it ought to be.) The main off-the-page pitfall seems to be the reply section — the coupon.

Obviously, the best form of coupon is one that you can easily remove, preferably without damaging the ad. In some magazines, you can pay extra and use either a tip-on or a bound-in. A tip-on is simply held in place with a blob of tacky glue. A bound-in is like a perforated mini-page that precedes your ad. Either of these can be extracted with great ease and leave your customer with a postcard in their hand, ready to go. Not surprisingly, they can increase your response levels by up to 10 times.[8]

They can also deliver free samples of your product and are widely used by fragrance companies.

However, there are two practical drawbacks to the use of these techniques. The first is budget — they can treble your production and media costs. The second is flexibility — for instance you can't use them in newspapers.

That means that you often have no choice but to create the coupon *within* the space of the ad itself. Unfortunately, this is where things begin to go awry.

If you think back to what I said about navigation leading design, it's quite clear that the same principle applies to ease. If you're putting a reply device *in* your ad, presumably that's the main purpose *of* your ad. (If it isn't, you're probably trying to achieve too much at once — and you should drop it.)

You want your customer to be able to glance at your ad and see that it's easy to respond. (Remember that this automatically helps with the navigation process.) This objective should be at the top of your design brief. Otherwise your art director may create an ad that looks pretty but doesn't work.

Compare and contrast. Figure 20 is based on three real ads for investment funds, found in the same edition of a consumer money magazine. In each case, to progress toward purchase, the next step for the customer is

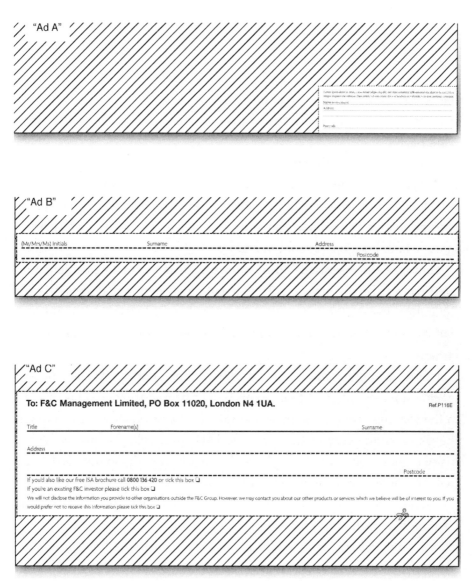

Figure 20 *The reply coupons from three ads for investment funds, placed in the same publication. While they share the objective of generating a customer inquiry, their respective designers clearly did not attach equal importance to ease.*

to send for more information. This, then, would appear to be the main objective of each ad.

Back in the mists of time, marketers found out by trial and error where the best place was to get maximum response from a press coupon: bottom right-hand corner. (Making sure, of course, that your ad is on the right-hand page.)

Common sense, of course. (As usual.) Two snips of the scissors and you've got it. You can even *tear out* a coupon from this position quite easily.

What is more, from a tracking point of view (and by tracking I mean the journey that your eyes and thoughts take as you peruse the ad again in more detail), it's a logical spot to end up.

However, the disguised "ad A" in Figure 20 was actually positioned on a left-hand page. If you've ever tried to cut out a coupon that's placed near the gutter (the center, where the pages are bound together), you'll know that it's tricky. In fact, the coupons in all three ads shown run close to the gutter.

I have examined thousands of applications sent in by customers. I would estimate that more than 90 percent of people are incredibly diligent in the way they cut out coupons and tokens. If you design your coupon in the shape of an octopus, that's how it will come back. You just won't get many replies. Your customers like to do things properly, so the harder you make it, the fewer of them will bother.

Graphic designers, left to their own devices, will often relegate the coupon to a small strip of space that they grudgingly give up. See the disguised "ad B," also in Figure 20. To all intents and purposes, this is unusable.

But when it came to developing "ad C" (the F&C ad, shown in full in Figure 21), I reckon someone stepped back and thought first about ease. The large space allocated to the coupon tells you — at a glance — that the advertiser is serious about wanting a reply. The bold dashed line is printed in red to make it stand out even more, and there's a pair of scissors urging you on. And — unlike ads A and B — there's actually room to complete your name and address in normal-sized handwriting.

Finally, what about the *back* of coupons? I'm surprised that you never see an advertiser buy the space on the reverse of their coupon. Not only is

Why the best way to **avoid the risks** of the stockmarket is to invest in it more often.

its

We're not talking about every day. Once a month is enough.

But by drip feeding your money into the stockmarket, you won't have to worry about whether you've picked the right time to make an investment.

You see, by investing in our Private Investor Plan savings scheme, you're not putting all your money into the market on one day. So, should things take a turn for the worse, you get the chance to buy more shares for your money the following month.

It's called spreading the risk. And investing a little at a time, month after month, is the best way to protect yourself from the volatility of the stockmarket.

But don't think this approach to investing brings boring returns. Far from it. Although past performance is not necessarily a guide to the future, if you'd invested just £100 a month over the last 15 years in Foreign & Colonial Investment Trust, you'd now have £41,481*

Find out more and you too could discover how regular investors can turn out to be rich investors. Just return the coupon below, contact your Independent Financial Adviser or call

0800 136 420

or visit our website at **www.fandc.co.uk/pip**

F&C

FIRST IN INVESTMENT TRUSTS

To: F&C Management Limited, PO Box 11020, London N4 1UA.   Ref: P116E

Title   Forename(s)   Surname

Address

                                            Postcode

If you'd also like our free ISA brochure call **0800 136 420** or tick this box ☐

If you're an existing F&C investor please tick this box ☐

We will not disclose the information you provide to other organisations outside the F&C Group. However, we may contact you about our other products or services which we believe will be of interest to you. If you would prefer not to receive this information please tick this box ☐

Issued by F&C Management Limited, previously Foreign & Colonial Management Limited. The value of shares and the income from them can fall as well as rise and you may not get back the full amount invested. *All figures sourced Standard & Poor's Micropal: 27.02.87 – 28.02.02, total amount invested £18,000. Value of investment over five years: £6,474 (28.02.97 – 28.02.02), total amount invested £6,000. Investment trust figures based on Foreign & Colonial Investment Trust PLC; using mid-market prices, net income reinvested, including 3.5% notional expenses. (Actual Plan charges 0.2% commission and 0.5% Govt. Stamp Duty). F&C Management Limited (regulated by the FSA) or its subsidiaries are the Managers of the investment trusts (except Graphite and SUIT). For your security, some calls may be recorded and randomly monitored.

See page 3 • Fastrack number 14

Figure 21 "Ad C" from Figure 20. Clearly, the design process was led by ease of response. Reproduced by kind permission of F&C Management Ltd.

it a second chance to get your message across, but also it makes sure there isn't something more important overleaf that your customer doesn't want to lose by cutting out your coupon.

Conventional advertising

In conventional advertising, no immediate action is required or asked for. So it would be tempting to think that ease doesn't matter. This could be a critical mistake. I believe that your customer thinks about ease even when their purchase may be several months ahead.

In Figures 22 and 23 are two ads featuring binoculars and telescopes, respectively from Opticron, a manufacturer of high-quality optical equipment, and In Focus, a successful optical retail chain. I think it is interesting to analyse how they have dealt with the "upstream" and "downstream" ease challenges in their particular market.

The ads shown were placed in the RSPB's *Birds* magazine, circulated to its more than one million members. These are interested customers who almost certainly take time over each quarterly issue, reading it thoroughly. Navigation should not be too much of a challenge.

However, when it comes to ease, if you've ever bought a pair of binoculars or a telescope (or any technical gizmo, come to that), you'll know that it can be a fraught experience. For what may be a once-in-a-lifetime purchase, and a costly one too, you don't want to make a mistake.

The problem begins with the fact that the average customers — I'll use binoculars as an example — don't know what they need. From personal experience, I'd say that this even applies to relatively experienced users of optical equipment. This raises all sorts of hurdles in your mind.

Take a look at the Opticron ad. Immediately you are reminded that this is a technical product category. Therefore, in a sense by necessity, it's populated with jargon and shorthand (and each company has its own peculiar dialect).

I've been using binoculars almost daily since I was a kid, but there's no way I could confidently order a pair of Opticrons based solely on the coded information available in the ad (although the consolation would be that I'd get an excellent product, whichever I bought).

Figure 22 How do you strike a balance between information and overload? Opticron recognizes this dilemma and integrates its advertising with that of its trade customers (see Figure 23). Reproduced by kind permission of Opticron.

Obviously, Opticron knows this. And while I think that the imperfections in its market make it impossible for it ever to produce perfect advertising, it does a pretty good job.

Working in its favor are the dynamics of the buying process. With an average inter-purchase interval of 10 years or more, typical Opticron buyers have probably read many ads before they get around to making a purchase. So any single ad doesn't have to do the job of communicating Opticron's entire 150-strong range and their attributes.

And when the customer's mind (or bank balance) moves into a more active binocular-seeking mode, Opticron is ready with a catalog and a website packed with facts. In this way, Opticron takes responsibility for tackling the 'upstream' ease challenge.

But now, two of the market imperfections I mentioned suddenly raise their ugly heads. The first is that you're still unlikely to spend £649 on a pair of 10 × 42s unless you've looked through them. The second is the task of looking through them. What I mean is the pressure-selling situation that this might entail: at a camera shop that you may never have visited before, with a salesperson of questionable knowledge literally breathing down your neck, in the High Street, in the rain, with suspicious passers-by looking at you askance. Aargh!

In Focus to the rescue. Not only does In Focus have branches at or near popular bird reserves, but it also runs a continuous program of informal field events at similar venues nationwide. You can simply turn up and basically help yourself to an eyeful of a whole range of kit in a real but relaxed setting, and get as much or as little no-obligation advice as you need, both from expert staff and from other customers just like you with whom you can exchange information. Indeed, you don't even have to go out of your way. Expensive binoculars are neither an impulse purchase nor an entry-level product. They are mainly bought by active birders who frequent the very places that In Focus has chosen to present its wares.

As you can see from Figure 23, In Focus devotes a good half of its advertising space to this aspect of the buying process. As a retailer, it has addressed the "downstream" ease challenge head on, and made it central to its marketing and communication strategies.

Figure 23 Successful independent retailer In Focus concentrates on convenience – a vital point of leverage in the optical equipment market. Indeed, more than half of the space in this ad is devoted to the process of getting trial products into the customer's hands. Reproduced by kind permission of In Focus.

Read the two ads in tandem — which you often can in the same publication — and they dovetail neatly. The critical hurdles have been identified and presented as solutions to customers long before they buy.

So the lesson? My view is that it's really important to do this sort of "perceived hurdle analysis" on your particular market. (Just ask your customer how they feel, having read your ads.) It could have a radical impact on the way you design your communication. If your customer reads your message and turns the page with more hurdles in their mind than when they began, your marketing is actually "unselling" your products.

Unease on the internet

Your customer won't visit your website just because you've got one. As Seth Godin points out, there are over 2 million corporate websites and — on a good day — about 50 million people surfing the web. That's 25 people per site.[9]

Obviously this average is meaningless in practice, but it does put things into perspective. The vast majority of websites are, to all intents and purposes, completely ignored by their intended audiences. All those marketing budgets lost in cyberspace.

I know of a well-established website, belonging to one of the 25 biggest grocery brands, which by late 2003 was attracting fewer than 5,000 actual visitors per month. (Compare this to the site for *The Sun* newspaper, with 3 million unique visitors per month.[10])

A friend of mine is in charge of the reception services of a borough council catering for over 100,000 citizens. I have visited the operation and it is absolutely inundated — besieged even — by members of the public, jamming the switchboard and arriving in person, all hungry for information. They want to know about stuff ranging from the abolition of water rates to the preservation of water rats. And the team does a sterling job in furnishing answers and directing enquiries to the corresponding rate and rat experts within the council.

There is obviously a huge demand for information and resources provided by government, yet a recent survey by ICM showed that *less than 3 percent of* the population use the internet for this purpose (while more than two-thirds of adults currently have internet access).[11] Part of the blame has been attributed to the poor design of websites, but I think it's much more basic than that.

For many customers, for many things, the internet is not the easiest route. Why would it be more comfortable to seek out and then wade through a strange website, when you can speak in person to someone you or your brother or sister or aunt or neighbor went to school with?

Books and banks

Searching for books (though not random browsing or deeper consideration) is much easier on the Amazon website than in a conventional bookstore. Amazon is open 24 hours a day and has a seemingly endless list of publications. So if you know what you want and don't need it right now, Amazon's the answer.

Compare this to my branchless bank account. It started with telephone-only access, and I've generally been impressed. I've timed it and it takes under two minutes to make a cash transfer by calling and speaking to a customer service adviser.

More recently I was also given access via the web and encouraged by mailings to use this route. But the site doesn't like my usual browser (a detail I always forget), so I have to exit and go back in using different software, then I have to change my settings so the site fits the screen, and finally go through all the various steps to locate my account. It takes about 10 minutes from going online. (So I generally don't bother.)

If your website can make something your customer already does easier, they'll use it. Otherwise, you're inviting a lower response. If you can go with your customer's flow and speed it up, all well and good, but think twice before you try to divert it just to suit your own purposes.

Ease and the mobile phone

One of the most successful product launches in recent years must have been BBC Radio Five Live, which began in March 1994. I believe a key factor was that it coincided with the explosion in ownership of mobile phones. (It's difficult to imagine now that in 1990 hardly anybody had one.) What makes good radio is good content: quality information and opinion, from authoritative contributors. In the past, many of these people were at work, maybe on the road — sure, listening to the radio, but with no easy, instantaneous means of making contact.

Before the advent of the mobile (and, to a lesser extent, email), the callers to radio phone-ins were, how can I put it, not very listenable to. Bring on the mobile, and suddenly the *people who know* can tell us how it is. The much-berated referee from a Premiership soccer match, driving home, can call the 606 fans' phone-in to explain his decision. A politician, in her limo between functions, can blow the gaff on the opposition spin. You or I can help other motorists by reporting in real time the latest jam at Spaghetti Junction.

It no longer has to be a phone-in, as such. Recently I heard Peter Allen, the co-presenter of the *Drive* news show, mocking someone for saying "the west coast of Norfolk." Within minutes he'd been flamed by scores of listeners pointing out that of course the county of Norfolk has a west coast — it borders the Wash. Now when the presenters want to know something, they just ask — and Encyclopedia Britain answers in a flash.

The mobile has created ease. If you can tap into it, it's a powerful marketing tool. Here's a simple example concerning beer.

Text 'n' win
Over the last few decades the drinks industry has poured millions of pounds down the on-trade promotions drain. (The on-trade means bars, clubs, restaurants, and hotels with a license to serve alcohol on the premises.) A couple of years back I remember a discussion with the managing director of Carlsberg-Tetley, Vincent Kelly. He said to me: "You don't want to know how much we spend on in-bar marketing." Then he added, with a large measure of cynicism: "But have you ever actually seen a promotion in a pub?"

Of course I had, but I knew what he meant: The majority of kits lie gathering dust in the cellar. The problem goes like this: The publican won't feature your brand unless your salesperson goes in with a promotion kit. But in practice, the bar staff often won't run the promotion if it involves any work or admin on their part (such as handing out scratchcards, or stamping a collector card for each drink purchased, or judging winners and giving out prizes). And resistance grows during peak sales periods – just when you most want to promote.

More recently I was chatting with Stephen Crawley, managing director of Edinburgh's Caledonian Brewery. The company had just won the CAMRA Champion Beer Award for its delicious Deuchars IPA brand. It wanted to promote this great triumph during the time of the Rugby Six Nations Championship, when the city's pubs become inundated by thousands of visiting drinkers.

I said I was concerned about the ease issues and my suggestion was that we should create an in-bar *advertising* campaign, rather than a promotion that nobody would run and nobody would enter. (At best it would get stomped underfoot.) Of course, this needed to *look* like a promotion, else the trade wouldn't take it in the first place (what a conundrum!). So we included a simple text 'n' win offer in the body copy of a series of large poster ads (see Figure 24 overleaf). This meant that the sales guys were able to say "I've got an in-bar promotion for you" (because you can't walk into a pub and ask the landlord to display your advertising), with the extra selling benefit that there was no hassle involved for barstaff.

Very few customers entered the promotion. But that wasn't the point. Some 90 percent of targeted pubs displayed the campaign (and were literally plastered with posters for Deuchars IPA) and thousands of drinkers participated in the beer and its advertising at the busiest time of the year. A record 50,000 pints were despatched in Edinburgh on the weekend of the Scotland v Wales game.

The mobile phone made this possible: it elegantly removed the hurdles as part of a considered strategy. The publican knew that most of his customers owned a mobile, therefore the entry mechanic was plausible. But that does not mean that the mobile is a promotional panacea. There has been a rash of text 'n' win promotions as brand managers have raced to tick the box. New, different, and fashionable, however, do not automatically

Figure 24 *Caledonian Brewery managed to get 90 percent of pubs to support its Deuchars IPA at some of the busiest times of the year. The trick? The introduction of the mobile phone as a promotional entry device. Reproduced by kind permission of Caledonian Brewery Ltd.*

equal *effective*. Indeed, in many cases, the introduction of the mobile as an entry mechanic simply serves to divorce the customer from the product and reduce the chances of an actual purchase taking place. Be vigilant — showmanship lurks around every corner.

Ease equals *convenience*

Ease is a key factor in effective marketing communications, and what is more — as I hope this chapter demonstrates — it permeates right into the heart of marketing itself. So if the process of analyzing your communications for their "easiness" takes you deeper than expected, then surely that's a good thing.

The more hurdles you can anticipate — and remove — the more participation and repeat sales you'll get. This principle applies across the spectrum, from advertising for binoculars to promoting beer in a pub.

As the faxback and try-me-free case studies illustrate, the tipping point can be remarkably unobtrusive when it comes to customer response. We naively tried to make our faxback mailing easier, and almost killed off response. A small detail that you might easily overlook could make the difference between profit and loss. (Your small detail could be your customer's insurmountable hurdle.)

Your customer gets — by one of the more conservative estimates I have seen — 254 commercial messages every day,[12] over 90,000 uninvited intrusions into their already busy life every year. How much effort can you realistically expect them to make on your behalf?

The answer, of course, is not a lot. But get navigation right and the interested customer will take a first step in your direction. Remove the practical hurdles — and do this at the start of your thinking — and you can maintain your customer's momentum.

To paraphrase Paco Underhill, chief exponent of the "science of shopping": make life difficult for your customer at your peril, for "amenability and profitability are totally and inextricably related."[13]

Steps you can take

So far in this chapter I've made little mention of direct marketing — or, at least, of direct *mail*. Yet of course, there is probably no other area of marketing communication more obsessed with ease than direct mail. I say obsessed, because if you read between the lines of any direct marketing handbook (and there are some very good ones[14]) you'll find that a significant proportion of the advice concerns ease: simple things you can do to make it easier for your customer to respond.

Indeed, John Watson, a leading direct marketing practitioner for over a quarter of a century, goes so far as to say (and I paraphrase):

"If there is a secret of successful direct mail, it is to devote your mailing to the action you want your reader to take."

People in the business of making mailings tend to call the physical elements of a mailing the *format*. This is the size, the shape, the material, the various pieces, the layout, the color, and so on. When it comes to ease, it's the format that can make a real difference for your customer.

Clear your customer's path

A good place to start is with the envelope. Can your customer open it? If your customer is a little old lady with arthritis and it is a tough polythene envelope, the answer is probably not.

In fact, not only are they awkward to open, but polythene envelopes or shrinkwraps always seem to transfer a film of grime to your hands and clothes. In a recent mini-survey I conducted, the average account executive's wastebin contained 2.7 unopened items of polythene-wrapped mail.

Next, can your customer read your writing? If they're over 40 and you've set some of the text in 5-point type, then I doubt it. If they don't have their reading glasses handy, you're in trouble.

But surely nobody would send out a mailing with essential instructions set in 5-point type? As you'll recall, the UK National Lottery did.

OK, your customer has found their specs. What about a pen? Even in the office pens go walkabout, and at home I can only put it down to the Borrowers. I'm especially amazed that more pen makers don't include free personalized samples in their mailings to businesses.

While a pen should not generally be too much of a hurdle, it can make a difference. The Cancer Research UK mailing shown in Figure 25 contains a free pen. The charity's experience is that this can create an uplift of 50 percent. Of course, a free pen in these circumstances is not just something to write with — it's a small gift and an indication of the urgency of the appeal, both of which may additionally influence the recipient's feelings and inclination to respond.

You should also ask yourself whether your customer needs a pen at all. If you have sent customers a personalized mailing (i.e. with their name and address lasered on it), then why not just ask them to send it back? (Or part of it, or a separately personalized slip or card.) If all you need is a "yes," you

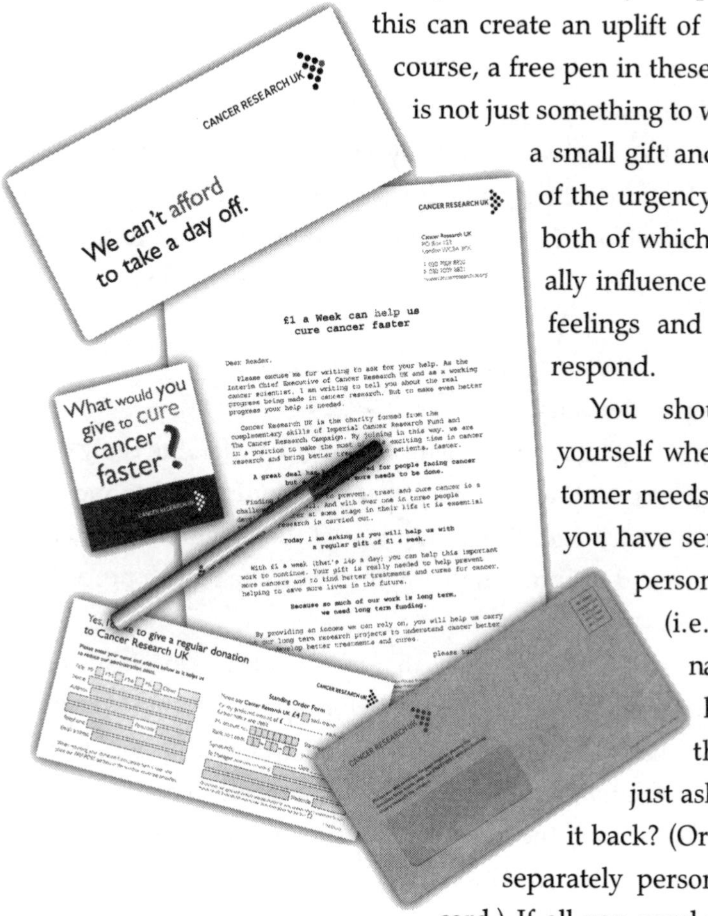

Figure 25 A mailing from Cancer Research UK. It contains everything the customer needs to reply. The charity's experience is that the inclusion of a free pen can create an uplift in response of 50 percent. Reproduced by kind permission of Cancer Research UK.

can make life as simple for your customer as placing a postage-paid card into their out-tray.

Then there's the issue of allotting your customer enough space in which to write. Given that this is usually the object of the exercise — as I highlighted in the earlier discussion of reply coupons — it's remarkable how often marketers make it a trial.

Confidentiality is an invisible factor, but nonetheless one that could prove to be a tipping point. Some people just don't like the idea of their details going naked through the post, even for the most innocuous of requests. We discovered that we could get a better response from very senior managers (to our win-a-prize mailings) if the subject matter wasn't obvious from the completed reply device. So we provided reply-paid envelopes. More lowly staff had no such inhibitions when it came to getting their names in the hat — and a reply postcard worked fine.

Design the reply device first

There is a range of explanations for why you might design the reply device first. One argument goes that your customer — intending to respond — will remove the reply device and discard the rest of the mailing. Later, if they can't find all they need to know on the reply device, the buying process will break down.

American adman Fred E Hahn says that busy readers, especially in business, often go straight to the reply device. Before spending time learning all the details, they want to discover what the offer will cost in dollars, time, effort, or other commitment. In response to this behavior, copywriters now load the reply device with the key benefits, and summarize the offer, the guarantee, and the conditions. Often, they design the reply device first.[15]

If you recall my counsel to "think tabloid," you'll recognize a great similarity in the way Hahn's logic acknowledges the busy customer's demands for information. It's as much of a navigation as an ease issue, but nevertheless valuable.

For me there's an even more basic reason why you should tackle the reply device first. Simply, it puts ease high on your agenda. It gives ease a chance to stake a claim before all the space is gobbled up by images, graphics, headlines, and copy.

It forces you to consider how your customer will respond, and how you can help them. So even if you don't actually have a physical reply device (response may be by phone or internet), it ensures that ease is not an afterthought. I find it useful to make a range of blank, actual-size mock-ups of an ad, mailing, or leaflet before I begin to write a single word.

Say "This is the reply device"

It can be as simple as putting the words "order form" in bold at the top of the order form. Or, "bring this card with you." Or, "ring here for beer." Or, as I illustrated earlier (and see Figure 26), "tear-off reply card" — which, productively, is not only a description but also an instruction, give or take a hyphen.

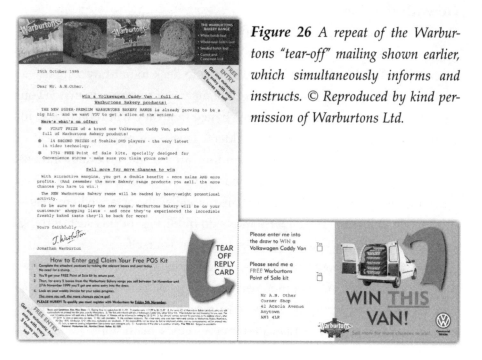

Figure 26 A repeat of the Warburtons "tear-off" mailing shown earlier, which simultaneously informs and instructs. © Reproduced by kind permission of Warburtons Ltd.

The tipster's mailing that I mentioned in the introduction started to work once we emphasized the reply device. The latter was originally an integral part of the main letter and had to be cut out, so I recommended a more involved arrangement, in which it became a separate slip ("return this to register and claim your three free tips") held by two paperclips over the front of the letter, roughly in the middle. To read the letter the customer had no choice but to interact with the reply device. As I stated earlier, response increased by more than 750 percent.

Straight-talking British direct marketer George Smith gave this equally direct advice:

> "You are not selling computers, copying machines or whatever. You are selling reply forms!"

I like it.

Go with the flow

Our faxback mailing patently did not go with the flow. It required our customer to make a significant detour. Our mailback cell worked because it stuck to the tried-and-trusted route: in-tray to desk to out-tray.

The more closely you can engineer the means of response to match your customer's usual behavior, the more chance that they will reply. Take, for example, the buzzphrase "traffic builder." This is an offer that is sent or communicated to your customer when they are outside an establishment, to encourage them to go inside. The customer constitutes the traffic. (And outside may mean literally outside on the sidewalk or anywhere else — most likely at home.) The supermarkets do quite a lot of this sort of thing, and here's an analysis you might like to try for yourself.

I live six minutes from Sainsbury's, eight minutes from Tesco, and ten minutes from Safeway.[16] My shopping pattern is about 80 percent Sainsbury's, 15 percent Tesco, and 5 percent Safeway. (A recent study indicated that 40 percent of shoppers travel less than 10 minutes to their main store.[17])

Sainsbury's feels the easiest to get to (there's only one unpredictable junction). A trip to Tesco involves a drive through a busy commercial bottleneck (or alternatively winding rat-runs mined with "sleeping policemen", those annoying road humps that slow down traffic). To reach Safeway, I actually have to drive past Sainsbury's.

I buy pretty much the same brands and products in each chain. Indeed, I can't really distinguish between their offerings, so my shopping pattern must be determined by the inherent physical obstacles, relatively insignificant though they may seem: Tesco plus two minutes, Safeway plus four minutes.

The great Claude Hopkins went so far as to state: "No one can profitably change habits in paid print."[18] I think these are salutary words for the modern-day marketer. Going against the flow is one of the toughest challenges you can tackle. (What would it take to turn your shopping habits on their head?)

Think carrots

Occasionally Tesco sends me traffic-building mailings with coupons — some of which are based on my meager spend (and therefore not of very high value). For Sainsbury's I get a low-key ongoing discount via my loyalty card at the store.

Every week while I was writing this, Safeway took the trouble to deliver a promotional leaflet through my door. When its much-publicized 20p-off-a-liter petrol promotion was introduced, I began to take notice of the leaflet. There were some good offers. Plus a £5 off coupon if I spent over £30. I decided to set out on a serious discount-shopping experiment, and planned a big list and an empty tank. I made a one-quarter saving on my grocery bill and saved £21 on petrol — in total over £76 in one trip.

The less you are able to engineer the means of response to match your customer's usual behavior, the bigger incentive you'll need to offer. Rather than build a dual carriageway direct from my house to its car park, Safeway went for the carrots big style: "Save 20p a litre on petrol and get BOGOFs[19] on lots of long-life household goods." It worked. Not surprisingly, my shopping pattern changed.

There are two lessons here. First: All is not lost if you can't remove the hurdles. Second: Can you afford the carrots? (Remember that Safeway was bought out by Morrisons.)

A last word about ease

I'll leave this to Drayton Bird (of whom David Ogilvy said: "He knows more about direct marketing than anyone else in the world"). In describing the attributes of *Reader's Digest* mailings he writes:

> "Note how careful they are to tell — very often at the beginning of a letter — how easy it is to respond and exactly how to do so."[20]

EASE — SEVEN TOP TIPS

1 Think ease before attention.

2 Define and mirror the natural flow.

3 Design the reply device first.

4 Dismantle all possible hurdles.

5 For advertising, identify future hurdles.

6 Test and research for tipping points.

7 Be prepared to dangle carrots.

KEY QUESTION
"Can my customer see that it's easy?"

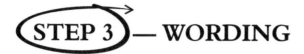

STEP 3 — WORDING

Make conversation with your customer

I spent over two years in charge of a team of five salesmen covering much of Scotland. Part of my job was to accompany my reps, in order to appraise their performances and develop training programs. I recall one trip (with George, a long-established salesman from Inverness) that lasted three days, when we did calls in Wick, Thurso, and the island capitals of Kirkwall, Lerwick, and Stornoway — primarily visiting the major wholesalers in each area. Though my grasp of Scottish dialects had improved, I have to confess that I missed much of what went on. Whatever it was, however, did the trick, because George took orders that I could only describe as astronomical. He sold so much that not only was he the top salesman in my area, but we won the top area prize too. Thanks to George, we both went on that year's incentive holiday to Hong Kong.

George knew his customers and could slip effortlessly into their idiom, whether it be that of the isolated north coast or the differing micronations that make up the northern and western isles. Obviously there was a bit more to it than a superficial switch of dialect — George had worked hard on building a deeper empathy and mutual respect with his customers — but it began with tuning in at the first level of contact, a common language.

All good salespeople are taught to speak the language of their customers. This metaphor is an old principle and a fundamental driving force behind the new "science" and growing business practice of NLP (neurolinguistic programming). In NLP it's referred to as *matching*. Matching is used to build pace and rapport, by mirroring and complementing aspects of the other person. When you match, you show that you are willing to enter the other person's model of the world — intuitively, they feel more at ease with you.[1]

It's such an important principle because it works. And we all use it in our daily lives — not just with customers, but with colleagues, friends, relatives, children, and even pets.

Reach the crowd, address the individual

Stop for a moment and consider this question: Why do we have advertising and its many cousins? One answer, when you think about it, is because it simply isn't feasible to speak to all your customers personally. If you could — if it were cost-effective and practical — you would. (Or you'd employ a talented advocate like George to do it for you.)

Instead, you have to resort to the intermediary of the mass media: which, depending on the scale of your business, may range from a postcard in your local newsagent's window to a full-blown national television advertising campaign.

But that doesn't mean that you have to start acting daft. (And I use this expression because that's what it seems like to me.) The inability to speak in person to your customer isn't a reason to adopt the manner of a traveling player. I call it "playing to the world." Using the mass media doesn't mean that you can't be yourself.

When I moved from sales into marketing, I remember that one of my first jobs was to organize some trade press advertising, to be placed in magazines like *The Grocer* and *Super Marketing*. I soon made myself unpopular with my agency. Having spent most days for the previous six years in the company of our customers, I just couldn't come to terms with the self-important oratory that I was expected blithely to approve. No one likes a show-off, especially one who's selling to you. It was the sort of speak that would get you thrown straight out of the buyer's office.

Trade press advertising is viewed as rather unglamorous, and I assume that it was assigned to the agency's most junior and inexperienced copywriters. Maybe these guys had never done a sales call in a corner shop, or been to a presentation at the likes of Asda head office. Whatever their excuse, it showed in their soapbox style presumptuously aimed at some great unseen yet miraculously enthralled crowd.

And it still happens. Trade magazines, in particular, are littered with ads that play to the world. My latest copy of *The Grocer* sports headlines like "Grab some mighty tasty profits!" and "The sky's the limit!" You just wouldn't say this sort of thing.

Just because in marketing you're trained to *think* audience, that doesn't mean that you should *speak* audience.

Almost invariably, your marketing communication will be consumed by one customer at a time.[2] As far as I know, my thoughts only happen in my head; I'm sure it's the same for you. If you've ever sat beside a friend and tried to "share read" the same newspaper or magazine, you'll know that it's impossible to move at the same pace. Thoughts are as individual as it gets.

I have always found it a valuable discipline to think "one customer" in this way. You may have noticed in this book that wherever it makes sense, I have referred to "your customer" in the singular, not to "your audience."

This one-to-one approach helps stave off the temptation to lapse into ad speak. As one writer put it:

"If your sales talk sounds like the public's conception of a 'sales talk', it needs revision."[3]

Which customer?

But what should you do when you are using a mass medium to talk to many *different* customers at once?

For example, if you sell tires in the UK, your audience is made up of almost 30 million vehicle owners. Something a bit more specific like diapers still gives you a potential market of around two million households at any one time. Even in a business-to-business context (say copiers, printing, or stationery), you're quite likely to have a diverse customer base numbering in the hundreds or thousands.

If you are unable to adapt or personalize your message, even two customers are more than enough to give you a problem.

Our own mailings were regularly sent to staff at all levels in our client companies, ranging from secretaries with very little marketing experience to managing directors with, er, very little marketing experience. In between were folk of all disciplines — marketing, sales, computing, underwriting, production, distribution, finance, personnel, and so on.

But for any given mailing — which may have reached 1,000 customers — when I wrote the copy I had *one person* in mind. This was a real person, and usually it was Mr A, the managing director of a multinational insurance company for which we worked.

I knew Mr A quite well and had a good business relationship with him. He was not from a marketing background, though he was making great strides in fostering marketing in a culture where historically it had been the poor relation.

By writing my advertisement as though to Mr A personally, I knew that I would benefit from a range of built-in safeguards. First, I would use a minimum of marketing speak. Second, I would adopt a businesslike yet friendly tone. Third, I would keep to the point (he was as busy as they got). And fourth, there would be nothing embarrassing at any level (since it was fit for consumption by an important managing director).

Most importantly, though, it was real speak to a real person — if you'll excuse my wording. I would write a letter just as though I were sitting in his office having a businesslike conversation with him.

It might have been coincidence, but over a 10-year period Mr A was our best responder. (I can't believe it was coincidence.) And overall — as I have said — we regularly got responses in excess of 50 percent across the entire database, so our mailings were clearly well received.

So what's my answer to the "which customer" dilemma? Certainly it's find your Mr A, because I do know that you can't write well to more than one person at a time. If you've ever sent an email to a group of friends (perhaps trying to arrange a trip), or led a three- or four-way conference call, you'll know how tricky it is to get the right tone.

Logically, it would seem sensible to write to the most numerous type of person in your audience — Mr Average. But I would counsel against this as a starting point. Our Mr A was far from Mr Average. In fact, there were probably no more than a dozen like him (of his status) on our database. And he was certainly not our bull's-eye target — that honor went to more lowly minions who were custodians of marketing communications budgets.

So there's no hard-and-fast rule here. You must use your judgment and then get whatever feedback you can. But *do* write to a person and not to a crowd.

In praise of wing nuts

At one time there was a marketing trainee in my department who made himself unpopular around the building owing to his love of the sound of his own voice. When the day came for him to depart for his six-month stint in the salesforce, somewhat concerned for his chances, I rather unsubtly presented him with a giant pair of false ears and the following blunt maxim, known to many a salesperson:

"God gave us two ears and one mouth. Use them in that proportion."[4]

Pick up any decent book on modern sales techniques and you'll find a section on listening. It might even be the more adventurous-sounding active listening. However, there's nothing new under the sun. This quote is from a text on commercial traveling written over half a century ago:

"Determine to listen to buyers. Talk far less and listen much more."[5]

In my experience, the best salespeople are nothing like the talkative stereotypes that verbally batter their victims into submission. In fact, they are often quietly spoken people who ask questions and pay attention to the answers. (And they invariably have a good sense of both humor and humility.) Listening is probably the single most important skill a salesperson can possess.

But if advertising and marketing really are just the same as selling, surely there is a great paradox: How on earth does an ad or a mailing *listen*?

I can't answer that, but here's a thought: If you can't actually listen to your customer, you can at least avoid the habits of a bad listener. One of my little training rules, for instance, concerns "you"s and "we"s.

When you write copy for an ad or a mailing, try to make sure that it contains at least two "you"s for every "we."[6] It's not always easy to do this while you're writing, but you can certainly check afterwards and make any necessary adjustments. For example, compare these two sentences:

☆ "We have more branches than all our competitors put together."
☆ "You're never more than half a mile from your nearest Post Office."

It's not difficult to tell which one sounds like it's operating in listening mode. In the first sentence the advertiser lectures its reader, with two "we"s to boot (actually a "we" and an "our"). In the second the advertiser looks at the matter entirely from its customer's perspective (and two "you"s).

This approach also has the advantage of magically converting features into benefits. (More about this in Step 4, Attention.)

The granny test

When I was learning to write direct-mail copy, I was amused by a frequent piece of advice: Get your granny to read your work before you inflict it on your customers. It still crops up in handbooks on copywriting today. (David Ogilvy's version is that you should talk to a farmer in Iowa.[7])

The idea behind this is that it provides a screening process to ensure you write in plain English. If your granny (or the farmer from Iowa) can understand it, then so will your customer.

I disagree. I think the granny test is a bit of a red herring. (I can't speak for the farmer.) Most grannies I've met seem pretty literate, have accumulated huge vocabularies during their long lives, and leave me standing when it comes to crosswords.

"The reading age of the average supermarket shopper is 11."

A Safeway buyer told me this, following some research she had conducted. A reading age of 11 is not as bad as it might sound (for instance, you would be able to read though not necessarily understand words such as atmosphere, binocular, and circumstances[8]), but it should make you stop and think about the words you use in your marketing communications.

You may have heard David Ogilvy's anecdote about the choice of words, but it's worth repeating. Having researched a particular ad he discovered that most housewives did not understand the phrase "Dove made soap obsolete." He changed obsolete to "old-fashioned." On another occasion, a journalist rang him to ask what the word "ineffable" meant in an ad he had written for Hathaway shirts. Ogilvy was forced to admit that he hadn't the faintest idea.[9]

Marketers sometimes use the word *complimentary*, when they are giving away something free. They also use the word *complementary*, when they are selling two things that go together. (You can even imagine an offer using both words, though it would be a devil of a job to get it to fit on the packaging.)

While I was writing this chapter I ran a simple test on a group of bright 12-year-olds. I showed a card with the two words in question written on it, just like this:

complimentary

complementary

I asked if they knew what the words meant, and what the difference was between them. I got blank looks, apart from one youngster, who said: "Angles that add up to 90 degrees." Nice answer, but not what I was after.

If intelligent 12-year-olds don't know what these words mean, what about the average supermarket customer with a reading age of 11? To confuse them further, marketers often get the spellings of complimentary and complementary mixed up. Is this bottle of tonic free, or does it just go well with this particular brand of gin?

Copy checking? I'd say it's a P45 for the granny, and a quiet word with your local primary-school teacher.

Don't blame the English

When the English landed in Britain some 1,500 years ago, little did they guess what impact their language would have on the world. (Linguists call it Ingvaeonic — the Angles and Saxons left us no name for it, and it evolved into separate branches of Frisian, Dutch, Afrikaans, Low German, and modern English.[10])

English is now the most influential and widely used language on the planet and has more words than any other (numbering in the hundreds of thousands — over 615,000 in the revised *Oxford English Dictionary*). Only in English are there proper thesauri — or is it thesauruses? (Guess what? It can be either.)

In fact, it's the French we marketers have to blame for our problems. (Strictly, the French-speaking Vikings who ruled England after 1066.) Norman French became the lingua franca of the Court, thus carrying great prestige among higher society. It was a good 300-odd years before we had the blighters back speaking decent English, and by then the language too had been well and truly invaded.

Today, borrowing from French poses an interesting dilemma for the copywriter. There are two ways to express many sentiments: in "Saxon" or in "Latin."

Saxon words tend to be short and their Latin synonyms long. (For writing purposes this doesn't mean that their origins are strictly Saxon or Latin, but it is a useful shorthand for the two families of words.) For example, you could mean the same thing and yet use either of these phrases:

☆ In Saxon: "great buy"
☆ In Latin: "excellent purchase"

Old English versus a mixture of Latin and Old French. Two syllables play five. Who wins?

The answer is that common currency wins. Time and again. It's reckoned that of the 100 most common words in English today, every one is Anglo-Saxon in origin.[11]

It doesn't stop there. One study found that 43 words account for half of all those in common use, and just 9 for a quarter of *all* the words in any sample of written English. Here they are, monosyllabic and Anglo-Saxon to the letter: and, be, have, it, of, the, to, will, you.[12]

I've occasionally been told by clients: "We say *complimentary* — we don't use the word *free* here, it degrades our brand image, we're far too *premium* for that." (I think: then why are you giving away free gizmos?)

I'm with American copywriting guru Herschell Gordon Lewis. He puts it simply: "use demotic language."[13] (Demotic, of course, means "of the people," democracy and all that. Ironically, it's a Greek word.)

"Complimentary" is a word from Old French, based on a Latin root. "Free" — as you'll no doubt have guessed — comes from an Old English word: *fréo*. When it comes to selling, my money's on *fréo*.

Jargon buster

Another common pitfall is the ill-considered use of jargon. For one insurance client, I spent years trying to avoid words like endorsement, indemnity, premium, sum insured, and warranty. It's all very well to use these terms in the office, but you may as well speak in a foreign language as put them in your consumer communications. Even on a business-to-business basis it's a risk: How can you be sure that the person reading your ad or mailing isn't a trainee?

Many people who run their own businesses come from a technical background. (And even in large firms, it's common for marketing staff to have trained initially in technical areas.) So it's not surprising that jargon creeps in unnoticed.

Look in your local paper and you can find people offering to supply you with rebate. They mean wood.

Grammar rules, not

There is a world of difference between grammatical rules (which you can't break) and opinions about grammar (which you can chose to ignore). For instance, here's a rule you know:

a   Before Harry went shopping, he went to the bank.
b   He went to the bank before Harry went shopping.

Both sentences contain an identical set of words. Yet only in the first sentence could Harry have gone to the bank. You automatically use this rule about word order every day without so much as a moment's hesitation. In fact, I don't even need to explain what it is (which is a relief).

Now here's an opinion about grammar, which you also probably know:

a   When you need to really think...
b   When you need really to think...

Of course, it's a split infinitive. Sentence a) is what most people would say. Sentence b) is what some "experts" think people should say. (Even though the phrase loses some of its meaning and intensity of expression.)

Thankfully, modern-day linguists are championing a far more enlightened approach. To paraphrase Professor R L Trask of the University of Sussex, writing about the dogmatic insistence on not splitting infinitives, it's astounding, bizarre, curious, insane, nonsense.[14]

Professor Steven Pinker of MIT says of such prescriptive opinions:

"They have no more to do with human language than the criteria for judging cats at a cat show have to do with mammalian biology."[15]

His fellow American Bill Bryson gets to the root of the problem. He points out that the early authorities decided that the rules of English grammar should be based on Latin — a language with which it has little in common. It's akin, Bryson says, to making a baseball team play to the rules of football.[16]

But what should you do when you are writing copy to sell with? You may have been taught never to start a sentence with a conjunction, like but. Or to end one using a preposition, like with. Yet this is just how people speak.

In 1995 I was the copywriter on a year-long campaign for Scottish & Newcastle that achieved a 72 percent response (and subsequently won three Gold Awards). I began to think that I must be getting something right. So my humble advice is: Write what you would say.

And if your boss or colleague or customer or client finds fault, here's a further, more profound reason.

The sound of words

Poet and essayist Alexander Pope wrote about writing:

"The sound must seem an echo to the sense."[17]

There is a school of study within psychology that says that readers are actually *listeners*.[18] Experiments monitoring brain activity have established that when people read, they hear the words in their minds. (Put crudely, the same parts of the monitored brain light up as when the subject is listening to spoken words.[19])

This doesn't surprise me at all. I don't know about you, but hearing is how it feels to me. A word doesn't really come to life until I've heard it spoken — think of tricky gaelic names like Sean and Siobhan. (How are you pronouncing AIDA in your head? Aider? Aye-ee-dah?)

A while back Lever relaunched good old Jif cleaner as Cif (presumably for the purposes of pan-European packaging, with English Jif losing out in the average-difficulty-of-pronunciation stakes). Personally, though I'm in a minority, I struggle with this: I see Cif and hear *kiff*. But phone the number on the pack and a voice says: "Thank you for calling the *siff* careline."

I know that in English we've got circle and city and cider (and virtually every other word beginning "ci" starts with a "s" sound), but my brain pronounces Cif like café and coffee and cuff. There are no words in everyday

English that begin with the letters "cif," so my processing system opts for the next most familiar sound pattern.

Now consider these points[20]:

☆ Spoken language is believed to have developed more than 100,000 years ago.

☆ Since the spread of agriculture 10,000 years ago, there has probably been little biological human evolution (nor much time for it, anyway).

☆ The first records of true writing date back less than 6,000 years.

☆ Little more than a century ago, the world's population was, to all intents and purposes, illiterate.

☆ The majority of the world's 6,000 languages still have no written form.

Put these "facts" together and what do you get? What they tell me is that human brains are designed to *hear* language. We've been listening a thousand times longer than we've been reading. Writing is just a convenient, if clumsy, means of conveying language in a complex modern society. We train our brains to convert it back into sounds when we read. To paraphrase the great lexicographer Samuel Johnson, written words are but the daughters of Earth.

So for marketing communication purposes, writing should be treated not as the written word, but as the *spoken* word. And surely this means a simple, conversational style.

After all, you want your messages to be most acceptable to your customer and easily understood by them. So why be hamstrung by some rigid, pompous system, or equally the notion that writing is an art form demanding highfalutin execution? Write what you would say.

Grammatical preferences

Having implied that you can more or less break the rules (opinions) as you wish, I'm now going to backtrack a little. If you break rules, you may irritate your customer. If I were to write an ad or mailing aimed at professors of English, I certainly wouldn't split my infinitives. (In fact, I'd find a friendly professor and ask him to thoroughly vet my copy first.)

Its so easy to distract your customer away from the delicate stream of buying thought into which you have carefully drawn them. Just make what they consider to be an error. If, like me, you're fussy about getting its/it's right, you're probably already distracted by the error that opens this paragraph.

(There's a simple rule: Only if you mean "it is" should you insert an apostrophe in "its." Remember: "It is an apostrophe.")

Hyphens (or, rather, the lack of them) also drive me bonkers. Without them, it's harder to create an easy to read effect. (Try an easy-to-read effect. Much better.) Sometimes, their absence can even affect the meaning of a phrase. Earlier in this chapter I wrote about a growing business practice. Is that a practice to do with growing businesses, or a business practice that is growing? (Only a hyphen could remove the confusion.)

ENCORE.

Pick up any newspaper or magazine and I challenge you to find a headline which ends with a full-stop. You'll look a long time. Operating in markets of near-perfect competition, what do editors know that many an advertiser does not? On a similar note, why when an article runs from the front to an inside page does it invariably break mid-sentence, instead of ending neatly? Of course, it's all about keeping the customer reading. David Ogilvy concluded that editors communicate better than admen.

Dispense with full stops — at least the ones at the ends of your headlines. The only possible effect a full stop can have is just that: to stop your customer from reading on. (Figure 27 shows a rather ironic example based on a real ad.) Next time you buy a newspaper or magazine, see how many of the headlines end with a full stop — excluding the ads, of course.

Figure 27 Unless your headline contains two sentences, the only effect a full stop can have is to deter your customer from reading on.

A while ago I noticed a card on the message board in my local Sainsbury's. It was like this:

```
want to earn some
    extra cash
tel: 123-123123
```

I wouldn't fancy phoning this number. Is the person at the other end of the line a potential employer or employee? You would normally expect a question mark to create ambiguity, but in this case it's the opposite.

Marketing myopia

At any time in a typical supermarket, 17 percent of customers can't read the signs above the aisles. A similar number can't read the labels on the goods.

This is not about illiteracy (in fact, I'm not even counting illiteracy) but eyesight: 60 percent of the population need specs.[21] And in a recent survey by the AA, 17 percent of people were found to be motoring about in a state of significant uncorrected short-sightedness (for instance, they would fail the requirements of the driving test).[22] Meanwhile, since many of the over-40s don't bother to take their reading glasses shopping, there's another sizeable chunk of customers on whom your brilliant words could be wasted.

If you don't need specs, it's perhaps easy to overlook the significance of this issue. I'm slightly short-sighted. As I write I can see a bird on a wire about 25 meters away, and though it's blurred I can tell it's a woodpigeon. But I can't read the type on the spines of books six feet away. It's the words that go first! It's no coincidence that opticians do eye tests with rows of letters rather than pictures of our feathered friends.

Received wisdom has it that 11-point type is about optimum for most people to read "in the hand." This book is set in 11-point type. So why do editors insist on draft manuscripts set in 14.5-point type *and* with double line spacing? (Because it's easier to read like that.)

I think the most important thing you can do is to test, and watch and listen to your customer. If your product is bought by the elderly and mainly stocked in supermarkets, you need to decide what information takes priority. If you're thinking of placing poster ads inside the local leisure center and pool, remember that there'll be a bunch of short-sighted people wandering about without their specs. (And long-sighted ones who won't be able to read your hand-held leaflets.)

In a drugstore study, Paco Underhill found that 91 percent of all customers read the front of the pack before buying a product. And 42 percent of them also read the back. The average reading time, even for something as innocuous as a moisturizer, was 16 seconds — during which interval most people can comfortably deal with 100 words, provided that they can read them.

A friend recently passed me a small ad from a newspaper that had amused him. I measured it and found that it was set in 6-point type. Here is a section of the text, at that size:

> If you have difficulty reading the printed word, the *Daily Blah* can still be enjoyed on both audio and electronic format. A taped digest of the publication is available every week on subscription, while each day's edition is available through e-text.

It's hard to believe that somebody actually produced this ad. But I can imagine the process: It's your job to manage the talking newspaper, you get allocated a small area of free space by the editor, so you fit the message to the space. (No guardian salesman, you see.)

Pictures and recognition

Back to the woodpigeon (now flown). I recognized it by a combination of its size, shape, gray plumage, blurred but distinct white collar, and the likelihood of its being in the area. It puts an interesting slant on the subject of wording: Use pictures instead.

I was in a McDonald's recently when a small boy in our party pointed over my shoulder and said: "I want one of those." After replying "Is that: I want one of those, *please*?", I looked round to see that the item in question was a giant-size chocolate-covered doughnut, on a window poster. At the age of three-and-three-quarters, any words would have been wasted on the wee chap. McDonald's knows this.

Many print ads have images or graphics that seem to serve little purpose. It's as though the marketers concerned have thought: "It's an ad, so it must have a picture in it." (This is showmanship making an unwelcome appearance.) Look through a few magazines — especially trade journals — and see how often you could take away the picture with no detriment to the message.

If you find yourself with this feeling about one of your own ads, think woodpigeon (or doughnut). Let the visual part of the ad do something useful: to enhance and dramatize recognition for your customer — of their need, or the category, or your product. (See Figure 28 for an excellent example.)

Research in the bread market has confirmed the importance of visual cues in the buying process. A supermarket's bread fixture is one of the most dynamic and heavily shopped in the entire store. There is a vast range of different brands and varieties (perhaps 100 or more in a large supermarket) and products can change places by the hour, never mind from week to week. For the busy shopper wishing to find their normal loaf, visual cues (color and graphics) are essential. Indeed, there's anecdotal evidence to suggest that some customers will stick to a particular brand simply because it's easy to find.

Much of what you sell will be to a customer who already buys from you. They know a lot about you and understand the buying context (like they're in your restaurant and they're hungry). Thinking about wording — at the outset as you develop your communications — will help your messages work harder, even if it means taking away words and using pictures instead.

Wording equals *conversation*
Edward de Bono says that 90 percent of errors in thinking are in fact errors in perception.[23] If he's right (and I'm not going to argue), it only emphasizes the challenge faced by the marketer.

Figure 28 *An ad in which the headline would work fine on its own, but with a visual that engages the reader through humor, and thus quickly clarifies and dramatizes the proposition. Reproduced by kind permission of Brown-Forman.*

Poor wording is to communication what lazy clutch control is to driving. Your marketing efforts can stall before your customer moves even an inch in your direction. And the journey — if it happens at all — will be a bumpy ride. The message just doesn't get home.

But good wording is your secret synchromesh system. With it you can match your revs to those of your customer's mind. In harmony together, you'll get on just fine.

And good wording is based on a simple principle employed by every competent salesperson. Write what you would say, to a person you know: the everyday art of conversation.

Steps you can take

Avoid the seven wordly sins

I've already touched on some tips that I have found useful in creating effective headlines and copy (for instance two "you"s per "we" and my remarks on grammar and punctuation). In this section are "seven wordly sins" — seven common pitfalls that litter the marketing communications motorway, but that you can ready yourself to steer around.

The seven wordly sins:
1 Hyperbole
2 Clichés
3 Platitudes
4 Plays on words
5 Riddles
6 Writer's fog
7 Designeritis

I have witnessed many (probably hundreds) of marketers trying to come up with ideas for ads. And I believe that most people can write perfectly good ads. But for some reason, common sense often gets left at home.

Consider these two statements:

☆ Because it's an ad, people will take notice of it.

☆ Because it's an ad, it needs to be clever, or grand.

You know what I'm going to tell you. These assumptions are incorrect; they are fallacies. Quite right. But give me two minutes at a magazine rack and I will find you a marketing communication that treats them as tenets of advertising.

You should not be afraid of writing ads, whatever your job or level of experience. But do think about it as a process of personal communication. Get feedback. Find out if you are being ignored or disbelieved. And watch out for the following pitfalls.

Hyperbole

Hyperbole is "the use of an overstatement or exaggeration for effect."[24] It's the long version of the much maligned expression "hype," and is generally less blatant.

Here's an example that happened to me. A short while ago I heard a radio ad for Edinburgh Zoo. The endline of the commercial exclaimed: "Edinburgh Zoo... wild about animals... wild about you!"

This was news to me. Next morning I grabbed one of my kids and set off. What did they mean, wild about you? Not a lot, as it turned out.

At first, I thought something promising was afoot. On arrival in the foyer, we were intercepted by a girl with a clipboard. Maybe she was going to find out what we're interested in and give us some advice? But no. It was to persuade me to sign a covenant form, so that the zoo could reclaim the tax on the entry fee. (Can't argue with that, but not what I'd hoped for.)

So we passed unadvertised-to into the grounds, in our ignorance missing the half-hourly open trailer that would have conveyed us painlessly to the top of the steep hillside on which the zoo resides. Still, it was a bracing autumn day, perfect for hauling a wobbling kid on your shoulders.

There were lots of staff about, clearing up and tending to the animals. On two occasions we stood right at the door of a pen and actually had to move aside to let a mute keeper enter. At the Harry Potter Snowy Owl enclosure, I think we must have been wearing our invisibility cloaks. Not one zoo-person spoke to us, in spite of our vocal dialog with the animals, which was a source of continual amusement to other visitors.

And maybe it was the time of year, but about half of the pens seemed to be empty (unless you counted the jackdaws). All of the refreshment kiosks were closed, and the output of the main cafeteria was reminiscent of a 1970s motorway service station. The education center had a sign up saying "Not open to the general public."

Wild about *who*?

At Disney they *are* wild about you. Giant cartoon characters constantly approach your kids. There are friendly helpers at every turn. There's more to do than you can shake a stick at, and you're never further than a scone's throw from the nearest snack stop.

Don't get me wrong — we had an OK time at the zoo. Rights and wrongs of zoos aside, they are amazing places to take small children. And I really do believe that Edinburgh Zoo is wild about animals. But why did they have to spoil it with the hyperbole?

I'm sure that a significant proportion of their visitors are, like me, repeat buyers. Previously, I was happy to find my own way around and accept a fairly passive experience. But now they've highlighted a missing aspect of their offering that I'd never considered before.

Sadly, hyped headlines are all too common. Think how often you've seen: "Win a fantastic holiday!" I reckon that in the customer's mind the code word "fantastic" is subconsciously translated as "not fantastic" and "probably a bit of a con."

You'll never read: "Win a fantastic Ferarri!" Why? Because plain "Win a Ferarri" does the job. (It doesn't even need an exclamation mark.) If something's fabulous, great, or superb, then it should either be self-evident, or the copywriter's job is to explain why, without recourse to showmanship.

So think twice before you use hyperbole. Ask: Will your customer notice a reality gap? Will they even believe you in the first place?

20 TIMES
MORE INTEREST
on your current
account than most
other banks

Figure 29 Hyperbole: A customer can spot it a mile off and will immediately adopt a cynical stance.

Clichés

Here's the dictionary definition of a cliché: "A once striking and effective phrase which has become stale through overuse."[25]

In English, apparently one of the oldest known clichés is the expression "hither and thither," which is believed to date from about 725 AD.[26] In fact it's so old and out of use that I'm not even sure if it's still a cliché. (On a similar note, Sam Goldwyn said: "Let's have some new clichés."[27] Nice one.) However, for marketing purposes, I prefer this version, from Bernard Taper:

"A cliché is a truth one doesn't believe."[28]

Ever seen an ad with the headline "We mean business"? How about "We deliver"? (Of course you have.) So overused are these phrases that they've become marketing clichés in their own right.

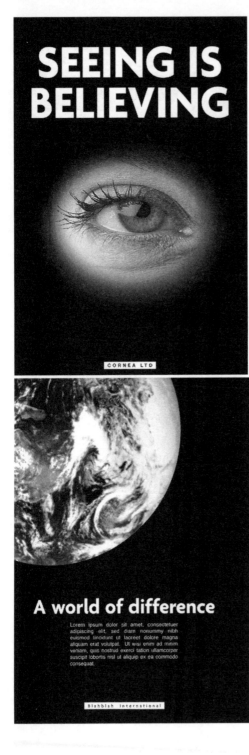

Figure 30 Print advertising abounds with clichés. These are some disguised examples from recent ads.

My observation as to why clichés are so prevalent in advertising comes back to the dangerous word "creative." When people sit down to write an ad or get round the table to generate some ideas, they feel that they must be creative.

This is a big mistake. The word they are looking for is "interesting." (That may have a creative outcome, but it will start by being relevant to the customer.)

Most basic brainstorming techniques are based on association. Typically, people begin with the product, its name, what it does, whom it's aimed at, and so on. This approach can be fine, but it's also a great source of clichés.

Call the tune. Put yourself in the driving seat. Pocket the difference. Make waves. Cash in. Peace of mind. Quality of life. Seeing is believing. A world of difference.

The marketing communications ether positively hums with tired exhortations like these.

A good cure for cliché creation is to use Edward de Bono's *random input* technique.[29] Quite simply, you attach a randomly selected noun to your subject and see what ideas it provokes. For instance, if you are searching for a way of promoting your brand of candles, you go: "candles + (let's say) sausages" and see what happens. As I'm writing I'm making this up (i.e. both candles and sausages), but immediately the idea has popped into my head to create special outdoor candles and lanterns for Halloween, or perhaps a campaign in supermarkets to promote sales for Bonfire Night. Surely a better approach?

If you recall what I said about readers as listeners, it's easy to understand why hackneyed phrases don't work. In fact, I'd go so far as to say that clichés fall on deaf ears.

Platitudes

Chambers describes a platitude as: "an empty, unoriginal or redundant comment, especially one made as though it were important."

While hyperbole breeds cynicism and disappointment, and clichés just don't get through, platitudes bore your customer into not buying. ("We deliver" and "We mean business" started as platitudes and have also become clichés.)

A good place to spot platitudes is underneath company logos at the foot (or end) of their ads. These so-called corporate straplines are meant to summarize what the organization or product stands for. Usually they are dull, self-centered generalizations with little reference to the customer.

I'm not against straplines, and have been charged to come up with a few in my time ("Soften the blow" for Kleenex tissues, "Play on" for Pro-Sport's athletic bandages, and for OVD Rum's soccer campaign: "They think it's all OVD!"). But straplines can have two detrimental effects.

The first is where they conflict with, or distract from, the main message of the ad. For instance, you watch a thought-provoking automobile commercial about an attractive couple getting it together, only to be told at the end that the lion goes from strength to strength. Lion? What lion?

The second is a more dangerous creature still. It's the strapline that usurps the headline. I'll give you an example:

"Release the power"

A well-known investment company has been using this headline across a series of ads for some time. But it's not a headline, is it? At best, it's a strapline.

How do you know it's not a headline? Well, you just wouldn't say it. It's a platitude.

Picture yourself handing out leaflets in the street, or even at a financial services exhibition. If you invited passers-by to "Release the power," what sort of reaction would you expect? They'd either look at you blankly or pretend they hadn't heard and scarper.

Yet this ad regularly competes with 60 others, in magazines packed with paid-for information. Does it cut through? I doubt it.

Surely what you would say to your passer-by is something more like: "Sir, 16.35 percent return from Brand X investment." (A more persuasive fact, currently tucked away in the body copy.)

Platitudes seem to invade headlines and body copy in equal measure. Once you're alert to their existence, you'll find them by the score: ads offering you reduced costs, greater efficiency, more flexibility; ads promising they listen to their customers, they understand your needs, they'll be your partner. These are ads that should make you want to pick up a loudhailer and shout: "Prove it to me then!"

If you can't find interesting specifics, you should really question why you are advertising at all. And if you still must, then perhaps it's best to stick to some simple, strong branding.

Plays on words

I love plays on words — especially in the sports pages of the tabloids. In Scotland we had the infamous (and now clichéd) soccer headline "Super-CaleyGoBallisticCelticAreAtrocious," when then-minnows Inverness Caley (north of the border conveniently pronounced Kally) disposed of Glasgow Celtic in a Scottish Cup tie.

Indeed, writing subheads for the tabloid sports pages has become a minor art form. And plays on words work well in this context. I've paid for the newspaper and it's part of the entertainment.

Not so in advertising.

If you're thinking of using a play on words in any of your marketing communications, you must ask a key question. Will my customer be ready for it? If not, they probably won't get it. (The joke, or the twist, that is.)

Busy readers of financial or business publications strike me as bad targets for plays on words. In this environment ads are intrusions into a sober and efficient news-gathering exercise. I doubt if you'd tell even your mate in the pub a joke without first warning them.

And what's the big risk of telling a joke? That your mate's heard it. Plays on words have nearly always been done before.

Much of my work has been in fast-moving consumer goods. I've read *The Grocer* for 25 years. I can't tell you the number of times I've seen the headline "Christmas Presence" as seasonal suppliers brag about their "heavyweight" (hyperbole, platitude, cliché) support campaigns. Then there's always "Get your Stockin'." Last year I saw "Season's Eatings," which did make me laugh (albeit used by both McDonald's and Pringles).

Seriously, though, it's a risk. When a good proportion of your target audience doesn't have English as a first language (I'm thinking of independent retailers here), why would you advertise to them in

Figure 31 *Four platitudes in one headline. Phrases like this dull the reader's mind. Add a bland visual and weak branding, and it's the perfect recipe for an invisible message. Sadly, many trade ads serve up this menu.*

gobbledegook? I think it's even slightly naive to assume that native speakers know the correct plural of the word present.

Imagine a salesperson walking into a call and speaking in some unintelligible tongue. In this context it seems so ridiculous as to be unimaginable... yet "printed" salespeople do it every day of the week.

Herschell Gordon Lewis told me that, in the US, the equivalent is the ad saying: "You know it makes cents." He said that the great danger of plays on words is that your customer will simply take you literally, and miss the point of your ad.[30]

He's right. Plays on words almost always require a second, subheadline to explain the message. This is your real headline.

Psychologists have long known that people have a strong tendency to organize their perceptions into elementary patterns. They will opt for the simple view, even when a more complex insight can be derived from a stimulus.[31]

NOUGHTY BUT NICE

lowest-ever rates
with up to 12 months'
interest-free credit

Lorem ipsum dolor sit amet, consectetuer
adipiscing elit, sed
euismod tincidunt u
aliquam erat volutp
minim veniam, qui
ullamcorper suscipit
ex ea commodo con
eum iriure dolor in
velit esse molestie co

YOU

KNOW

IT

MAKES

CENTS

transatlantic travel

at less than half the price

Figure 32 *Plays on words. Note how you have to read the subheading to understand the proposition. Readers are very literal in their take-out, especially in a serious medium where humor may be unexpected.*

CHRISTMAS PRESENCE

Heavyweight £5m seasonal
TV advertising campaign

Where plays on words could succeed is in ads placed in, or mailings or promotions for, the tabloids. Say that you're advertising your baldness cure in the sports pages. You're just as likely to connect with your customer using a headline like "Here Wig-Go, Here Wig-Go" (get it?) as with a serious approach. To boot, humor creates a sense of peer-group acceptability for the product being marketed.

Riddles

A common technique used by advertisers is to set up a problem and then show how their product solves it. There is nothing wrong with this. As already mentioned, virtually all Procter & Gamble commercials open in this fashion.[32]

What P&G doesn't do, though, is dwell on the problem any longer than necessary. As soon as it can (usually within eight seconds), it moves to the solution and emphasizes its benefits.

However, most of the time, most marketers don't have the luxury of television advertising (i.e. where the viewer gets to see the solution simply by sitting still). In most other media, you have to manhandle your customer through your communication.

Armed with this knowledge, it's obvious that riddles are not a good idea.

By all means in your headline ask a question or make a provocative statement — but make certain that it's not in riddle form. A riddle is basically anything that doesn't make sense. Your customer won't bother to decipher it just because you've put it there.

Figures 33 and 34 show two long-headline ads that fall into this general category. Figure 33, from a business magazine, still leaves me baffled, while Figure 34 — for the Royal National Institute for the Blind, placed in women's press — makes perfect sense, even though the provocative conundrum in the headline remains unresolved (until you read the body copy). Indeed, this is a great example of the use of a storytelling technique, demanding that you read on. But for this to work, your customer has to be able to understand the headline in the first place.

Figure 33 An ad with a riddle in its headline – this one is disguised to avoid embarrassment and I'm still trying to work it out.

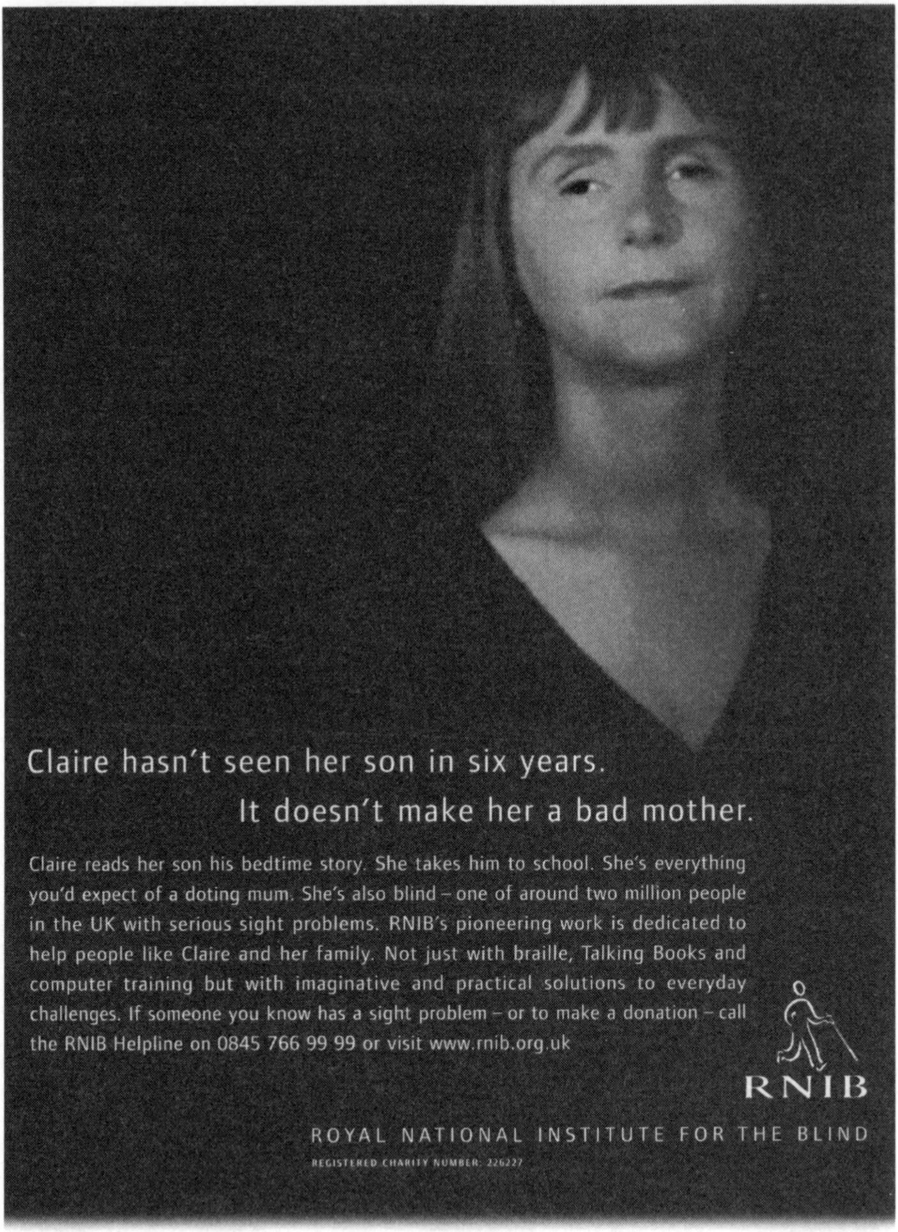

Figure 34 An ad with a riddle in its headline that provokes my curiosity. Reproduced by kind permission of RNIB.

Writer's fog

Most copywriters develop their own *structural* style through a mixture of trial and error, observation, imitation, and coaching. A simple method is to limit yourself to one thought per paragraph, broken into three short sentences. Use brackets for interjections, Saxon wording, and edit out disruptive "thats."

It seems to work.

And don't be afraid of really short paragraphs to make points of strong emphasis or contrast.

(The word *that*, by the way, can often be excised from copy without anybody noticing. For example, "It was news to me we'd won the contract" has a *that* removed, with the positive effect of jamming the two clauses more actively together.)

One thing's for sure: Long sentences and long words make text more difficult to understand. And that means fewer sales.

There's a well-established way of measuring the clarity of writing, called the Fog Index.[33] The higher you score, the cloudier your message.

Here's how to work it out:

1 Take a section of your text and count 100 words (exclude proper names, and treat hyphenated words as one word).
2 Count the number of sentences in this 100-word block.
3 Divide 100 by the number of sentences. Call the answer X.
4 Count the number of words with three or more syllables. Call the answer Y. (Exclude words that reach three or more syllables by a part of speech, e.g. plurals: message ➔ messages = two not three; or verb tenses: listen ➔ listening = two not three).
5 Fog Index = $(X + Y) \times 0.4$.

Clear writing has a Fog Index of between 9 and 12. For some tabloids it can be as low as 5. Certainly, for most advertising copy you should aim for less than 10.

The excerpts from ads shown in Figure 35 overleaf have respective Fog Indices of 9 and 16. These were real ads, placed in the same publication. See if you can tell which is which.

A RETURN OF
120%
ON YOUR SAVINGS
COULD HAVE BEEN YOURS

For example, if you'd invested just £60 a month over the last 15 years, it would be worth £23,829 today. That's nearly £10,000 more than a building society would have paid. So you can see, investing in a with-profits savings policy could make your savings really grow. That's in addition to built-in life cover and protection from the ups and downs of the stock market.

Simply pay in as little as £20 a month, or invest a lump sum of at least £1,000. Either way, you'll boost your savings with the company that one million investors already rely on.

Figure 35 Excerpts from two ads placed in the same busy magazine. One has a Fog Index of 9, the other 16. Read the copy and it should be easy to tell which is which.

DECISIONS...DECISIONS...

Investors have an overwhelming level of choice and information to consider when constructing their portfolios. That is where the premier funds service may help. Instead of looking at the entire fund universe an option is to simply choose from one of the five strategies we offer, therefore leaving the hard work to us.

The premier funds service is designed to provide investors with the benefits that a diverse and flexible range of investments should offer, along with access to the expertise and experience of and international fund management company. Along with your IFA, the only thing you would need to do is decide which strategy fits your requirements best.

This book, on a random 10-section sample, just scored 9.3 — which I hope is not bad, as it's saddled with phrases like "marketing communications."

Certainly, if you can, keep your sentences short. One Australian study concluded that learning declines as the number of words in a sentence increases beyond seven.[34] (And this correlates to George A Miller's famous paper entitled "The magical number seven, plus or minus two: Some limits on our capacity for processing information."[35])

Designeritis

As Oscar Wilde said, "No great artist ever sees things as they really are; if he did, he would cease to be an artist."

Many small firms use design agencies to produce their ads, brochures, and mailings. Designers are very skilled at making things look nice — awesome, even — but sometimes less skilled at *selling*. And boy can they mangle text!

If you treat text as a graphic device of course it can appear more pleasing when set, for instance, in fully justified blocks of reversed-out sans-serif upper-case type. But wait until your customer tries to decipher it.

If you've ever read bedtime stories to a small child, you'll know there's a moment when they start identifying words. "Look!" they exclaim, pointing excitedly, ahead of where you're up to. When you do look, you find it's the word "look" — one of the first they learn to recognize by its shape.

That's how we read. We learn the shapes of words. But not words set in upper case (i.e. CAPITALS).

I'm not sure anyone knows which is the chicken and which the egg here. Do our brains prefer words set primarily in lower case and so we have surrounded ourselves with them? Or do we grow up to prefer words set in lower case *because* we are surrounded by them?

Intuitively, and I think logically, the former seems to make more sense. A word has a more distinct visual identity set in lower case. Typographers (a rare breed nowadays) believe that serif typefaces enhance this effect.

INTUITIVELY, AND I THINK LOGICALLY, THE FORMER SEEMS TO MAKE MORE SENSE. A WORD HAS A MORE DISTINCT VISUAL IDENTITY SET IN LOWER CASE. TYPOGRAPHERS (A RARE BREED NOWADAYS) BELIEVE THAT SERIF TYPEFACES ENHANCE THIS EFFECT.

As you can see, I just repeated the last paragraph using capitals and a sans-serif typeface. (Serifs are the little curly bits that help letters glide into one another. Sans serif means without serifs.) I could go one step further and reverse out the text, i.e. use white lettering on a black background. But in the easy-to-read stakes, it's already no contest.

So don't let your precious words be press-ganged into service as reluctant graphics. If we were meant to communicate with pictures we'd all carry sketch pads. Deaf people use sign languages that are every bit as rich, complex, and structured as spoken languages.[36]

Twelve typographical tips

Much has been learned about the presentation of words to make them sell better. Here are some of my favorite soundbytes of received wisdom.

1 DO put your headline below the main image, and the body copy beneath this. It mirrors the natural eye flow and gets 10 percent more readership than a headline set above the image.[37] (In a series of direct marketing tests, response increased by between 27 and 105 percent.[38])

2 DON'T set text over pictures. (It can reduce attention value by about 20 percent.[39]) You wouldn't write a report to your boss and then doodle all over it to make it harder to read.

3 DO use a large initial drop capital to start the text. (This means a big first letter — look in your newspaper.) It telegraphs to your customer where to begin and increases readership by 13 percent.[40]

4 DON'T juxtapose red and blue text — these colors are at opposite ends of the spectrum and the eye finds them a strain to deal with.[41] (Avoid colored text in general.)

5 DO set body copy in a serif face, minimum 11 point, in narrow columns of about 40–50 characters.

6 DON'T set body copy in reversed-out type (i.e. white text on a black background). It's much harder to read. Short headlines, reversed out, are OK.

7 DO put a caption underneath the main image — it will be read by twice as many people as read the body copy.[42]

8 DON'T put your logo in the headline or body copy. Your customer won't read it as part of the sentence. Use normal type for your brand name.

And some DOs specifically for direct mail:

9 DO pull out your main headline at the top of your letter (e.g. into a "Johnson box").[43]

10 DO tell a synopsis of your message via the subheads above each paragraph — make it easy for the scan reader.

11 DO use a large typeface, narrow columns (average 10 words per line), and plenty of line spacing.

PS 12 DO use a PS to repeat an important fact — it gets high readership because your customer looks to see who's writing to them.

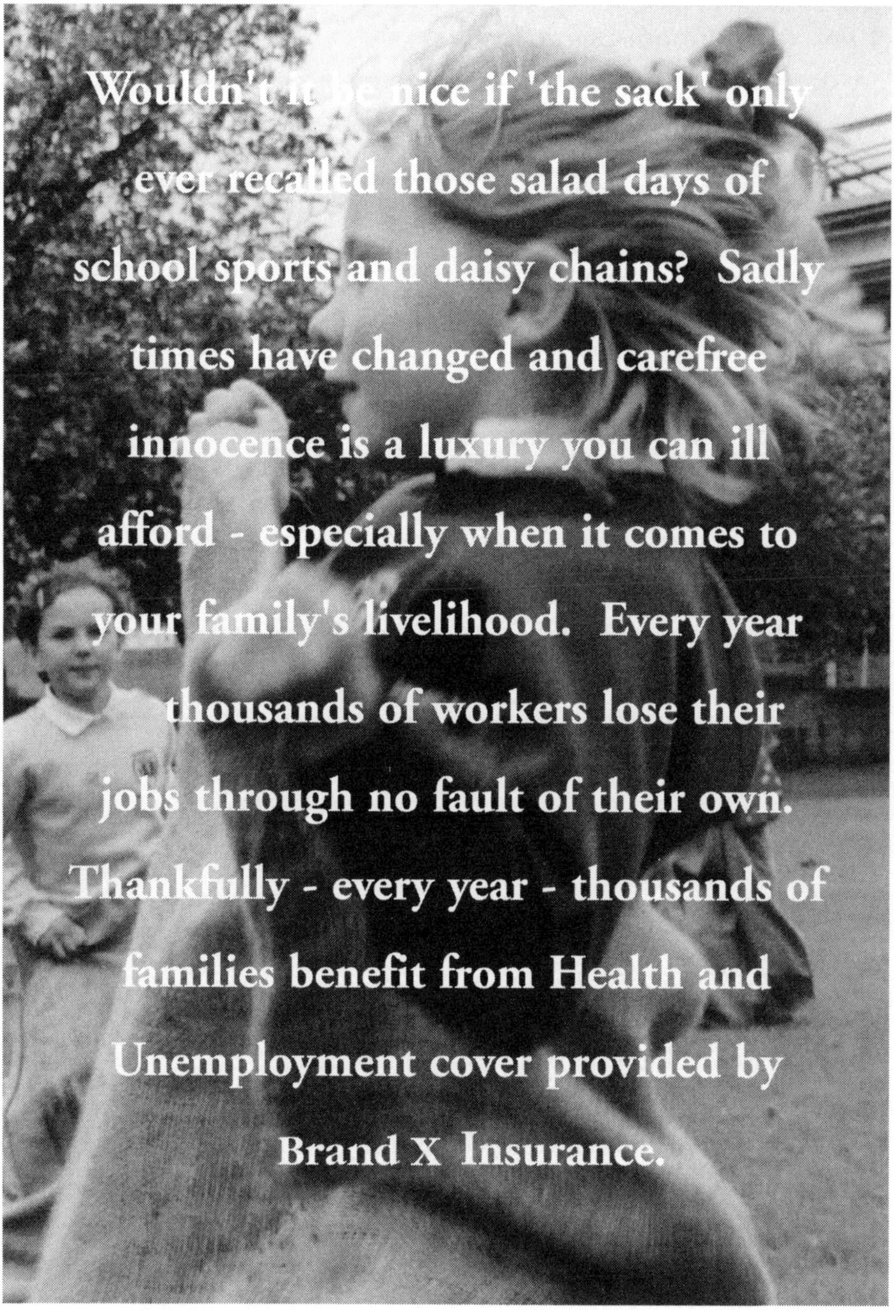

Figure 36 Designeritis: no headline; text used as a graphic device; type reversed out and set over the image. And there really was an ad that looked like this.

A few words about negatives

I've occasionally read that you shouldn't use negative expressions in ads, especially double negatives like this sign I spotted at a well-known fairground:

"If you are not as tall as me you cannot ride on the mini dodgem."

The argument goes that your customer will be confused by a statement containing double negatives. I can certainly buy this. If you're not careful, your headline won't make sense.

David Ogilvy cautioned against straight negatives, such as this one:

"Our salt contains no arsenic."

He said the danger was that the reader misses the negative and comes away with the opposite opinion (i.e. that the salt does contain arsenic).[44] This I find harder to agree with, although it's worth being alert to the possibility.

Steven Pinker is far less prescriptive when it comes to negatives and confusion. For instance, he argues that the well-known line "I can't get no satisfaction" is both perfectly grammatical and unequivocal in its meaning.[45]

John Caples recommends you avoid headlines that paint the gloomy side of the picture.[46] For instance:

"Is worry robbing you of the good things in life?"

His advice is to take the cheerful, positive angle. Intuitively this feels right, and is supported by a generally known phenomenon within the sales promotion industry: that positive rewards get a better response than negative ones. For example, a free box of chocolates should pull more responses than a free first-aid kit of the same perceived value. Claude Hopkins found that positive ads outpulled their negative counterparts by four to one.[47]

James F Engel states that people are less likely to enjoy buying and using what he calls "negative-reinforcement" products, are less receptive to advertising for them, and spend less time and effort in buying them.[48]

However, in the battle for share of the quitting smoker's newly found disposable income, "It needn't be hell with Nicotinell" has been used to good effect for some years. It contains both a negative and the dark side of the story. The brand is the UK's longest-established nicotine patch.

And then there's "I can't believe it's not butter." Double negative, yet immensely successful as a new product. It must be one of the few brands with a name that's actually a headline. And I don't imagine it would have done as well had it been called "I can't believe it's margarine." Perhaps this bears out Ogilvy's view: The word *butter* acts as an embedded command, so the customer subconsciously takes on board the notion that it is butter — or at least that it has buttery qualities.

My advice would be to take note of these authorities, and then to use your common sense. Avoid negatives as a general rule, but don't worry about going with a strong line just because it ain't positive.

WORDING — SEVEN TOP TIPS

1 Find your Mr A.

2 Match with your customer.

3 Think and speak one to one.

4 Adopt a listening mode.

5 Use demotic language.

6 Put conversation before grammar.

7 Remember the sound of words.

KEY QUESTION

"Am I talking my customer's language?"

ON REFLECTION

What's N–E–W?

How about this fact? You're some 28,000 words into a book on marketing communication, and there hasn't been a single reason why your customer should buy. No selling points, no persuasive techniques, no fancy "creative" tricks.

For instance, in the previous section when I talked about ways to make your words work better, I barely made mention of the single most important and effective thing you can do. (Put a benefit in your headline.)

That's because the NEW of NEW AIDA is, by and large, a structural matter. It's to do with the *way* you prioritize and present your message to your customer, rather than *what* it is you say in order to persuade them to choose your product. Think of it like those sensible words (sadly now a cliché) that precede every successful story: Are you sitting comfortably?

So if your reaction to what you've read so far in this book is "That's obvious," then I'm delighted. If you've been nodding your head and thinking it's hardly rocket science, then great. It means you can do it.

John Stapleton, writing about salesmanship and the art of communication, made the observation that "common sense is comparatively rare."[1] Indeed, when you look at some of the inept marketing going on around you, it's tempting to think of the expression "common sense" as a contradiction in terms.

However, this would be a bit unfair to us well-intentioned marketers. I prefer to put it down to a mixture of rush and exuberance. The job is always needed yesterday (so there's rarely time for proper reflection) and it's easy to get carried away with the glamor of marketing communications (and so choose something that looks like a good ad, but actually isn't).

Salesmanship — or NEW AIDA thinking — is a great antidote to this malady. Built in from the start, it makes sure you don't skip those steps that afterwards make it look like you had a temporary common-sense bypass.

It puts you on the spot when the time comes for your customer to meet your marketing.

I've worked in firms where the sales guys, on returning browbeaten to head office, were accused of disloyalty; of always taking the customer's side; of seeing the problem only through the customer's eyes. *Be glad if yours do.*

Whether you're about to create or evaluate, it takes just a few moments to ask yourself the key questions: Will my customer understand what to do or think about? Will it be easy for them? Will they engage with my message? Navigation. Ease. Wording. NEW.

Once your customer is sitting comfortably, the persuasion can begin.

(STEP 4) — ATTENTION

Think location and put customer benefits to the fore

An erstwhile client of mine had been – in a previous job – a buyer for Sainsbury's. Whenever he gave us a brief, just to remind us that he expected results, he used to trot out his customary challenge: "Look, I used to be able to *double* the sales of a product simply by sticking it on a gondola end."

No discounts, no special offers, no dancing girls. All it took was to move the item from its normal position on the fixture to the shelves at the end of the aisle. Sales at 200 percent.

You might argue that sales doubled because shoppers thought there was a special promotion – but I doubt it. Customers are naturally suspicious: You must have noticed how displays of unpriced goods don't sell.

No. It's quite simple. In the supermarket, attention equals location.

Down the years, surveys have consistently reported that over 50 percent of supermarket purchases are *specifically* unplanned.[1] I italicize the word specifically, because what this means is that shoppers let the products in-store prompt them as to what they need and what they would like. (Does this sound familiar?)

When I worked at Cadbury, we used to reckon that over 70 percent of all purchases of countlines (bars like Crunchie and Flake and Twirl) were *entirely* unplanned. In an impulse market like this, location is paramount. That's why the confectionery guys pump such massive resources into display materials.

In the late 1970s the feminine protection market was transformed almost single-handedly by a chap called Ted Connor. A former Co-op buyer, Ted moved to Kimberly-Clark where he took control of merchandising. In those days most stores grudgingly stocked "fempro" in a straggling run stretching for yards along a bottom shelf. Sales were sluggish. (As a salesman I can remember *dusting* our packs.) Ted's retailing instincts led him to pioneer the "blocked-fixture" theory, whereby products were displayed in a vertical block from top shelf to floor. It meant that you could comfortably preview the whole market from one spot, and that a greater number of packs were merchandised at eye level. Typically a switch from run to block led to a sales increase for the store of between 50 and 100 percent. Retailer after retailer adopted the policy, and indeed it spread to many other product categories. Today it is the standard method of merchandising.

Yet there is still much undone. Paco Underhill writes at length about watching the young, the small, the infirm, and the overweight as they stretch and bend and puff and groan in vain attempts to reach products targeted specifically at them.[2] One of Ted Connor's maxims was "Never place any of our products above 5'2" on the shelf" (the average female's eye level). Actually the hot-spot is a good 18 inches lower.

As every retailer knows, there is a direct, proportional relationship between site and sales. The more people bump into a product, the more buy it. I repeat: In the supermarket attention equals location.

Attention second

So putting attention first — as a task, in isolation — is naive, to say the least. Attention is inextricably related to the sales environment. And that environment can range from an office to an off-license, and from a sofa to a subway.

As a salesman it always felt rather uncomfortable and paradoxical when I did a sales call knowing I was supposed to start with attention. There I was, *in* the buyer's office, *with* the buyer. What next? Clap my hands? Stand on my head? (Surely I'd already got his attention?)

In old AIDA, attention is treated as a matter of impact achieved via design. Valuable advertising space gets eaten up by "Hey!" or "Boo!" or "Look!" or a nude or a celeb or a flying hamster or a talking camel. There is a formulaic approach, blinkered and obsessed, that pays little regard to the sales environment and the customers who inhabit it.

Profitable attention

In this regard I'm intrigued by vendors of *The Big Issue*, a street newspaper published on behalf of and sold by homeless people. Last year I wrote a cover ad for *The Big Issue*, for a Unilever tea brand, and I got to know a bit more about the publication as a result. Evidently there are a disproportionate number of buyers among younger women and older women.

However, this doesn't stop me (and, as far as I can see, every other passer-by) being assailed for £1. Often several times a day. Often by the same person.

I wish I could buy *The Big Issue*. It's hard not to feel guilty when you swing out of Starbuck's having spent £2 on a coffee you didn't need, and there's some guy in the rain trying his best to earn an honest living. But the trouble is, I don't really want the newspaper.

I want *Private Eye*, or *GQ*, or *Trail* — something I actually read. I'd happily pay an extra £1 for the convenience and feelgood factor. In fact, I don't know why *The Big Issue* sellers don't have a monthly guest publication — I'm sure magazine publishers would provide them free as a sampling exercise.

But I digress. Back to attention. In relation to *The Big Issue*, mine is random, irrelevant — indeed unprofitable. The vendor's marketing efforts are wasted on me.

Next time somebody hands you a flyer in the High Street, take a close (but suitably surreptitious) look in the first litterbin you pass. Odds on it will be crammed with copies of the same leaflet. I can't help thinking that a second message displayed at this point would be very effective.

Yet despite a skewed readership, *The Big Issue* vendors don't seem all that bothered about profitable attention. I suppose they've got time to spare and little to lose. And of course, they have one telling advantage over other forms of marketing communications: pressure selling — and sometimes the customer just gives in.

You can't use pressure selling when you're sitting at a desk in Hammersmith and your customer's watching your ad or reading your mailing in his lounge in Hinckley. You can't convert random, irrelevant attention into a sale. Your marketing will be binned before you've had the

Figure 37 The Big Issue *vendor. Gains random attention but has the advantage of pressure selling. Reproduced by kind permission of* The Big Issue.

chance metaphorically to draw breath.

This admission is really important: Profitable attention is that extended to you by an *interested* customer. And it's something I'll talk more about in the next chapter on interest. Here, it's a salutary reminder that the kind of attention you seek does not always come automatically: Location has its limits, and a few examples follow.

Habitual shopping

We carried out a number of large-scale observational studies at Blue-Chip to measure the impact of on-pack messages in a store environment. In one such exercise, looking at paper products, we discovered that the national equivalent of 6.8 million householders enter the paper aisle, pick up a pack of *own-label* bathroom tissue, and then leave the aisle without looking at a single other product. If you're a brand, aiming to convert own-label buyers, what does that tell you about location? (It says that the best place for a trial-generating offer is not on your packs.)

This result, by the way, is something I have seen repeated across a number of product categories. Many of the items that most supermarket shoppers buy seem to be selected out of habit. It would be one long trip otherwise.

Location on the web

If ever there were a place where the real-estate maxim "location, location, location" applied, it's on the internet. This becomes clear when you consider that over 90 percent of people use the major search engines.[3] (In fact, currently Google is reported as accounting for 60 percent of all searches.[4]) Your competitive advantage could lie simply in finding the most popular words that searching surfers use — especially those your competitors would want to lead surfers to their sites.

How do you do this? Research among your customers, lots of trial and error, plenty of testing (and keep testing) — until you find effective keywords. Some might be obvious, others might surprise you. (Think *Family Fortunes*.) Only the other day I watched my seven-year-old daughter type the following into Google: "pitcher of doiney osmand." The corollary? Register common misspellings, too.

Another key location factor is of course your url. That's uniform resource locator, by the way. I don't know why they can't say web address. And while I'm at it, who came up with double-yew double-yew double-yew dot? Ten syllables to confound the listener before they even get started on your name. Most brand names have one or two syllables. Ho, hum... whatever. Despite these in-built handicaps, you need to get your web address in your customer's face. And then into either their mind or, more reliably, their hand. Preferably on a piece of paper that they'll keep long enough to remember to visit your site.

This process involves a mini "sale" in its own right. Treat the sale of a visit to your website as seriously as you would any other direct-response activity. The most frequent observation I make is that lip service is paid to the communication of a firm's web address.

It seems naive beyond belief that 30-second television ads feature the web address as a tiny line of subtext in the endframe. (Compare this to the omnipresence of the web address that I described for DRTV ads in Step 2.) Is the advertiser just trying to tell us: "I've got a website, I'm cool"?

I have to say I admire the car manufacturers who enable digital TV viewers to select a brochure-request option during the ad. If only the contractor's technology lived up to the advertiser's vision. But it's one to watch.

Figure 38 *Advertising that takes the "sale" of the web address seriously. Reproduced by kind permission of elephant.co.uk.*

even cheaper car insurance!

save £££s on your insurance now, with the first Internet only car insurer...

it's easy, it's fast, it's...

elephant.co.uk
part of the Admiral Group

Sofa vs subway

A few pages earlier I used the expression "from sofa to subway." (And by subway I mean the tube, the underground.) These are two contrasting sales environments where your customer might meet your marketing.

Think of the subway. It's marketing heaven! In sight of your customer there'll be just three or four poster ads; maybe a cast-off *Evening Standard* or *Metro* newspaper they can salvage if they're lucky. Usually they've got nothing to read (85 percent of tube passengers don't carry reading material, while the average journey lasts 20 minutes, 13 of which are in the carriage[5]). Starved of stimulation, they're trapped until they reach their stop, surrounded by strangers they're reluctant even to make eye contact with.

On the subway, the location factors are firmly in your favor. Indeed, your marketing communication should come as a positive relief to your customer. It's a real opportunity to deliver a detailed and persuasive message.

Sofa-man, however, provides an altogether different challenge. Just think of the competition for his attention:

☆ Perhaps a choice of over 300 digital TV channels.
☆ Cluttering the coffee table, a backlog of magazines and newspapers (each potentially boasting 350 news headlines, 21 feature articles, and 85-odd ads[6]).

Fancy a corporate bond fund that's as good value as Sainsbury's, solid as the high street banks and trustworthy as the Government?

Good, solid organisations, all of them. And they're not alone. The M&G Corporate Bond Fund holds bonds issued by 110 establishments such as high street banks, newspapers and utilities. The kind of companies, in fact, that you could take home to meet your mother.

And just to make doubly sure, we've backed the fund up with a few gilts – bonds issued by Her Majesty's Treasury.

Better returns than the building society, safer than the stockmarket.

So if you're looking for an investment that minimises risk to your capital – this could very well fit the bill. In fact, 'Investors' Week'

> **5·2% Annual Gross Redemption Yield.**
> **5·7% Annual Gross Distribution Yield.**
>
> These figures are correct as at 22/07/02. Yields may vary and the level of income it provides is not fixed and may fluctuate. For the latest yield please call 0800 072 6154. The M&G Corporate Bond Fund aims to achieve higher returns than you'd normally expect from gilts (Government securities) by primarily investing in sterling corporate bonds issued by companies that the independent credit rating companies have rated very highly.

actually called it one of the safest corporate bond funds'.

Which is really saying something, because bonds in general are regarded as a pretty safe investment and are traditionally less volatile than equities. (Of course, if you're looking for total security, salt it away in the building society.)

The real difference they have over equities is that a bond is technically a loan.

We take no initial charge so you start earning from day one and the diminishing withdrawal fee disappears completely after five years.

One of the most tax-efficient ISAs.

Bonds are one of the most tax-efficient ISA investments you can make. Not only are all profits tax-free, but you also benefit from a tax reclaim of 20% on interest distributions (under current tax regulations, although this could change).

To find out more about our Corporate Bond Fund and for your free copy of our Guide to Investing call **0800 072 6154** quoting reference XXX. Lines are open 8am to 8pm, seven days a week; for

> *Okay, forget we mentioned the Government.*
>
> We're not talking politics here. What we mean is our Corporate Bond Fund invests a proportion of your money in bonds issued by Her Majesty's Treasury, which (this being a stable, G8 country), provides a pretty solid silver lining to any cloud that may heave itself over the horizon.

your protection calls may be recorded. If you prefer, you could return the coupon below, visit www.mandg.co.uk or speak to your financial adviser.

Please send me a copy of your Guide to Investing and information about the M&G Corporate Bond Fund.

Name:

Address:

Postcode:

Email:

Tel. No:

Are you an existing M&G customer? Yes ☐ ref. XXXX
No ☐ ref. XXXX

Please return to: The M&G Group, FREEPOST 9131 (There, you're 27p better off already), Chelmsford. CM1 1FB.

M&G may use your information for marketing purposes and we may disclose your information to our service providers and other members of the Prudential Group. The accuracy of this information will be maintained at all times. If you do not wish to be included in our marketing programme, please tick the appropriate boxes. By post ☐ by telephone ☐ by email ☐ You have the right to apply for a copy of the information we may hold about you.

M&G
INVESTMENTS

Reference to 'one of the safest corporate bond funds'. Source: Investors' Week. Reference to M&G Corporate Bond Fund yields'. Source: M&G Statistics as at 22/07/02. Issued by M&G Securities Limited and M&G Financial Services Limited. Both companies are regulated by the Financial Services Authority and together form the M&G Marketing Group which provides PEPs, ISAs and other Investments.

Figure 39 *Although this example was taken from a consumer finance magazine, it's also exactly the type of long-copy ad the average subway commuter is crying out for. Reproduced by kind permission of M&G Financial Services Ltd.*

☆ Social interaction — in one recent study accounting for half of the time spent by "viewers" during ad breaks.[7]

☆ Freedom to roam about the house — when I asked my daughter (the doiney osmand fan) what was the best thing about television ads, she said they're really good when there's a movie on and you're desperate for the loo.

The "permission" school of marketing would have you waving the white flag when it comes to gaining the attention of sofa-man. But for a good salesman, that's exactly the time to fight on. You just fight smarter.

Benefits: Let the selling begin

Five times as many people read the headlines of advertisements as read the body copy.

This well-known "fact" must be the king of communication clichés. I've seen it in articles on "how to write better ads" more times than I've had hot dinners. The argument goes that if you don't attract your customer with your headline, not even Shakespeare could have written you some body copy that would rescue the sale.

I think this is a bit of a red herring. As far as I can establish, it was David Ogilvy who first put forward the idea, over 40 years ago. He cited his source as the Starch Readership Service.[8]

Actually, I don't have any problem with the figure. For some ads it's probably many times greater than five. But why would anybody in marketing be surprised by this?

The standard argument continues that you must use your headline for all it's worth, else your ad will be wasted on 80 percent of your customers.

The *News of the World* has around 10 million readers. Does that mean if you buy a double-page ad that everyone must pass by, only two million of them will pause to read the body copy? (Is that bad?)

Maybe the 80 percent who won't read the body copy don't want your product? Surely the whole thing about using mass media like the press,

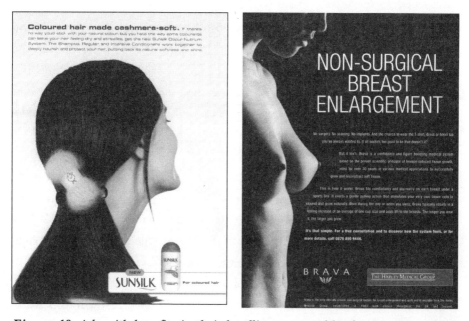

Figure 40 *Ads with benefits in their headlines are read by four times as many people as those without. Reproduced by kind permission of Lever Fabergé Ltd/JWT Paris and The Harley Medical Group.*

direct mail, or even the newsagent's window is that lots of people *not* in your target audience are exposed to your ads?

Flick through a newspaper and what do you see? Lots of headlines. It's almost impossible *not* to read them. Body copy you can take or leave.

OK, I'm playing devil's advocate. But I'm warning of the danger of getting sidetracked by a separate phenomenon. Targeting and random attention are not the same as what makes your customer think about buying.

Five times as many people might read headlines as body copy, but I think a more apposite description is that five times as many people *bump into* headlines as they do body copy. With that thought in mind, consider this ostensibly similar, but actually far more profound finding:

"Ads with *benefits* in their headlines are read by four times as many people as ads with no benefits in their headlines."[9]

Think about it. Why would anybody who has read the headline of an ad then go on to read the body copy? Answer: They must be interested in the product or service.

And it must have been the headline that made the difference. More specifically, the *benefit* in the headline. For profitable attention, you need a benefit.

True lies

A further warning. Take a look at the disguised ad shown in Figure 41. This was a full-page, full-color ad, placed in a popular weekly marketing magazine to which I subscribe. These are more or less the original words, with the company name changed to "Tupidus."

My first reaction was: "Welcome to Platitude City." And if you think back to what I said about platitudes in the last chapter (they bore your customer into not buying), this is a risky strategy.

And because there's no *true* benefit in the headline (or even anywhere else in the abbreviated copy), I haven't got the faintest idea what this ad is for.

I've never heard of the firm, so I don't know what they do. The real company name (as vague as Tupidus) didn't help one jot.

So what next?

Phone, or get on the net, to find out what business the company is in? Just on the off chance that it might be a service that's relevant to me or my clients? But I'm watching the late-night soccer show, which is when I usually manage to wade through all my trade magazines.

True benefits

What this ad demonstrates is the fine line between communication success and disaster. I'm sure that the person who wrote it did so with the best intentions: "I'll pack it with so many benefits that it's irresistible to my customer."

Flexibility, freedom, peace of mind, security. Trouble is, they're not benefits. They're general, abstract concepts that don't register with the reader until they're attached to specific, tangible facts.

FLEXIBILITY THAT SETS YOUR BUSINESS FREE

We take care of business today
helping you to take care of tomorrow

For further information on how to set
yourself free call 123 4567, email
sales@tupidus.co.uk or visit
www.tupidus.co.uk

TUPIDUS
Less con, more fusion

Figure 41 *The danger of mistaking platitudes for benefits. A disguised ad using the original text. Notice that unless you've heard of the company, the words give absolutely no indication of what service it provides.*

Imagine Tupidus is your firm. Say you sell telephone switchboards to small firms. Here's some copy that surely should work a bit harder:

> "The Tupidus Flexi-Exchange comes with 10 handsets as standard. It has built-in capacity to accommodate up to 100 lines with no software upgrade and no added cost. For Tupidus read *peace of mind* — you'll know you've invested in a system that will grow with your business."

The clichés-cum-platitudes are converted into meaningful benefits for your customer. From here it's not difficult to think how you might develop some ideas for an effective headline:

> **The telephone exchange that's as good as new**
> **when you're 10 times bigger than today**

And if you pop your navigation hat on, you'll note that a headline like this immediately signals to your customer what you want them to think about: telephone exchanges. (I was pleased to see that, a few months after the first "Tupidus" ad, a revised version appeared in the press that did indeed explain what service the company offered. I imagine it noticed the lack of response generated by the original ad.)

John Caples cited a modest yet typically authoritative example in this regard.[10] A maker of a hay fever remedy got a good response with a small ad headlined simply "Hay Fever." Navigation at its most basic.

But in a split-run test, "Hay Fever" pulled 297 sample requests, while the headline "Dry Up Hay Fever" achieved a 28 percent increase, pulling 380 sample requests. The simple addition of two words transformed a competent flag into a direct and persuasive promise of a benefit.

Effective headlines

In the mid-1920s, not long after Strong had apparently devised AIDA, Caples proved statistically that *self-interest* was the single most important requirement for an effective headline. After that he listed, in order, news, curiosity, and quick, easy way.

Many handbooks on advertising, copywriting, and direct marketing are packed with long lists, such as "headlines that sell." I'm looking at one now: "57 direct marketing offers." With so many alternatives, books like this become impossible to use. Just where do you begin?

For me, it all comes back to benefits (which I think is pretty much the same as self-interest). Analyze headlines that work, and usually they promise a benefit for the customer.

And it stands to reason that if you can make your benefit newsworthy as well as quick and easy, it will be all the more attention-getting and persuasive. Think about a real customer and what your product or service does for them. Be as tangible and specific as you can.

Testing

There just isn't enough testing. So much marketing is done from the "bunker," you have to be there to believe it. Billions of pounds worth of communications are fired off in hope and often nobody looks to see where they landed.

The military (whose budgets compare to those of the marketing community) have whole areas of the country set aside for testing. Not a bullet is fired without somebody checking to see where it finished up and what impact it had on its target.

You might ask why a book about effective marketing communications is raising the subject of testing. Surely the idea is to use the book and you'll get it right first time? True (I hope) — but I don't think the two sentiments are incompatible. After all, without testing in the first place, nobody would know what works and what doesn't.

More intriguingly, what Caples went on to demonstrate was that even the so-called experts can't always tell which headline will work best. He prescribed that once you have developed some "good" headlines, you'll actually need to test to find which will be most effective. And you need to keep testing to make sure the winner keeps working.

Here's an example, two versions of an ad designed to generate applications for a free book, *The New Way to Grow Hair*.[11] Which of these propositions do you think was the most effective?

A *Illustration*: Man (with hair) pointing his finger at another's bald head.
Headline: "60 days ago they called *me* Baldy"
Copy plot: Story of man who got excellent results from hair-growing remedy.

B *Illustration*: Hair specialist offering a blank check to the reader.
Headline: "If I can't grow hair for you in 30 days you get this check"
Copy plot: You get your money refunded if you are not satisfied with the results.

And the winner is...? The answer was in fact proposition A. This is interesting, since both headlines promise benefits, and B even offers a refund. (You wouldn't be alone if you found it hard to judge this — both were considered good enough by the advertiser to be worthy of testing.)

Why did advertisement A succeed? There are several suggestions. Perhaps proposition B implied the remedy might fail? Maybe the picture and the word *baldy* in version A did a better job of navigation?

Of course, with hindsight it's easy to come up with reasons like this, but less so beforehand. While from a copywriter's perspective I find the idea of testing mildly irritating (aren't I paid to know best?), it's hard to argue with its value. The fact is there's no reason why any given proposition can't be bettered. As an old marketing boss of mine used to say, rather cryptically, there are more ways than one of skinning a cat.

Claude Hopkins, who became fabulously rich through his copywriting skills, said:

"The wisest, most experienced man cannot tell what will most appeal in any line of copy."[12]

If you work for a large firm, the chances are you have the resources and systems in place to test your marketing communications. If your business involves direct marketing, no doubt you will be testing as a matter of course. What always surprises me, though, is the number of major companies that conduct very little testing — perhaps because much of their output does not ask for a direct response from the customer.

This is not good logic. Starch concluded (and I paraphrase) that ads that pull best sell best.[13] In fact, I think that's worth highlighting, in case you're scanning:

Starch concluded that ads that pull best sell best.

So if you want to get a feel for whether or not your ads are selling, why not see if you can get them to pull? This is quite simple in practice. If you're running a press campaign, design an A/B split[14] and within the body copy of each version "bury" an identical offer of perhaps a free recipe booklet or coupon or whatever is appropriate. (But make sure you can tell which ad your replies come from.)

If you get a *significant* variation in response between your two propositions, that suggests one ad has a higher readership than the other. Which means it's doing a better job of getting your customer's attention. (And I use the word *proposition* rather than headline here, to indicate that the overall "appeal" may comprise imagery, headline, and copy.)

But what if you work for a small firm? Is testing beyond your means? Far from it.

As the faxback vs mailback case study demonstrated, invaluable testing can be done on a small scale — in fact, it's often easier. The main thing to remember is to test only one variable at a time. Otherwise you won't know what has made the difference.

At a less scientific (but no less valuable) level, there's not enough common-sense asking and watching going on. Many of the anecdotes I've related in this book are simply the result of acting the guardian salesman. But how many brand managers spend even an hour a week loitering in supermarkets and watching their customers in action? Who ever flyposts their ad in the tube and rides to and fro watching fellow commuters' reactions? I loved the fake poster campaign aimed at anglers, for "magic worms" that were guaranteed to catch fish — apparently there were thousands of inquiries. (The idea was to prove that poster ads get noticed. I'd put it in a slightly different way: True benefits get noticed.)

Attention equals *serendipity*

So two main levers work together to gain attention. The first, location, mainly concerns *random* attention. The second, the benefit, moves up a gear to *profitable* attention — which is where the selling really begins.

Yet a remarkable number of ads don't even contain a clear benefit in their headlines. I recently made a painstaking survey of 1,028 ads (from 28 magazines) and an astonishing 71 percent offered no benefit.

It's all the more surprising when you consider that, according to research by Roper Starch Worldwide, half of the readers of women's magazines claim not to notice the average packaged-goods ad[15] (a phenomenon that I prefer to blame on the ads, not the readers).

Nevertheless, while your customer may claim to be oblivious to the wall of marketing white noise that assails them, they have a little radar secretly monitoring inbound messages. (Call out their name and you'll see.)

And although they may insist that they aren't influenced by television ads, or that they never read direct mail, I bet they'll still be able to talk knowledgeably about products they've never used, and will grudgingly admit that they're among the 72 percent who've ever responded to direct marketing.[16]

The fact is, we are all *accepting* of the marketing radiation that envelops us, and we tune in to it from time to time when we get a bleep from our radars.

In more academic terms, James F Engel puts it like this:

"Attention can be defined as the allocation of processing capacity to the incoming stimulus. Because that capacity is a limited resource, consumers are very selective in how they allocate their attention.

The reality of selective attention means that, while some stimuli will receive attention, others will be ignored. The marketer's job is to achieve the former."[17]

And that's why ads with benefits in their headlines are read by four times as many people as "non-benefit" ads. Location first puts your benefit in your customer's path. Then, as your customer meets your marketing, the benefit creates a fleeting moment of "stickiness" — for the customer a moment of serendipity. ("Oh! Just what I need.") They engage with your marketing just long enough for you to nip in and deal with navigation and ease. (Using, of course, wording that speaks their language.)

Profitable attention is created not by a nude or a loud noise, but — as every good salesperson knows — by a benefit.

Steps you can take

10 ways to improve your location

Clearly you should strive to get the most favorable location for your message. Even if your marketing communication is a card in the local newsagent's window, you want it to be at eye level, just above the door handle. Why settle for less?

You want your leaflet dispenser next to the till. You want your door-drop alone on the mat. You want your press ad on the back cover of a magazine.

Starch found that an ad on the back cover of a magazine attracts 65 percent more readers than a middle-section position. The inside covers perform 30 percent better. But studies have found only minor differences between left- and right-hand pages, and front, middle, and end locations in the body of a publication.[18]

Research has shown there are numerous tactics you can employ to enhance your location dynamics. While these have a random effect (i.e. they are non-selective in terms of whom they attract), their purpose is obviously to increase the absolute number of "relevant" customers who meet your marketing.

10 ways to improve your location

1   Size
2   Color
3   Intensity
4   Contrast
5   Directionality
6   Movement
7   Isolation
8   Novelty
9   Celebrity
10 Conditioning

Size

Larger ads attract more attention.[19] So do larger images within individual ads.[20] Equally, more shelf space in-store means more attention.[21]

Starch found the relationship between ad size and readership to be directly proportional, but not linear. So if a half-page ad is read by 20 percent of readers of the publication, doubling it to a full-page size will attract a further 20 percent of the remaining 80 percent.[22]

Color

The ability of a stimulus to attract attention can be sharply increased through the use of color.[23] In a study of black-and-white newspaper ads, the addition of just one color produced 41 percent more sales.[24]

Direct marketers have long known that color can influence response. Drayton Bird cites a 20 percent uplift achieved by changing the color of an envelope, and a 50 percent uplift by changing the background color of a mailing (although in this case it was thought to make the text easier to read). Equally, though, he cautions that in four cases out of five, the increased response that full color delivered did not offset the higher costs.[25]

Starch reported 85 percent greater readership for half-page color ads (compared to their black-and-white counterparts) and a figure of +50

Figure **42** *Starch found that ads with a large single image and a dominant focal center were more successful in attracting readers, as demonstrated by this ad reproduced by kind permission of* TIME *magazine, created by Fallon Worldwide. It also unerringly exploits the ancient principle known as the Golden Section or Mean, in which the graphic focus is located at a mathematically calculated point to where the eye is naturally and irresistibly drawn. (See the later discussion of isolation.)*

percent for full- and double-page ads. He found that color ads generated 45 percent more inquiries.[26]

If color *in general* works better, then what about specific colors? Physicists and biologists tell us we see red first, and this is also the received wisdom in direct marketing circles. George Smith reckons that for envelopes, red outpulls yellow, which outpulls gold, which outpulls black, which outpulls full color.[27] Next time you fly over the suburbs of a city, notice how the red cars stand out. Or flick through *Yellow Pages* for the same effect. If you want to attract your customer's eye to a certain point, red seems to help. (It can be as simple as a red underline.) But beware red overkill.

Intensity

This basically means that loud sounds and bright colors attract attention. But I believe it also applies to message content. Ex-P&G man Charles Decker notes that most Procter & Gamble television ads open with a robust "Hey, you!"[28] He characterizes the opening of a commercial break as a battle for attention between the ad, the other channels, and the bathroom. By "jump-starting" the ad, the aim is to engage the viewer immediately. On a reverse note, I often suffer the frustration of daydreaming through an ad (particularly on radio) that I have wanted to hear for professional reasons, but find I have consciously tuned in only at the very end when the brand name is mentioned.

Contrast

We're taught for fun at an early age to pick the "odd one out" (if, indeed, it's not an inherent hunter-gatherer trait designed to help us spot ripening fruits before some other creature nabs them) and tests have shown that people pay more attention to stimuli that contrast with their background.[29] Contrast is a particular speciality of the sales promotion agency. While designers strive for visual harmony, the SP guys will create a promotional flash with the sole aim of violating your packaging. In a typical supermarket, hundreds of thousands of facings clamor for the attention of your

Figure 43 A good on-pack offer gets noticed by disrupting the usually harmonious design of the packaging. This dominant flash can be removed ("easy-peel") if the product is intended as a gift. Reproduced by kind permission of Kraft Europe.

customer. If your on-pack offer doesn't stand out from the crowd, you need to ask why.

In the design of press ads, Starch made a fascinating discovery that, for me, falls under this subheading of "contrast." Quarter-page ads designed as a single column (i.e. a strip down one margin) attract 29 percent more readers than traditional quarter-grid-shaped ads. His conclusion was that the browsing reader's eye sweeps across the top of each page, and so is more likely to cross an ad that has a footprint covering the entire height of the page.[30]

Directionality

The eye tends to follow visual cues such as arrows, fingers pointing, or a person's glance or demeanor.[31] I think the most important tip here is not to signpost somebody "out" of your ad. Bill Cather, an NLP practitioner, believes that ads are more effective at gaining and holding attention if the directional image (e.g. a side-on photo of a face) is placed on the left of the space, looking to the right.[32] This stems from the NLP theory that the layout I have described conveys an underlying sense (a "metaprogram") of "moving toward," a positive energy of achievement, of looking to the future.

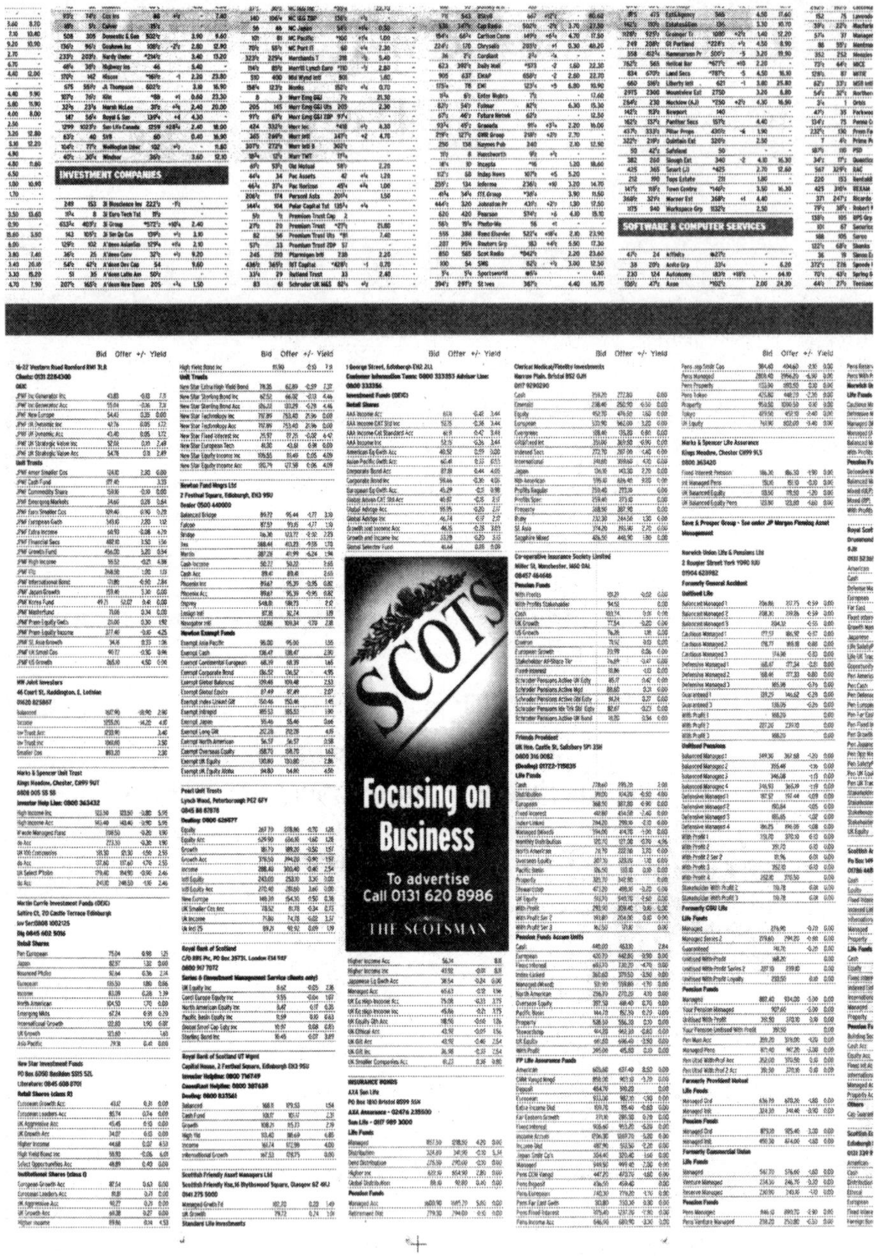

Figure 44 Small ad, big contrast. Against a controlled, mainly white background, this reversed-out ad by The Scotsman *achieves a striking effect. Reproduced by kind permission of The Scotsman Publications Ltd.*

Figure 45 NLP teaches that right-facing images convey a more positive message. Reproduced by kind permission of Clarks.

Take a look at your brand or company logo. Are you "moving toward" or "moving away"? Cather even suggests that when you present to a group you should stand on the left of the flipchart (as the audience sees you) to communicate moving toward. Once you're convinced by this theory, it's hard to believe anybody would set an image facing in a contrary direction to the text in an ad. It rather reminds me of the watchmakers' protocol always to show the hands in a "smiling face," ten-to-two position.

Movement

Now literally to movement. As an ornithologist, the one thing I know that birds notice above all others is movement. You can wear an Arsenal strip and bright yellow wellingtons, but stand perfectly still and they'll ignore you. Twitch, and they're off. Observing from a car, you can wriggle about as much as you like — but break the "horizon," and it's bye-bye birdie. The same rules apply pretty much to fishing and hunting.

Given that it's recently been declared we share 90 percent of our genes with the humble mouse, I think it's fair to assume the "movement rule" applies to us humans too (i.e. if it moves, better look quick in case it's coming to eat you — or maybe you can eat it). It's a reflex that is almost impossible to resist — although, curiously, it has been largely resisted by the marketing industry, which remains in the stone age as regards what is probably the most powerful attention-getter going. (In one Californian retail study the use of movement in display generated nearly three times the sales of static display in food stores and nearly twice the sales in liquor stores.[33])

Isolation

This is the lateral thinker's approach to standing out from the crowd. You remove the crowd. A simple example is where you pay for a full-page ad, even though you could communicate your message perfectly well in half or a quarter of the space. In fact, I think the technique is probably most valuable where you can only afford a half- or quarter-page ad (or smaller). By building plenty of space around your message, you enable it to stand out amid the melee.

Figure 46 One way of standing out from the crowd is to remove the crowd. An
effective technique that is much underused in smaller-sized press ads.
Reproduced by kind permission of British Airways plc.

Clearly linked to this phenomenon is what Starch described as "the one most important characteristic of an ad in stopping readers." And that characteristic is a *dominant focal center*.[34] Give your customer's eye and brain an obvious starting point, so their mind can relax into the flow of your message.

Artists and photographers often place a point of focus in the "north-east" quadrant (i.e. the top-right section) as you look at a picture. This is based on the concept of the Golden Section or Mean, which you may remember from the *TIME* ad in Figure 42. It has been known at least since the time of Euclid (3rd century BC) and may be discovered in most works of art.[35]

To find the Golden Section in your ad, simply draw a horizontal line across at a height of 61.8 percent up the page, and then a vertical line down at a distance of 61.8 percent across the page. The lines intersect at the point of natural visual focus.

Novelty

Wear a red nose and walk down the High Street and, most times of year, people will stare at you. Anything unexpected is capable of gaining and holding attention. Once more, this seems to be a part of human nature: The unusual can induce curiosity.

Celebrity

The old chestnut. Do celebrities get attention? No question. Are they a good idea? Sometimes. (But probably mainly not.)

I'll talk a bit more about the potential role of celebrities in Step 6, Desire. As far as attention is concerned there's an obvious risk: The celebrity takes the limelight while your product withers in the shadows. This is a common occurrence.

In 1997, as part of a campaign for a brand of Scottish lager (surely a contradiction in terms?), we enlisted the help of former British Lions captain Gavin Hastings and quicksilver Rangers and Scotland striker Ally McCoist. They were dropped by helicopter at major Scottish superstores, where they made pre-advertised guest appearances. While they drew the crowds and toiled admirably as brand ambassadors, it was soon apparent that their stardust was not rubbing off onto the cans of beer.

Nevertheless, the activity was successful for another reason. The trade — and by this I mean the managers and staff of superstores chosen for visits — *were* starstruck, ordered extraordinary quantities of stock at the expense of competitive brands, and built gigantic off-shelf displays that remained in place for weeks afterwards. (At this point you should be thinking *attention equals location*.)

A further pitfall is that your carefully chosen star can get in the press for the wrong reasons (and not necessarily of their own making). In December 2003 alone, brands as illustrious as Bacardi, Nike, and Sony found themselves having to review major campaigns and sponsorship deals due to adverse publicity surrounding their celebrity endorsers.

Conditioning

Conditioning is a proven phenomenon. We get trained to respond by reflex to sounds, smells, sights, and other stimuli.

You must have noticed your own reaction to a ringing telephone in the background of a television drama or movie, or even during a radio interview. It's very distracting. Yet like movement, sound is underexploited as an attention-getting marketing tool — particularly in the retail environment.

One notable exception, where retailers do attempt to exploit conditioning aurally, is in the relentless playing of pop carols in the ever-lengthening run-up to Christmas. The theory goes that by awakening warm feelings in their customers, sales resistance will be overcome and shoppers will jostle all the harder for those must-have gifts.

Conditioning and sex appeal

By all means consider the techniques listed above. Indeed, you could try the challenge of using all 10 of them in a single communication. What you must guard against, though, is "a stimulus that dominates viewers' attention, while leaving the remaining message ignored."[36]

Figure 47 *Classical conditioning is commonplace in fashions and fragrances: products which can justifiably use sexual imagery in their appeals. Reproduced by kind permission of Jones Bootmaker.*

Marketers' efforts to capitalize on conditioning often take the form of sexual imagery. While this can be perfectly justified for some products, it's probably the most overused and abused shortcut to irrelevant attention in the communications business.

It's one thing to attract the random attention of a passer-by to whom you were never going to sell in the first place, but quite another to waste the profitable attention of a potential customer. It has been proved beyond all reasonable doubt that benefits are the key to effective marketing communications. If you block the route to the benefit, or at least divert your customer's mind elsewhere, your ad may be self-defeating.

"Safe Sex Dangerous Cheese." As you may recall, this was a campaign theme for Seriously Strong Cheddar. The Häagen-Dazs-like ads showed various couples cavorting and kissing. But in December 2002 the marketing press reported its replacement by a new campaign with "all-round family appeal" (a quote from the firm's joint managing director).[37]

It's food for thought. Compare the early sexually charged Häagen-Dazs ads and their cheesy lookalikes. While both grasp your mind in a similarly striking fashion, the marketer should question where they lead. For Häagen-Dazs, the imagery was perfectly consistent with an aspired-to consumption occasion (bit of a mouthful, sorry), and arguably was also an understandable metaphor for the pleasurable experience of eating luxury ice-cream. So for Häagen-Dazs it makes sense. For Seriously Strong Cheddar... well, there's a tenuous after-dinner connection, but it's much harder to see how this campaign exploited conditioning. Thus the drawback of the gratuitous use of sex appeal is that the communication stops dead in its tracks.

Seven ways to stimulate profitable attention
1 Something good gained or received.
2 Use the picture to enhance the story.
3 Consider curiosity.
4 Make your ad newsworthy.
5 Quick and easy.
6 Sensory language.
7 Combat adaptation.

Something good gained or received

This subheading is *Chambers'* primary definition of the word "benefit." Next comes "advantage." Caples, as I mentioned earlier, preferred the term "self-interest." Semantics aside, a clearly stated benefit will have two related practical effects:

☆ It will connect with customers for whom your product or service is relevant.

☆ It will increase (by 400 percent) customer involvement in your marketing communication.

So how do you make sure that what you're proposing is a benefit? First, you might try this. Take a copy of a magazine that's well padded with ads, thumb through it, and write out the headlines.

With ease in mind, here's a selection from a recent edition of *Stuff* magazine:

☆ Picture perfect
☆ Talks a good picture
☆ Work smart, live smart
☆ Gimme
☆ Personal stuff
☆ Perfect compatibility
☆ Hot sound
☆ Upgrade your life

What do you think about these headlines? Spot any of Caples' magic ingredients? (Self-interest, news, curiosity, quick and easy.) Or are they just an assortment of clichés, hyperbole, and platitudes?

Put simply, a headline that contains a benefit tells your customer why they should buy your product. At a glance, it enables them to identify your offering as something relevant to their life. Like Dry Up Hay Fever.

So if you provide a really meaningful and distinctive benefit, put it in your headline. If your promotional offer is your strongest benefit, don't be shy — *put it in your headline.* Here's an example, again from an ad in *Stuff* magazine:

"The big screen EPSON projectors now come with a free Xbox"

Eureka! Two benefits *and* news, *and* it instantly navigates the customer. Plain and ordinary though the words are, of the 60 or so full-page ads in the magazine, this is the one I'd like to have written. Why? Let me return to the headline exercise.

Can you, by reading any of the headlines in the list, work out *what* the product might be and *why* you should buy it? I think you'll agree that at best there are a couple of vague clues.

Then would you as a reader — as a customer — take the trouble to stop and work out the answers? Remember, you're wading through 100-plus pages packed with hundreds of new products.

So how about your firm's last ad? When it was finally approved, did your boss look at it in splendid undistracted isolation, or did you make her pick it out from scores of others while she was busy trying to do something else? It's worth thinking about.

If your customer has to take on the task of asking *what* and *why*, then your ad or your communication will underperform. As a rule of thumb, it will operate at 20 percent effectiveness. That's the difference between an ordinary and an extraordinary response.

An ad I know for sure was effective was a job ad for my own company. We mainly recruited graduates and trained them before they'd adopted someone else's bad habits, but occasionally we needed a high-caliber go-getter with a few years under the belt. These were hard to find, and even harder to attract, especially to the dismal North. Rather than the standard feature-oriented approach, I wrote the ad to appeal to my own frustrations that I'd experienced as an employee. As you can see in Figure 48, the plagiarized headline inquired "desperately seeking promotion?" and the body copy told facts about the success of the agency and how every single member of staff had gained a promotion within the past year. We soon got our person. (And, in due course, our person got promoted.)

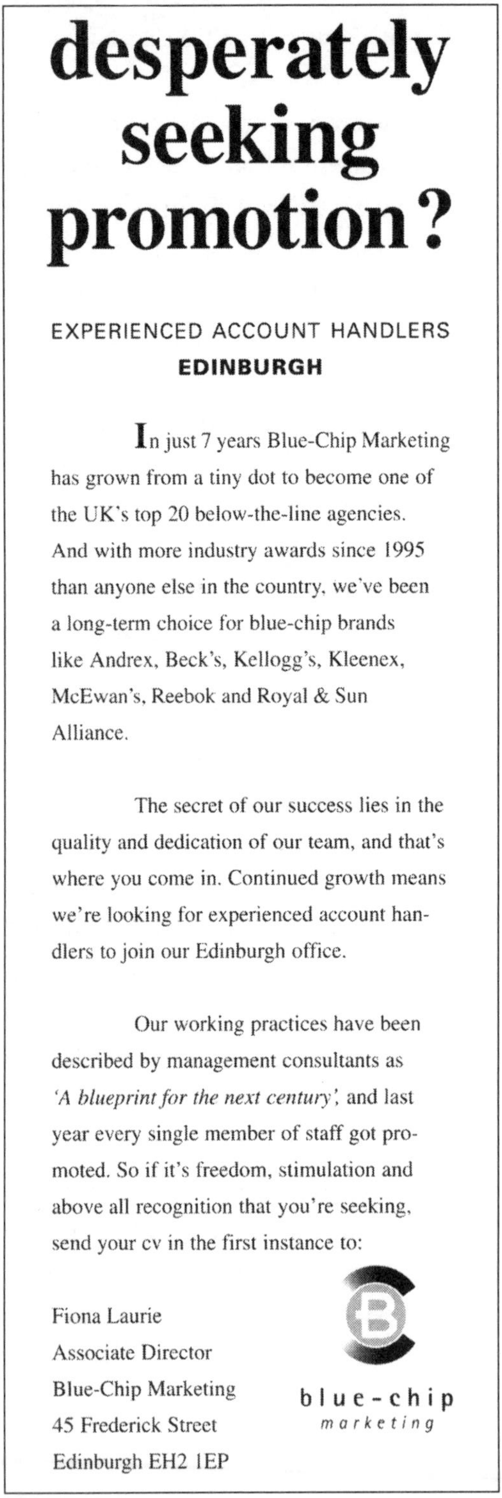

desperately seeking promotion?

EXPERIENCED ACCOUNT HANDLERS
EDINBURGH

In just 7 years Blue-Chip Marketing has grown from a tiny dot to become one of the UK's top 20 below-the-line agencies. And with more industry awards since 1995 than anyone else in the country, we've been a long-term choice for blue-chip brands like Andrex, Beck's, Kellogg's, Kleenex, McEwan's, Reebok and Royal & Sun Alliance.

The secret of our success lies in the quality and dedication of our team, and that's where you come in. Continued growth means we're looking for experienced account handlers to join our Edinburgh office.

Our working practices have been described by management consultants as '*A blueprint for the next century*', and last year every single member of staff got promoted. So if it's freedom, stimulation and above all recognition that you're seeking, send your cv in the first instance to:

Fiona Laurie
Associate Director
Blue-Chip Marketing
45 Frederick Street
Edinburgh EH2 1EP

blue-chip
marketing

Use the picture to enhance the story

I expect you've been thinking there's more to an ad (or any marketing communication, but especially an ad) than just the words. Quite right too. What about the picture?

The oft-misquoted F R Barnard said that a picture is worth 10,000 words.[38] On the other hand, philosopher Bertrand Russell said, "Do not feel absolutely certain of anything." I'm with Russell, I think.

If a picture's worth 10,000 words, why don't we communicate with friends using quickdraw Rolf Harris-like sketches? Or read cartoon books instead of novels? Or watch television with the sound turned off?

Because pictures are not the medium of human conversation.

As eminent psycholinguist Steven Pinker has argued at length, we're programmed to communicate via language — via words spoken and heard.[39] And while mental images

Figure 48 A recruitment ad headlined by an emotive benefit.

might be the stuff of memory (see below), when it comes to selling the words have it.

That's not to say pictures aren't important. At this point I'm talking about attention. When I get to *desire* I hope to show a vital and unique role for pictures.

And they can do a fine job for attention too. Pictures can work with your words to create relevant — and therefore active — attention. For instance, take a look at the Garmin ad in Figure 49 overleaf. The body copy tells you why you want a GPS, and this ad could run reasonably well without any pictures at all. (In which case the headline would obviously need to elaborate on the product category and what it does.)

However, the inclusion of the two images — the product and the matchbook — in an instant brings the benefits to life. First and foremost is the size — the GPS is obviously tiny and the matchbook tells you that. At a secondary level is the direct association with simplicity and necessity, claims backed up by the body copy.

For me, the art direction in this ad is at least as important as the copywriting (good though the copy is). Together they are additive and make a whole greater than the sum of the parts. Here, I'd say the picture's well worth its weight in words.

I think many ads of the no-headline genre get approved because they *look* cool and trendy and make the people working on them *feel* cool and trendy. Unfortunately, this isn't the best recipe for making ads that sell. Navigation gets neglected and benefits appear more by luck than judgment.

So an ad is designed as a fashion statement, at the expense of essential communication. It might *look* great, but the only role it performs is to contribute to the overall lifestyle feel of the magazine in which it appears. Cutting-edge chic makes for blunt communication.

But as the Garmin ad illustrates — and others I'll show you later — fashionability doesn't have to be abandoned. An ad can be perfectly stylish and still have a hard-working headline.

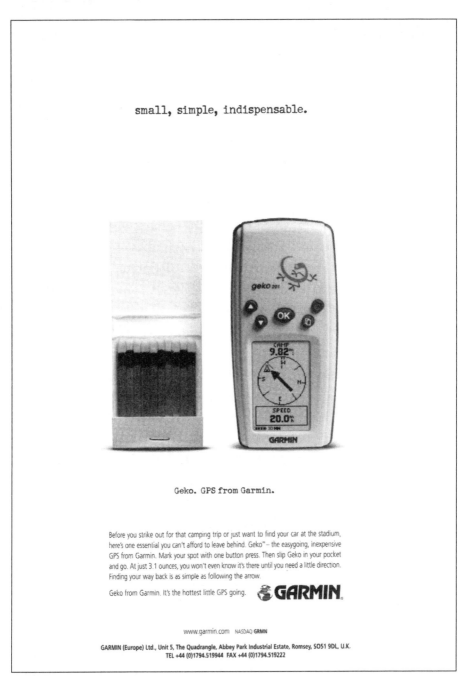

Figure 49 How the right picture can help create relevant attention. The choice of a matchbook placed alongside the tiny GPS dramatizes the primary benefit. © 2003 Garmin Ltd. or its subsidiaries.

Consider curiosity

Of course, what marketers are relying on with ads that don't make immediate sense is curiosity. That is fine in principle. Caples found curiosity to be the third-best means of creating an effective ad.

However, the risk you take when you appeal to your customer's curiosity is that they won't bother.

Why should they, when they've got a trillion other things to do? You might say they will "because they're interested" — but they can't be interested if you haven't navigated them in the first place. And navigation means giving the game away and so spoiling the "reveal," so you can't do that. Catch 22.

The Kenwood ad in Figure 50 I also found in *Stuff* magazine. I like this, it's art directed with good communication in mind, and would probably pass Ogilvy's test for an effective layout. Look at the U2-inspired headline:

"Still haven't found what I am looking for"

On its own, it doesn't make sense. No benefit, no self-interest, no news, no quick, easy way. Yet it's OK.

Of course, it's a little puzzle for you to solve. A quick glance around the ad (with no great strain on the eye muscles) and you soon get the idea. The Kenwood radio's so good you just want to keep on driving. (I think.)

It's a nice clean ad, with a simple appeal to curiosity. The reward for curiosity is a piece of useful "information" about the product; moreover, one that you have "discovered" yourself.[40] Here again, the headline and pictures work together to make a whole bigger than the sum of the parts.

So where's the risk in curiosity? Let's revisit the word *bother*: Will the customer bother?

If they're interested in radios and they notice the image of the radio or the logo at the bottom of the ad, they might. If they don't... I'm not so sure.

To reiterate a point I've been making at regular intervals, they're busy. They've only got so much processing capacity and, with a copy of *Stuff* magazine in their hands, they're probably experiencing stimulus overload.

To unravel the riddle in this ad, the customer has to switch their attention from the passive to the active mode. They have to read and comprehend the

Figure 50 *An appeal to curiosity can create deeper involvement between ad and customer, but runs a greater risk of being passed by. Reproduced by kind permission of Kenwood Electronics.*

headline, relate it to the scene in the picture, and then resolve the conundrum by reference to the radio.

Having done this, they "get" the benefit. (Curiosity is just a curvy route to a benefit.)

You can see that, even in a simple ad like this, an appeal to curiosity builds a delay into the communication process. And a hurdle for the customer. So there is a risk.

Always remember that placement of an ad does not guarantee readership of an ad. Tucked innocuously in Caples' *Tested Advertising Methods* is the almost throwaway remark:

> **"For every curiosity headline that succeeds in getting results, a dozen will fail."**

Engel put it another way. He called the customer a "cognitive miser."[41] He makes this common-sense observation:

> **"A reality of the marketplace is that many products are simply not important enough to warrant a significant investment of 'cognitive resources' i.e. mental time and effort. The customer does not take the trouble to find the *perfect* solution for all of his needs, but is forced to settle for the *acceptable*."**

Make your ad newsworthy

If you haven't got something new to say, you might like to stop for a moment and consider why you are spending money on marketing communication. (I'm not saying you should advertise or promote *only* when you've got news to divulge, but it's a useful reality check. It helps you say something meaningful.)

After self-interest, Caples found news to be the second most effective motivator. Ogilvy reported that ads with news in their headlines were recalled by 22 percent more people than those without.[42]

News, too, is a route to a benefit — but a much faster one than curiosity. It's another way of appealing to your customer's natural self-interest.

Figure 51 *News: a route to a benefit, and one the marketer can make happen.*

And news is a handy category for the marketer because you can make it happen.

You can improve your product, create a new flavor or model, or offer a special deal for a limited period. You can link up with another product or service, you can piggyback someone else's news (like a big movie premiere), or you can invent an event of your own (like National Paper Clip Week). You can even launch a brand new product.

If you work in a market in which all products are basically similar, news could be your communication mainstay. Better, faster, cheaper. The power of news shows no sign of waning.

And it doesn't always have to be big news. Procter & Gamble's Tide detergent has been improved more than 70 times.[43] Many of these changes were no doubt small adjustments to the formulation and the packaging, but each meant P&G could take a "new improved" message to its customers.

For existing customers this can say "Look, we don't take your custom for granted." For former customers it provides a reason to consider the brand afresh. And in every market there's a constant flow of new customers, perhaps setting up home for the first time, who will have few preconceptions and be open to suggestion.

But if news is a conduit to a benefit, you must make sure it's a benefit that your customer hears. I refer you back to my two "you"s per "we" rule in Step 3, Wording. Your customer doesn't want to know *you've* got a new fuel-injection system (feature), they want to know *they* can drive all week on a single tank (benefit).

Quick and easy

Most of us would like to do things more quickly and more easily. Study for a degree. Learn a new language. Clean the loo. Get a loan. Cut the grass. Lose weight. Conjure up a six-pack. Write a book.

But what did Caples mean by quick and easy? Well — again — it's really just another form of benefit. You get something faster and with less effort, perhaps something you previously thought was impossible. Here's an example he gave of a quick-and-easy headline that proved very effective:

"How I improved my memory in one evening"

Quick and easy can be applied to any walk of life (or business). Recently at the Good Food Show I watched a team of craftily unassuming salespeople demonstrate at close quarters a cleaning product that, at a touch, magically restored charred oven trays on which a wire brush had no apparent impact. Suckers (me included) were disappearing with armfuls of the stuff.

The great thing about convenience is that it's a synonym for price premium (or, to look at it another way, competitive advantage). Every marketer should be seeking this angle, yet in a survey I conducted of *Yellow Pages* ads, only 8 in 100 small businesses emphasize quick or easy in their messages.

This is remarkable. When you pick up *Yellow Pages* it's usually because you want your troubles taken away, a claim many businesses could make.

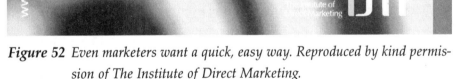

WHAT CAN YOU LEARN
ABOUT DIRECT MARKETING
IN JUST ONE DAY?

"The Absolute Essentials"

ONE-DAY COURSE

www.theidm.com

February 2001
Bristol, London, Glasgow, Leeds, Birmingham

The Institute of
Direct Marketing

Figure 52 *Even marketers want a quick, easy way. Reproduced by kind permission of The Institute of Direct Marketing.*

Sensory language

I think comedian Frank Carson has a point when he says, "It's the way I tell 'em." While the *content* of a marketing message will always be more important than its *form*,[44] good content works even harder if said well. (I say, clumsily.)

But it's not just me who thinks this. Advertising "wizard" Roy Hollister Williams states:

"The secret of writing memorable ads is to use language that creates a vivid first mental image."[45]

He believes that an intrusive and intriguing first mental image will cause your customer to abandon the thought they had previously been thinking. Passive attention becomes active attention. Your customer is all eyes and ears.

What does Williams mean by "first mental image"? The idea here is twofold.

First, memories are stored in the form of mental images. Hence it's much easier to remember someone's name if, when you meet them, you create a picture. (Try it: Next time you're introduced to a Peter, think of him in green tights, flying through the night sky.) It's on this reservoir of images that your customer draws when your message evokes a need in their mind.

The technique was put to good effect during the heavily advertised launch of the new 118 directory inquiries numbers in the UK. The campaign, which focused on distinctive visual imagery (the twin "David Bedfords" in their 118 running vests), scored almost twice the recall of its main competitor, which majored on a rather mournful ditty and largely eschewed pictures.[46]

The second part of first mental image is sensory language. Writers of fiction know to let their reader see, hear, and feel the story. Sensory language engages the reader because it makes them create specific pictures, sounds, and feelings (i.e. mental images). Conversely, abstractions, like understand, think, education, put the reader in a trance.[47]

Ahem.

Research has found that readers exposed to a list of "concrete" words (like tree or dog) and abstract words (like necessary or usual) demonstrate greater retention of concrete words.[48] In the US, sales of a rust inhibitor called Thixo-Tex rose from $2m to $100m in four years following a change of name to Rusty Jones.[49]

Metaphors are an excellent way to use sensory language. As you'll recall from schooldays, metaphors are literal images, in which the subject is described as if it really is the thing it merely resembles. Metaphors can conjure vivid images in the mind of the reader or listener. For many years Esso boasted it would "Put a tiger in your tank," while Castrol GTX was

Figure 53 *The power of the metaphor. Why say calorie when you can say war?*
Reproduced by kind permission of The Ryvita Company Limited.

described as "Liquid engineering." However, I can't think of a better example that the famous Ryvita ad, headlined simply "The Inch War." Instantly it engages your mind: Why say calorie (who's ever seen a calorie) when you can say war? It also demonstrates that sensory language need not mean highfalutin language.

Combat adaptation

Psychologists have observed that people share a tendency to become "habituated to a stimulus." Eventually they don't even notice it. Traffic noise is a good example. (Or the pictures around your house — have you noticed them lately?) This phenomenon is known as adaptation.[50]

Marketing noise can suffer the same fate. Your customer is probably familiar with your product or service. You may find it hard to find something new to say about it. These are the perfect conditions for adaptation.

Whether your company runs big-budget television campaigns, or — like the vast majority of enterprises — employs more modest media, the war on adaptation is one you must fight. Show your ad too often and your customer will metaphorically switch off. (Don't show it often enough, however, and it may not reach them.)

The rule here is to keep your marketing communications fresh. (This doesn't mean you can't be consistent.) Just don't spend all your money on production if it means you have to keep using the same execution. And employ the 10 tips to improve your location.

Salesmanship not showmanship

By now, I hope I'm beginning to convey the difference between showmanship and salesmanship. To my mind, and in my experience, it's what in turn makes the difference between an ordinary and an extraordinary response: to your advertising, mailings, and any other form of marketing communication. Old AIDA trains marketers to use showmanship: It suggests you should jump in with size 12s to make the biggest possible splash. But NEW AIDA says this is not the best way to engage your customer: In practice it's not how the effective salesperson operates, because it's not how a customer thinks.

This chapter also begins to show how a NEW AIDA approach brings out the best of old AIDA. By first thinking about navigation, ease, and wording, you can employ good salesmanship to get your customer sitting comfortably. Showmanship becomes superfluous. What matter now are benefits, and NEW AIDA enables you to focus on why your customer should buy, without unnecessary distraction.

ATTENTION — SEVEN TOP TIPS

1 First think location.

2 Maximize random attention.

3 Put a benefit in your headline.

4 Inject news and make it quick and easy.

5 Employ sensory language.

6 Make the picture enhance the benefit.

7 Test for effectiveness.

KEY QUESTION
"Will my customer meet my benefits?"

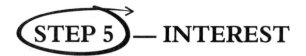

STEP 5 — INTEREST

Remember your customer is already interested

For 12 years, drumming up what the agency world calls new business was a key part of my job. I kept a record of all the new clients who came my way. On analysis, an intriguing statistic emerged:

Only 5 percent of them could be classed as truly new. For 95 percent of new projects there was a previous, personal contact.

So-called "new" business in fact came from people who had worked with us before and had moved to another company or division or department; from people who knew me or one of my staff from earlier jobs; from people at firms with whom our clients co-promoted (and so had seen us in action); and from people who knew people who knew us!

They were already interested.

As I began to realize this phenomenon, I radically changed our new business strategy. We moved away from cold calling. We stopped pitching for projects unless we were paid a fee. We actively avoided pitches where we could not identify a contact (i.e. when we suspected we had been put on the pitch list to make up the numbers, just because someone had heard of us).

Instead, we focused our efforts on increasing the frequency and depth of communication with our existing clients and contacts, led by our intensive and interactive mailing program.

That we grew from zero to become one of the top 20 marketing communications agencies in seven years suggests our strategy was right.

"It costs five times as much to gain a new customer as it does to retain an existing one."

This is another maxim-cum-cliché that you can find in most books on business and sales. Its source is direct marketing, in which acquisition and retention costs can be calculated to the penny.

Indeed, I came across a fascinating case study in which a weekly business magazine began a mailing program to re-solicit lapsed subscribers[1] (i.e. people who had canceled their subscriptions). The publication created a separate database of former customers, and compared the re-acquisition costs of this list against the costs of gaining new customers from "cold" rented lists.

> Remarkably, it took *five years* from the original expiry of a customer's subscription before it became cheaper to ignore them and recruit a new subscriber from a cold list.

The equally ubiquitous 80:20 principle tends to bear out findings like these. Ask anybody who sells anything and they will tell you about their own 80:20 situation: 20 percent of their customers account for 80 percent of their sales. (Ask your local publican about his regulars.)

I can't think of a brand, product, or service I've worked on where this rule of thumb doesn't apply. Airlines, banks, cars, detergents, eyedrops, fish fingers... I could plow on through the alphabet. Often the ratio is more extreme than 80:20.

During the 2003 wildcat strike that stranded some 87,000 British Airways passengers at Heathrow airport (at a time when the airport was at its busiest with holiday traffic), 17,000 of them belonged to the company's frequent flier program: a shade under 20 percent. No wonder the firm went to such lengths to apologize "in person" to this vital core of customers.[2]

A further perspective is provided by a phenomenon in direct marketing known as "merging and purging." When you compile a master mailing list from several sources, one of the first things you do is "dedupe" it — you get rid of the nuisance names that appear twice or more. This makes sure individual customers only receive one copy of your mailing — it eliminates waste and annoyance for the customer.

3 FREE ISSUES of *Money Observer* and free access to moneyobserver.com

Dear Mr Sample

19 March, 2003

It's been some months since we last sent you an issue of the magazine, and I'd like to tempt you back with this special re-subscription offer.

Reply now and we'll send you three issues of the magazine and we'll give you three months access to the restricted area of moneyobserver.com - absolutely free. Exclusively for the benefit of subscribers, the site lets you read *Money Observer* online well before it's available in the shops and gives you access to our internet archive, an invaluable library of financial information.

Money Observer magazine continues to provide the expert analysis and independent practical information that has won it so many awards and which, more importantly, has helped boost readers' wealth. You benefit from expert opinions, the experience of our award-winning team, and in-depth research designed to save you time and effort

Add to this the regular supplements that give you in-depth knowledge of key areas of your personal finances and the free email bulletins with up-to-date share tips and you have an unbeatable package that helps you and your investments prosper.

I hope that we can welcome you back, and look forward to hearing from you shortly.

Yours sincerely

Will Ricketts

Will Ricketts, Publisher

PS To take advantage of this special offer, please reply within the next 14 days.

Money Observer Subscriptions, FREEPOST LON21183, Manchester M3 9LS ☎ 0870 870 1324 money.observer.subscribe@guardian.co.uk

---

Please extend my subscription by quarterly direct debit (tick one)
- ☐ *Money Observer* magazine and moneyobserver.com (£11.50) or
- ☐ *Money Observer* magazine only (£8.50)

My account will only be debited once my current subscription has ended. I can cancel my subscription at any time by writing to my bank.

☐ As a subscriber, I would also like to receive the free *Money Observer* email newsletter

Email address

MREN9/MRC.J009/10821503/19 March 2003

Mr A Sample
1 The Street
Anytown
AB1 2YZ

If your details are incorrect, please amend them above

Instruction to your bank / building society to pay by direct debit

Name(s) of account holder(s)

Branch sort code

Bank/building society account number

Instructions to your bank/building society. Please pay Guardian Magazines Ltd direct debits from the account detailed on this instruction subject to the safeguards assured by the Direct Debit Guarantee overleaf.

originator number 910040

Money Observer Ref No. (office use only)

Name and address of your bank/building society

The Manager .... bank/building society

Address

Postcode

Signature .... Date

Return completed form to: *Money Observer* Subscriptions, FREEPOST LON21183, Manchester M3 9LS

Figure 54 *It can take five years from the original expiry of a customer's subscription before it becomes cheaper to ignore them and recruit a new subscriber from a cold list. Reproduced by kind permission of Guardian Newspapers Ltd.*

In the early days of computerization the duplicate names were simply erased... until it was discovered that if a name appears as a duplicate across several lists, that person is *more likely* to respond to a mail offer than someone who appears as a purchaser on only one list.[3] Duplicates, far from being a nuisance, should be gobbled up with glee. Non-buyers, in contrast, are tough nuts who might just ruin your teeth.

Old AIDA, new slant

By the time you gain your customer's *profitable* attention, you should have them in a vicelike grip. They know what you want them to do (or think about). They know how to do it (and that it's easy) and they feel you're bang on their wavelength. They've got the time and space to listen, and they like the sound of your offer.

Old AIDA makes the presumption that now it's the marketer's job to make the customer interested. NEW AIDA recognizes that the customer is already interested. This makes a big difference in what you should tell them.

And by "already interested" I don't even mean that you've made them interested. I mean that they always were going to be interested. They were interested *before* they met your marketing.

This comes down to a fundamental law of selling: The customer has needs, the marketer makes them aware of those needs. As Engel puts it:

"The need must already exist even though it may be dormant and largely unrecognised: it is not created by the marketer. It is true that marketing communication stimulates desire to buy a product or service to satisfy that need, but the need itself lies beyond the influence of the business firm."[4]

So you don't have to haul your disoriented customer across some artificial — and probably non-existent — chasm that lies between attention and interest. At worst, think of it like leading them lightly over a crack in the pavement. And they should come willingly.

Instead, it's time to acknowledge that, when you analyze customers in any market, the overwhelming majority share this one pervasive characteristic: They're already interested. This might at first sound like it's from the school of chicken-and-egg logic, but the facts say ignore it at your peril. You don't need to *make* your customer interested, you need to speak *to* their already existing interest.

"Just looking, thanks"

Your customer may not know about your product, but they are certainly interested in the solution it provides. And, to repeat, statistically it's the "interested customer" to whom you're most likely to be able to sell. They're the one who's metaphorically come off the street to browse in your store (perhaps even literally so).

And you know yourself, when you're "just looking" you're secretly aching for a really good salesperson to make the right approach and help you reach that solution (even if the solution is to postpone the purchase). The idea that we go "just looking" without reference to some need (past, present, or future) is patent nonsense. We'd no more go "just looking" in complete isolation than we'd do "just cooking" and then shovel the hot food straight into the wastebin.

There's an elementary logic about this that is often overlooked. John Watson, a founder of direct marketing agency WWAV to whom I referred earlier, calls it the "magic margin" — the small percentage of people who can be persuaded to respond at any given time.[5]

And the operative word here is *persuaded*. Watson says the most effective mailings are written to the customer who is interested but wavering. He argues you *can't* persuade people who get your mailing by mistake or at the wrong time of year (they're just not in the market), and you don't *need* to persuade people who are going to buy anyway. (I say you can only *deter* the latter group through poor communication.) So it's the small margin in between that you should aim for.

The mathematical precision of direct marketing makes Watson's magic margin a simple concept to grasp. But I believe it's a universal principle. It reinforces my entreaty that you shouldn't *play to the world* in your marketing communications.

Some might say the weakness of this theory is that it will lead you to ignore lots of *potential* customers: You'll exclude all those metaphorically walking past the door of your store. But that's missing the point: This is not about targeting, it's to do with how you address your interested customer in order to maximize the chances of a sale.

Latent interest

In any event, the knowledge that you will only sell to an interested customer doesn't mean you have to sit and wait for them to come "just looking."

I can sketch to a dangerously mediocre standard, and one hot summer in the 1970s I spent several weeks hawking watercolored line illustrations door to door. My bestseller was an idea I have to admit to pinching. It was a series of cartoon bulls that I could turn out quickly, and I framed and strung them so they were ready to hang.

I targeted new housing estates, where I figured there would be plenty of bare wall space. Then it was just a question of going from house to house with as big a stack as I could carry. Each picture was priced at £1.50 — or about £5 in today's value.

Almost exclusively the door would be answered by a woman, and I would say that about 50 percent of them purchased — usually just one picture, after looking through the range. I tried to be excruciatingly polite, simply explaining I was a student, so I don't think there was much of a pressure-selling factor (unless it was to get rid of the spectacle of my sail-like Oxford bags).

The watercolors were genuinely funny (I repeat, not my idea), and I could see my customer's eyes instantly light up. Basically they were the sort of informal thing you might put up in the kitchen or a bedroom or the loo, to take the mickey out of a lazy member of the household. Each had a caption like "Insufferabull" and "Incorrigibull." I think most of the women had their partners or offspring in mind as they considered the different versions.

Looking back, it was an enlightening exercise in interest. As I rang the doorbell I can't imagine that every second housewife was thinking, "I need a picture." Yet moments later I got an extraordinary response: a 50 percent strike rate.

Surely a case of interest created from nothing? Not really. When you think about it, several interest factors were actually at play.

First, imagine I was giving the watercolors away free. Most houses (though maybe not 100 percent) would surely have taken one. We all like amusing pictures, and you can usually find a space somewhere; failing that, they make handy presents.

Second, £1.50 (or £5 in today's terms) is a good deal for a cute, framed "original." And everyone's interested in a good deal. So having butted in on my customer's morning, I wasn't exactly making difficult demands.

Third, you can bet that not far below the surface of most housewives' thoughts was the notion of dishing out an ear-bending (good-natured or not) for some household misdemeanor or other. My watercolors fitted the bill as an indirect, tongue-in-cheek means of chastisement.

So when you think about it, my customer already was interested. She just didn't know it when I pressed the doorbell. But a combination of my short sales spiel and sight of the clearly price-marked pictures soon did the trick — her ready interest became activated.

Interest equals *persuadability*

So the customer your marketing can have most impact on is the one who is "just looking." They might be interested-but-wavering, or they might be interested-but-not-thinking-about-it-at-the-moment. And this poses a conundrum.

If you are marketing on a medium to large scale, you will be aware that your message is going to reach a much wider audience — people who are not "just looking." People who are not even interested. They're "just passing" (or rather, your marketing is just passing them) and they're never going to buy from you. They'll probably ignore your message.

There are obviously many options available for selective targeting, which is beyond the scope of this book. But targeting notwithstanding, marketers must accept that to reach customers en masse is inevitably akin to the proverbial blunderbuss: Collateral communication happens. So the trick is to aim for the bull's-eye.

Indeed, think about this piece of logic. Since every product is mainly bought by an entrenched minority (the loyal 20 percent who account for 80 percent of your sales), if you go out to market looking for new customers you take on an entrenched majority (the sum of everybody else's entrenched minorities). What looks like a seething mass of waving wallets is actually as impregnable, hard-nosed, thick-skinned, blinkered an audience as you'd have the misfortune to meet.

So don't feel obliged to entertain them. Don't play to the world. Stick to your guns: Write for your interested customer. To paraphrase Claude Hopkins: "It's sales you want, not applause."[6]

Steps you can take

Appeal to interest groups

"I could get more customers if only they'd give me a chance and listen to my message." (We've all said it.) I think it applies to every firm, business, product, and service.

But customers are just too busy and overloaded to try new things all the time. And, as I noted earlier, many products are simply not important enough to warrant a significant investment of "cognitive resources." If you work in fast-moving consumer goods (fmcg), you'll know all about this.

Fmcg brand managers spend much of their time organizing sales promotions in an effort to break the habits of their (not-very-interested-but-persuadable) customers. Aside from price cutting (which has wide customer interest but is proven to have no effect on long-term brand loyalty[7]), the main tactic used is what you might call an appeal to an interest group within the market.

When I was about 12 years old I won a bike in a competition. (It was one of those "chopper" contraptions — presented by Jimmy Hill, no less — which I confess I immediately swapped for a racer.) The promotion was organized by the Burton Stores Group, and my mum came home with the entry leaflet after buying me a new anorak or something. I had to select the "Best Current British Soccer Team" to match Jimmy Hill's choice. (I remember there was Moore at the back, Best, Law, and Charlton up front... and of course Banks in goal.)

Football and anoraks, then — no connection. (Unless you count the times my anorak served as a goalpost.) Yet clear proof to me that an *unrelated* interest can play a role in the selling process. My mum thought (correctly) that I'd be interested in the soccer promotion.

Thus you will find all manner of ostensibly unconnected offers plastered across the packs of many products in the supermarket (and elsewhere). Win a sports car. Win a cruise. Win tickets to the World Cup. Free trips to a theme park. Free cinema tickets. Free compilation CDs. 2-for-1 flights. 2-for-1 hotel accommodation. 2-for-1 meals.

Do these "bolt-on" offers work?

Answer: They can do. I'll talk more in Step 7 about what really makes an offer effective, but here I'd like to consider the interest factor.

Obviously, the idea of a bolt-on sales promotion is to get people who weren't about to buy a product to do so (whether they have been previous purchasers or not). Otherwise, it would be a waste of money. The theory goes that if you choose a reward that interests a segment of potential customers, they'll try your brand for the sake of the offer. If they like your product (or are reminded that it does a good job), hopefully they'll stick with it.

For the launch of the *101 Dalmatians* movie featuring Glenn Close, we set up a cross-promotion between Disney and Andrex. If you bought a nine-pack of Andrex you could get a free kid's ticket, no strings attached, no parent needed; just cut it out from the back of the pack and go straight to the cinema. (We heard of whole classes of kids going with their teacher for their Christmas outings.) This promotion won an Institute of Sales Promotion award. As the record shows, target household penetration of the nine-pack increased by a whopping 27 percent during the campaign period, and the movie took £5m more in the UK than expected.[8]

Was there an interest factor at work? I'm sure there was. While it's hard to tease out the effect of the value of the offer, there's no denying that you have to be in a special-interest group (i.e. roughly in possession of kids) to benefit from it.

Of course, the added beauty of a campaign like this one was that it effectively brought the brand's advertising into the grocery store and other environments. I'm sure you've made the connection between the two varieties of puppies — but you might be surprised to know that this was the first time (after 25 years) that the Andrex puppy had appeared on the packaging. Now it's a fixture. So it should be, when research has shown that even simple cues to advertising placed at the point of purchase can increase sales by as much as 15 percent.[9]

In my experience, a well-executed and properly funded bolt-on offer can pay for itself. Almost certainly it will have a greater marginal effect than spending the equivalent marketing budget on an extra sliver of advertising. For an extraordinary response, however, it helps if the offer refers back to the brand.

For instance, Reebok has been a long-term sponsor of soccer's flying winger Ryan Giggs. He has featured not only in television advertising, but also in a number of promotional offers (such as the chance to win Giggs-autographed Reebok merchandise).

Clearly, for the Reebok customer, ranking high among the benefits might be those qualities enhanced (e.g. product performance) or even endowed (e.g. peer-group status) by Ryan Giggs. Thus the promotional offer becomes virtually inseparable from the overall marketing proposition.

Effectiveness? We ran a retail campaign through JJB Sports stores called "Play Giggs in a Cage." Customers were invited to try out a pair of Reebok boots — actually kicking a football in a special protective cage — for the chance to play one-to-one with Giggs in the final. Stores sold out of Reeboks and the promotion won three ISP awards.[10]

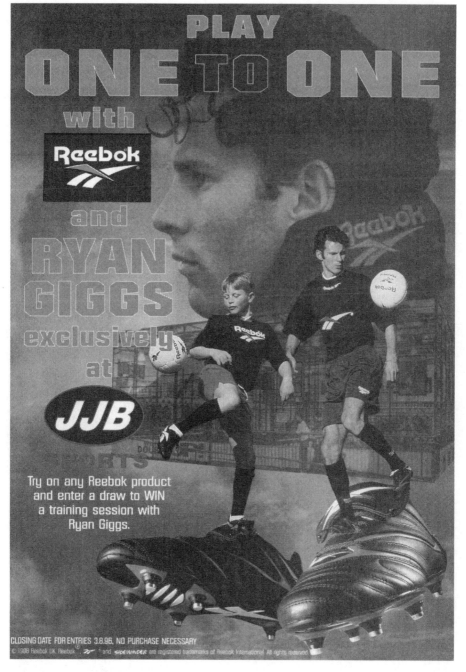

Figure 55 *Appealing to an interest group. An award-winning campaign exploiting Reebok's long-term sponsorship of Ryan Giggs. Reproduced by kind permission of Reebok UK.*

Obviously, a celebrity's influence can only extend so far. Reebok sells to many people who wouldn't recognize Ryan Giggs, and it also sells lots of gear that has nothing to do with football. But for the soccer interest group, he plays a blinder.

Put the interest group first

The decision to target an interest group with a bolt-on offer raises an important question: How much message space should it get? My answer — if you're doing it properly — is the *max*.

If you believe in your offer, and have made a significant investment, you should treat it as the most important benefit. Thus your offer must be given primacy throughout your marketing communication. (If you pay lip service to an offer, why bother?)

This means building the offer into your thinking right from the moment you put pen to layout pad. Navigation, ease, wording, and attention should all be focused on delivering communication of the offer: what it's about, how it's easy, why it's great.

From that reassuringly measurable world of direct marketing, John Watson is adamant that

Figure 56 Received wisdom says lead with your offer. You should expect at least to double your response rate. Reproduced by kind permission of Condé Nast Publications.

the offer must take over from what he calls the "marketing proposition," such is the power of a properly used incentive. This means in the headline, the copy, the art direction, and the format. In Watson's experience, an incentive will commonly double response rates, and often achieve increases of 500 percent or more.[11]

Real vs bolt-on

For every product there is a spectrum of customers who are already interested. Thankfully, for many, the real "marketing proposition" is sufficient. For some waverers, a brand-related theme like those I have described helps to secure the sale. And for others it's all about getting a free gizmo or widget, and to hell with the brand. (Theirs is mercenary carrot interest only.)

As Hoover's painful free-flights promotions demonstrated, customers are always interested if there's a big enough carrot. But big carrots are rarely sustainable. Your decision is much more likely to be about the extent to which you employ the middle way, i.e. the brand-related offer.

My advice is don't be shy of it. Sometimes you just know you should be communicating, but struggle to find something new to say. A well-thought-through promotional campaign may be the answer you seek.

It could even grow to into a significant branch of your communication strategy, like the Kleenex "survival" campaign we originated in 1990, which for well over a decade has been a biannual mainstay of news for the brand, targeting significant and relevant interest groups of hay-fever or cold and flu sufferers. Now it is a mature and valuable brand property.

Help interested customers in distress

You're probably familiar with the expression "distress purchase." Traditionally it's associated with products like car tires, paracetamol, and condoms. But I think it goes much wider than that, and offers a valuable insight for the marketer seeking new customers.

Indeed, many products and services share the "distress" characteristics of *infrequent* and largely *reluctant* purchase. They also share the problem of getting their customers already interested, especially at the level of brand-name recognition.

If you're a plumber, roofer, insurer, lawyer, maker of cough mixture or shoelaces or umbrellas or newborn-baby products or half a hundred other things, you must be familiar with this dilemma. When "distress" flashes up in your customer's mind, how do you make them be specifically interested in you? (And *already* interested?)

The facts say you won't sell to someone who isn't interested, yet you can't find anyone who *is*! Beforehand, nobody wants to listen. Hm...

Should you devote resources to what big-budget advertisers call "maintaining brand awareness"? How much should you spend to implant your name (and benefits) into the mind of your customer? To what lengths should you go to insert practical reminders into their life, for that rainy day?

If you're a plumber, every house in your district is a potential customer. But apart from a general clue like cold weather, it's almost impossible to predict which ones will need you at any given time. And how will they know to call *you*?

In my street of old terraced houses we have a guy called Bob the Painter. He doesn't live here, but he works here (full time, it seems). And while decorating is not ostensibly a distress purchase, there's a lesson in his method.

Bob is a smoker and a chatterbox. He takes his regular coffee breaks sitting on the front wall of whichever property he's currently beautifying. Sooner or later you bump into Bob... and sooner or later you book him. (Feeling grateful that he's free in only 15 weeks' time.)

A subsequent word-of-mouth check will confirm that he's good value and top quality — if you haven't already employed him (as most locals, of course, already have).

In fact, booking Bob has close parallels to a distress purchase. One day you make up your mind a room is looking tired, or maybe you notice that the outside window frames are peeling alarmingly. Then what?

Your infrequency of purchase of decorators means there's no ready solution. So you put off taking action. But now you're aware of it, the problem grows – by the minute the decor seems more dingy and the paintwork more flaky.

Then you spot Bob's car with his tell-tale ladders. "Ah," you think, "I could ask Bob." Next you spy him talking to a neighbor – aargh, *they* might be booking him! Off you sprint.

When it comes to distress purchase, your key role is to understand where your customer is, and what your customer does, when "distress" happens. Then you must adapt your marketing communications to match. In Bob's case, all he has to do is literally sit on the fence, in a paint-spattered overall. (And he knows this, because I've asked him.)

The man in black

The lion's share of Milk Tray sales take place in December. At the time I worked on the brand, it was big enough to merit substantial television advertising – I'm sure you'll remember the "Man in Black," a James Bond-like character who annually risked life and limb to deliver the chocolates to the boudoir of a mystery female.

Cadbury's distress strategy was quite simple. In October amass stocks and displays in the retail trade. In November kick off the advertising. In December... sit back and wait.

It was rather like fishing for salmon. The salmon only appear at certain times of the year and in certain conditions. This customer "run" meant marketing resources could be synchronized to achieve a cost-effective out-come. And it was effective. While Milk Tray as a product was not specifi-cally targeted at male buyers, unlike virtually all other boxed assortments at that time the majority of purchases were made by men, to give to women. Notorious last-minute shoppers, blokes found a perfect ally in the brand: a relatively inexpensive yet indulgent gift, which the advertising helpfully positioned as a symbol of love that the giver has gone to great lengths to impart.

So Cadbury's solution was indeed to create an army of short-term but already-interested customers, through a focused mass-media message aimed at a distinct and distressed interest group.

Smooth operators

A car is an infrequent and largely reluctant purchase. So how about motor dealers? No longer can they rely on the seasonality provided by the old August registration system. But even for the largest of dealerships, to maintain a high level of brand awareness throughout the year via television advertising is cost prohibitive.

Posters and press are more economical, but these obviously have a limited effect on the non-interested customer, who simply won't engage. Television is more effective at making people engage, but at risk of them enjoying the ad rather than absorbing anything useful about "future benefits." This is a further conundrum faced by marketers of many distress-purchase products and services: inherently, they tend to be uninteresting and often related to negative experiences.

So motor dealers have opted for a communication strategy with two main strands.

The first is to get in your face. Through sheer convenience and visibility, they improve their chances of capitalizing on distress interest. Notice they are rarely sited on quiet back streets, and are always very heavily branded, with plenty of flags and bunting and gleaming models on roadside display.

Secondly, they assume that every week, lots of customers pick up the local paper in problem-solving mode. So every week in the motor section you'll find a big ad directed at the interested customer — someone who needs a replacement car right now. That means full specifications, prices, offers, and guarantees.

Indeed, you won't find many ads for motor dealers that play to the world, trying to create a nice branded feel that anyone can enjoy. They rightly have little interest in the uninterested.

Act local

OK then, what if you're a plumber? What should you do if you can't afford to use the big boys' high-intensity, high-cost techniques? Answer: Copy their strategies on your own scale.

Figure 57 *Ready and waiting for the interested customer. Reproduced by kind permission of Arnold Clark Automobiles Ltd.*

If I were a plumber and had worked out my "patch," I think I'd first try to get an idea of which were the more productive localities. For instance, this might be areas of large, old housing where people can afford to employ tradesmen and where decrepit systems are forever springing leaks. (If I were just starting out I'd spend time on the streets looking for the highest concentrations of fellow tradesmen's vans.) Then I'd focus my marketing communications on these neighborhoods.

The Cadbury approach, fish when the salmon run, is perfectly valid given the seasonality of real emergency plumbing. Get some leaflets printed in advance and watch the weather forecast. The Met Office has a good record of forecasting cold spells, so you can time your deliveries to coincide with the flood of burst pipes and leaky radiators.

Then there's the automotive "visibility" tactic. This is basically what Bob the Painter employs when he hangs out in the 'hood with his Nescafé and Woodbines. His distinctive car does the same job in between times. A tidily liveried van is a good asset: I'd put my full marketing communication on mine — not just a phone number, but reasons why my customer should call too.

Next there's the "80:20" phenomenon. Like Bob, you can build up a circle of "regulars" by making sure it's you they're interested in next time the need arises. Bob's presence in the street serves as a timely aide memoire. This is more tricky if you're a plumber — you need a larger number of customers, over a wider area. But you can legitimately place strategic reminders where you've done a good job: a guarantee sticker or tag on the boiler or pipes you've mended (with your contact details, and perhaps the offer of a free 12-monthly service check). How about a handy LCD thermometer for your customer's noticeboard? At the very least a leaflet and business card in case your customer actually has a filing system, and perhaps a couple of stickers for their phone book.

Yellow Pages obviously plays a role here, too. But a first glance at Plumbers for my area reveals some 350 entries. It's a jungle out there. This is where a relevant and memorable brand name and visual icon for your business will help.

This seems such common sense, yet in my *Yellow Pages* over 85 percent of all plumbing firms are called after a person's name or a place, or are just initials. For instance, in quick succession there's PG Plumbing, PK Plumbing, and P&W Plumbing. A year on, how would a customer possibly remember which one they'd used previously?

Your interested customer needs to be flooded with reminders, not left to flounder helplessly as their memory ebbs away. (Today's buzzphrase for this ancient and obvious sales principle is CRM, or customer relationship management.)

Fill memory gaps

Curiously maintaining the plumbing theme, I think the same marketing communications problem faces the makers of loo blocks. (I mean the giant tablets you drop into the cistern to make the water blue.) How does the customer know which one they're interested in when the color begins to fade?

If you shop for these things, you'll probably know what I'm on about. Some of them last for ages, others seem to dissolve in a few days. But once you've removed and binned the packaging (as you have to do, to use the product), which one was it? I counted more than 10 brands in my local Tesco. Most people can't name the Chancellor of the Exchequer, so surely it's naive to think they'll devote much memory capacity to something equally uninteresting. Worse still, the longer the loo block lasts, the less likely the customer is to remember which brand. How ironic.

If I had a superior-performing product in this market, I think I'd increase my price by a penny and include a modest coupon off next purchase within the wrapper (solely to act as a branded reminder).

On a similar note, why don't the makers of loo rolls and kitchen towels print their brand name or an image from their advertising on the "core" — the cardboard tube that's left at the end of the roll? We ran one promotional campaign that involved placing winning stickers on the cores; as well as a reminder, I think this would be an ideal couponing method to get customers to trade up from smaller pack sizes.

How many brands spend a fortune cultivating interested customers and then let them slip from their grasp before they buy again? A lot, I'm sure. One of the great irritations as a Milk Tray brand manager was reading research reports telling me that one in four viewers thought my television commercials were for arch-enemy Black Magic.

At the end of each Milk Tray ad, the Man in Black always left his calling card (with just his silhouette) on top of the box. I'd had some of these printed for a trade promotion, and they were great fun to give out with the product. With hindsight, I think we could have made much more use of them at the point of purchase.

Virgin shoppers

The saying goes you can always remember the first time. So do you remember the first time you went grocery shopping? I mean shopping for real: to stock up *your own* fridge and larder and cupboard under the sink?

Every year in Britain about 200,000 new homes are built and occupied, there are 300,000 marriages, 750,000 teenagers come of age, and over 3 million people move house. The government estimates that by 2010 40 percent of homes will have just one occupant, many of them novices in the supermarket and DIY store.[12]

I'm surprised more firms don't have a special subplan to target virgin shoppers. Every brand or product or service needs a healthy flow of new customers (the grim reaper alone removes 1 percent of the population each year, and it soon begins to add up). Why not address this issue as a key component of the marketing strategy?

> Question: When is your product most interesting to your customer?
> Answer: When it's new. And no matter how old your brand, it's always new to a first-time buyer.

Sure, there are some products — like Heinz Tomato Ketchup — your customer's grown up with, packaging and all. But most fall into the loo-block category. For the majority of things your customer first buys as an adult, their contact will have been minimal. At best they'll have seen some advertising, which they'll largely have watched for entertainment value. (And no harm done, in creating a positive predisposition in the minds of future customers.)

Figure 58 *Bountiful: experts at targeting first-time buyers in the maternity and babycare market. Reproduced by kind permission of Bounty (UK) Ltd.*

One of the few sectors that takes this opportunity really seriously is that for baby products. Mums-to-be are systematically bombarded with free samples and coupons and information. But in every market there must be a steady stream of first-time buyers, unprejudiced, inquisitive, welcoming, just waiting to be made already interested.

And first-timers can pop up in all sorts of unexpected ways. For instance, when I was a lowly salesman I was lucky enough to be allowed to handle one of the regional key accounts: Leicester Co-op. This sounds like a shop, but was in fact Leicestershire Co-operative Society head office, where the buying took place for the entire county, and sometimes for other affiliated societies too. They could order titanic quantities.

Calling there was rather like taking part in a Dickensian drama. The buying office was reached via echoing stone staircases. You had to wait your turn shivering in a marble anteroom. Finally, a barked order: "Come!"

The buyer — Mr Walker — eyes bulging at your impudence for entering, scowled Squeers-like across a desk akin to the great oak deck of a schooner, in a room the size of a small dancehall. By the time you'd traversed the vast floor, you were convinced you were about to get the cane.

I'm being serious!

Getting a proposition approved for a product to be featured on a special promotion was not easy. Mr Walker rejected proposals on principle. It was a case of "over my dead body." Strictly speaking Leicester Co-op was my boss's account, but you can see why he let me look after it. (His excuse was that it was good for my development.)

Then one day — unbeknown to me — Mr Walker retired. Instead of the usual gruff summons, a much younger man actually came and opened the door, and introduced himself as Trevor, the new buyer. He said it was his first day, and even held out my chair for me. In a bit of a daze, I blundered on with my planned presentation.

Of course, my "pitch" was designed for Mr Walker. I'd learned that the best technique was just to keep throwing mud at the wall, and hope that tiny blobs occasionally stuck. So I went through my welter of promotion proposals... and Trevor promptly accepted the lot! I got just about *every one* of my company's key products featured during the next quarter.

When I phoned my boss that night (no mobiles in those days, remember) he did a lap of honor round his garden before coming back to the phone. I think we won every incentive going that quarter. And all because I found a virgin shopper.

I assume that morning Trevor had sat down to the realization that he needed a promotion program — and fast. Thanks to lucky timing, I managed to pile my goods into his hitherto empty shopping trolley. This is a business-to-business example, but I'd be willing to bet that whatever your line, there are first-time buyers to be found. And often, they're more obvious than meets the eye.

A friend of mine runs a management consultancy that specializes in providing human resources training to the public sector. He meticulously studies the job ads in the national press. When he comes across a vacancy for someone who would be his customer (for instance director of personnel), he diaries to contact the organization in four months' time — when the new manager is likely to be taking up the position and looking to make their mark.

At a more parochial level, a similar opportunity exists to find first-time buyers (in some cases literally so): in the conspicuous form of the real-estate "For Sale" sign. What a boon to the painter and decorator, landscape gardener, electrician, or plumber. A readymade mailing list of eager new-comers looking for local suppliers of domestic services. All it takes is a small investment in time, touring the neighborhood once a month and noting down addresses. Within a few weeks, most homes will be reoccupied by people keen to start making improvements.

If you're in alcohol or soft-drinks marketing, the chances are your brand share will soon wilt without a flow of new customers. In my experience most companies focus their research and marketing efforts on non-buyers who match *current* buyers — I think this could be a mistake. I'd be monitoring prospective new entrants long before they reach my age band, to understand the impact of my communications on them in creating ready interest.

If you're a charity, you need to capture first-time customers before your competitors do. Why? Because there's no more virtuous way of turning down a request for another donation than when you know you're already doing your bit. A long-term commitment to a particular charity gives you an exemption from all others; it's like being able to say "Got one, thanks" to a *Big Issue* vendor.

If you work in local or regional tourism, think about virgin holiday-makers: they've never visited your area before, yet are keen to spend money if only they know what to do. Some of the hotels in your area know who they are and when they're coming. A simple promotional partnership could benefit both of your businesses.

If you're thinking of setting up a shirt-ironing enterprise, you could seek out single males. Target your leaflets at modern flats and bedsits where the newly divorced or newly fledged come to rest. (You may also locate girlfriends who don't want to iron.)

DOES YOUR MARKETING SELL?

Poke about in a store like Currys or Comet and you'll notice that sample packs of Ariel have been quietly placed inside many of the washing machines. It's an obvious tactic, but few firms have the tenacity to turn it into a strategy. Perhaps it's got something to do with the short spin cycle of the product manager's job.

Humush for gardens

If you receive an envelope with the message "Fantastic Offer Enclosed" or "Important News Inside" or — worse — no message at all, you'll know by now what to think. This mailing could be about anything, for anybody. Here's a marketer playing to the world.

That most mailing lists *mainly* consist of uninterested customers (whose attention you would classify as random and irrelevant) is not a reason to direct your message at them. Remember — collateral communication happens. It would be a case of the tail wagging the dog.

Admittedly, it's often a very large tail wagging a very small dog, but that is just a fact of life when you use mass-media techniques to reach your customer. The limitations of targeting methods should not divert you from addressing your customer in a focused manner. Which means — in direct mail — starting with the envelope.

Figure 59 *Addressing the already-interested customer. (Note, no offer required.) Reproduced by kind permission of Next Retail Ltd.*

Drayton Bird cites an instance in which the simple addition of the product name and its function ("Humush for gardens") caused a 32 percent uplift in sales, followed by a further 27 percent rise when the incentive copy was also printed on the envelope.[13] When you think about it, mundane as "Humush for gardens" is, it immediately deals with navigation and flags up the subject matter for the interested customer. The incentive then begins to cultivate their active attention.

John Watson believes the most powerful way of using an envelope is to feature the incentive on it in full color. He says this consistently works best, whereas there have been cases of non-offer or non-incentive messages actually *decreasing* response.[14] Clearly, a message for a message's sake is not the answer — it must have the qualities of a good headline.

If you are a copywriter, or you are creating a mailing for your own business, spend half of your writing time on the overall proposition. Treat the envelope message like you would the headline in a press ad. Do it first, not last as an afterthought.

While there may be good reasons why you might on occasion have to send out a blank envelope, cost and time need not be among them. Why not? Because you can always use a window envelope.

As you must have noticed from your own correspondence, the modestly typed phrase Private & Confidential above your name and address is all it takes to make a significant impact. Even a standard-sized window in a stock C5 envelope (C5 fits an A4 page folded in half) allows plenty of extra space to laser in a message with your offer. We successfully used this unassuming technique for a year-long mailing program for Velvet bathroom tissue, and achieved a cumulative response of 41 percent. Content always beats form.

In business-to-business direct marketing, in particular, displaying your benefits upfront on the envelope is vital. Business people, by virtue of subscribing to trade publications, get lots of inappropriate mail. Binning becomes habitual. When in-tray and wastebasket are just a sweep of the arm apart, you can't risk waiting until your mailing is opened for your message to strike home.

I once ran a split-test mailing for a fast-fit company. It was aimed at getting small and medium-sized firms to sign up for a business account for new tires and exhausts. We hired in lists and sent half of the mailings to named contacts (in most cases the managing director or owner), while the other half were simply addressed to "The Fleet Manager."

The fleet-manager cell pulled more than *double* the response of the named-contact cell. (Explain that one!)

It's easy when you think about it. A named contact was in fact a shot in the dark — a guess that they dealt with vehicles. But when an envelope arrived addressed to the fleet manager, the person who sorted the mail simply passed it on to the manager responsible for the firm's cars and vans... an interested customer (and in most cases *not* the boss).

Apply this simple principle and you could save money. In many cases I believe it's more cost-efficient to send a single mailshot to a job title (like "incentives buyer") or to a section (like "promotions department") than to try to chase after individuals who've often long changed their jobs. Out-of-date commercial mailings — particularly those addressed to several ex-employees in the same company — are en route to the recycling skip the moment they leave your postroom.

And on this note, a further thought about the gatekeeper. If you send business-to-business direct mail, do you know what percentage gets opened in advance by a secretary or PA? Do you know on an individual customer basis?

This is easy to find out, yet few marketers bother. An understanding of the mail-handling process is vital (we're back to location dynamics). How can you construct an effective proposition without knowing which pieces of it will reach your customer, and in what order and condition?

Say your firm provides consultancy for managing directors in how to save money by cutting staff. Would you put this message on the envelope? Surely not without a clear idea of how the mail is handled. (What chance of it reaching your intended customer?)

And you should apply the same kind of thinking in a consumer context. Direct marketer George Smith reckons the average front door is 30 seconds from the bin. If your intended recipient doesn't pick up the mail, what chance of it beating the gatekeeper?

The first job for your envelope is to break through and engage with your interested customer — or their proxy. Bland platitudes and blatant hyperbole won't wash. For your mailing to avoid the wastebasket it must act like your best salesperson.

I just received a heavy, smart-looking letter with these words on the envelope: "Attractive benefits for busy directors." (I only retrieved it from the bin so I'd remember to mention it.)

Renowned copywriter Robert W Bly urges the marketer to start with "an irresistible message that compels the reader to open the envelope."[15] I agree. However, he goes on to advocate a blank envelope if the former is not possible. The idea is to "resemble personal mail" that the recipient will open, just to be sure. I disagree. If you've got nothing to say on the outside, you've got nothing to sell on the inside. Instead, spend your marketing budget on improving your product.

When the editor of *Who's Mailing What* analysed the 100 most successful mailings in the US, over 70 percent of them had envelope messages.[16]

Spam[17]

What can we learn from spam? I'd say a simple and universal lesson. Spam emphasizes the link between navigation and the interested customer.

A recent report indicated that spam already accounts for a hefty 40 percent of all emails.[18] Anti-spam groups claim that staff spend more than 10 percent of each working day dealing with junk emails. (Now there's a cost saving in waiting.) Apparently creatives in advertising agencies are the worst culprits.

A quick glance at my mailbox just now revealed a whole shelf of spam, including (verbatim): "ianmoore itis identical to the" from Evelina Morreale and "Get rid of it" (thanks, I shall) from Rachel. Typos and mumbo-jumbo from senders I've never heard of. When I last got back from a few days away I had 95 messages, of which 88 were spam. Why would I waste time on these? (Never mind the risk of viruses.)

If you think about an email that you would open, it will probably have one of two characteristics: either you recognize the sender, or you understand what it's about. Maybe both. (If neither, you'd probably just delete it.)

I don't need to spell out the rules here for addressing emails effectively, but what strikes me is the parallel for other media. By the minute, the new media spammers are training your customer to be more ruthless with your old media marketing communications: with your mailings and door-drops, with your ads placed in their favorite magazine or television program, and with any other spam-alike messages you care to send him. (The latest Mori survey suggests about a third of direct mail is binned unopened.[19])

Pure spam is a navigation anathema. Envisage how summarily your customer will dismiss it, and apply that same concern across all of your marketing outputs, virtual or actual.

Remember, you can only realistically sell to an interested customer. Tell them what to do or think about, or at least identify yourself to them. To avoid deletion, think navigation.

Beware of the newsletter

I have a folder bulging with first editions of company newsletters that I've received over the years. The *second* editions...? Many of them just never happened.

So if you get the urge to produce one, I'd advise you to think twice. Statistically, it may not be a good investment. And there's a lesson for websites in this regard, too.

In my experience, firms decide to publish a customer newsletter when certain events occur. These include: a new boss takes the helm (usually managing director or marketing director); there's a reorganization (or a merger or takeover); the firm has a rebranding exercise (whether or not related to the former); or several marketing initiatives coincide (and it feels like there are too many messages for the customer to absorb separately).

All of these events (and others like them) are short-term occurrences. There's the problem. A newsletter is a long-term commitment.

When the time comes for the unfortunate junior marketer to whom the project has been delegated to produce the second edition, there's precious little to say. The *news* is no more. The initial wave of enthusiasm was just that — a wave. (And now a wave goodbye would be the best tactic.)

But if you do carry on, there's an even more fundamental difficulty. Your customer isn't that interested. Fascinating as you think your story is, your customer is busy and your news is low down on their list of priorities.

I used to work with a guy who would insist on giving you uninvited lectures about how good his clothes were. It's not only rather bizarre, but also plain ignorant and, of course, you start taking evasive action when you spot people like this heading down the corridor toward you. As Claude Hopkins wrote, the two greatest faults in advertising lie in boasts and selfishness.[20] To my eyes, many company newsletters fall into this trap: "Look how wonderful our clothes are!" There's no reference to the poor customer; babble is thrust on them in a manner that will surely seem boring and rude.

However, unrequested newsletters *can* work. For over three years we published an internal newsletter for a division of Royal & SunAlliance. It was called *Centre Circle* and was the size of a tabloid newspaper, printed in black and white with the odd spot of blue. The "customer" was the employee, of which there were about 500 populating huge open-plan offices in Oldham.

I have to say, it was one of the more remarkable marketing communication experiences to stand on the buzzing and bustling office floor at the moment *Centre Circle* was distributed to everybody's desks. Suddenly... stillness. (It was like a scene from *The Office*.) For a few minutes the only sound was the gentle rustle of crisp, new pages being turned. Then gradually there would be the odd shriek of embarrassment or hoot of laughter. Next, phones would start ringing and little crowds would gather as people began to exchange their findings. Soon the whole place would be filled with lively banter. It was a great exercise in corporate-scale teambuilding.

Why did *Centre Circle* work when most unsolicited newsletters fail? I'm sure you know what I'm going to tell you. It was jam-packed to bursting with news about and (especially) photographs of the employees themselves. Yes, there was some company propaganda too, but it was couched in the same 'team-goes-forward' manner, and limited to about a quarter of the content.

The bulk of the publication was given over to reporting on company nights out (*especially* company nights out), sports teams (and their rather

Figure 60 Centre Circle: *a rare corporate newsletter that really worked, and made it past its first edition. Reproduced by kind permission of Royal & SunAlliance.*

NOA Newsletter

Norfolk Ornithologists' Association — Spring 2003

Spring Roundup 2003

March proved interesting with an early spell of dry warm weather in the third week producing many early first dates for spring migrants. At Holme 11 Stonechat were along the track on the 8th and a Tree Sparrow on the 23rd was very unusual. Winter visitors were still present with Snow Bunting, Shorelark and Twite regular until mid-month at least. Black Redstart were noted on the 18th and 28th. A Ring Ouzel was the first for the year on the reserve on the 24th. Sea-watching produced 6 Long-tailed Duck (8th), 4 Red-throated Diver (6th), up to 20 Red-breasted Merganser (7th) and two Gannet (15th). At Redwell the long-staying American Wigeon continued to show well daily until the 12th, and a flock of up to 50 Twite were seen regularly until the 17th. White Wagtail and Garganey quickly followed, however, and a significant passage of Meadow Pipits took place throughout the month with over 150 on the 31st. Sand Martin was first recorded on the 24th, and an Avocet was feeding on the scrape on the 26th. Walsey was graced by a singing Cetti's Warbler from the 18th, a Red Kite which flew over on the 24th was a bonus. Waders included Spotted Redshank (6th), Little Ringed Plover (11th), and up to seven Ruff (11th).

continued on page 2

INSIDE THIS ISSUE

1 Reserves Roundup – Spring 2003

1 Chairman's report

2 Reserves roundup continued

2 What a Tangled Web

2 Hempton Progress Report

3 Charity Begins at Holme – Events & Fundraising news

4 Questionnaire Results

CHAIRMAN'S REPORT

Spring, as always, is a time of major change and excitement in the bird community – summer visitors arrive whilst the last of our winter visitors depart. This time of year also brings first young birds into view – Mallard, Moorhen and later Blackbird, Robin and Starling – all a little earlier this year, thanks to the spell of warm dry weather, whilst many other species are busy establishing territories, nest building, laying and incubating. Hopefully, the damp and cold weather of the early summer last year will not be repeated this year and the birds will have a successful breeding season.

As mentioned in the last newsletter, our previous treasurer has resigned but, fortunately, we have been able to recruit a new treasurer who brings with him a long term professional background in accounting. The maintenance of the membership details is now being handled very successfully and efficiently in house.

The preliminary findings of the questionnaire sent to members in the last newsletter are briefly analysed on the back page. Please read these important results and any further comments would be most welcome. Please address these to the chairman. The council earnestly wishes to continue this critical two-way communication process with the membership.

I must mention the forth-coming cricket match – please attend if you can and support the NOA team in this major event in the sporting calendar. Any potential players please contact Jed at the Observatory. The association is holding another moth night this year – please see the article on page three for further information.

It would be very gratifying if members were able to support the sponsored Birdwatch, either by running their own sponsored event or by subscribing to Chris Mills effort, and please consider contributing to our new adopt-a-net programme, more details of which can be found on page three. I would be totally failing in my duty as chairman if I did not insist that each and every member returned their raffle tickets (and asked for more) thus boosting the association's finances whilst standing a good chance of winning a very worthwhile prize!

Mike Reed   *Chairman*

Figure 61 *Content always beats form. In a 2003 survey of its members, The Norfolk Ornithologists' Association found that its modest quarterly newsletter was read in full by an impressive 86 percent of respondents. Reproduced by kind permission of The NOA.*

alarming tours), charity events, unusual hobbies and achievements, staff promotions and awards, and anything else that enabled us to cover as many people as possible and make them local heroes.

The budget didn't run to a full-time (or even part-time) photographer, so much of the visual content was supplied by the staff themselves. The quality of pictures was terrible! But that didn't matter: content always beats form.

Centre Circle worked because it was about its customers.

If my tale of the perils of the newsletter is ringing a few bells, what about your website? Is it little more than an unsolicited electronic newsletter, first edition? Is it about you, or your customer?

Always remember, marketing communications are something your customer routinely rejects, not seeks out. And if, on arrival, all they get is a lecture about *your* clothes, it should be no surprise when they sidle quietly away.

INTEREST — SEVEN TOP TIPS

1 Write for the interested customer.

2 Don't play to the world.

3 Appeal to interest groups.

4 Anticipate distress behavior patterns.

5 Plant reminders to activate interest.

6 Seek out first-time buyers.

7 Think navigation.

KEY QUESTION
"Am I treating my customer as if they're already interested?"

STEP 6 — DESIRE

Give your customer the facts

"Sell me this pen."

Have you ever found yourself in this situation? The dreaded interview question, when all you want to do is talk about your latest BASE jump and the website you set up for your brother's bootleg record label and the novel you're writing about the meaning of life. He wants you to sell him his pen!

If it does happen, don't worry. It's dead easy. I'll show you.

First take the pen. Have a good look at it; think why you might use it. Then put it in your briefcase, out of sight. (No good salesman ever walks in and slaps his product down on the desk before understanding his customer's needs.)

So now you start asking questions. What line of work is he in? (He's probably a salesman, too.) What kind of impression does he like to make? Is a stylish signature important? How much writing does he have to do? Does he need to be able to write quickly? Vertically on a clipboard? On NCR forms? To turn pages quickly? To make alterations? Does he often lose pens? In the car? In the warehouse? Do people steal them from his desk?

And so on. (You've already got the job, by the way. The interviewer wanted to see whether you'd try to understand his needs, or blindly burble on about the features of the pen. Your task was to find out why he'd bought it, or — if it was a gift or a free sample — why he'd continued to use it.)

The moral of the story? You can't make your customers need your product, but you can find out whether they want it. The communication task, then, is to help them realize that they do.

Facts: The building blocks of desire

In the above scenario, I think it's pretty clear that you've been invited to begin selling at the "post-interest" stage. Call this desire if you wish, but to me it seems the task is to make the customer *more* interested. *Really* interested.

I introduce this semantic blurring for good reason. Since AIDA was invented it's given rise to — in my view — a comic-strip school of marketing thinking. It's as if your customer's brain was divided into little offices, where the tiny numskulls sit and wait to be convinced. Once you've finished in the interest department, you get a signature and toddle down the corridor to start working on desire.

It doesn't feel right, does it? Surely there's just a continuous spectrum of want? At any point the customer might buy — depending on their perception of hurdles (such as price, availability, and convenience).

If you tried to sell me a pen — if you asked the right questions — you'd discover I'm left-handed and like to write with an italic fountain pen. That means I have to fill in checks and greetings cards from the bottom up, right to left, to avoid smudging. Strange but true. So then you tell me about your patented ink that dries the instant it touches the page. Wanton interest takes over, and the sale is almost made.

So what's desire? And why is there a chapter on it? Answer: Because for you, the marketer, it's a very useful step.

For desire, read detail

I've mentioned several times David Ogilvy's maxim "content is more important than form." Most direct marketers would support this from personal experience. There's an even shorter way of putting it: "Facts sell."

Facts are what makes your customer know they want your product. The more they want it, the more trouble they'll take to buy it. Your job is to deliver the facts.

Facts, of course, equate to benefits. There are hard facts (like "I'll spend £10 less per week on petrol") and also what I call "soft" facts (like "I'll feel really cool and attractive").

So to create wanton interest (or *desire* if you prefer), you need to provide plenty of detail. You need to educate your customer. Only then can they make up their mind.

The numskulls fight back

But here's a paradox. Worldwide, marketers spend billions on advertising and other forms of marketing communication, yet the average college psychology textbook will tell you that people ignore messages they don't agree with. (Picture the numskulls, fingers in ears, chanting: "We can't hear you, we can't hear you.")

The thinking behind this theory of "cognitive consistency" is that we all naturally strive to maintain a consistent set of beliefs and attitudes.[1] Any challenge to this creates adverse psychological tension. (I think that means it does your head in.)

You only have to listen to opposing politicians on *Question Time* to witness cognitive consistency in action. In politics, the stakes are high and hence the dogmatism extreme. But we all do it in our daily lives, even at the most mundane level.

Figure 62 Cognitive consistency in action. Reproduced by kind permission of The Scottish National Party.

We're receptive to information that maintains or enhances consistency, and we avoid information that conflicts with our beliefs and attitudes. This appears to be instinctive and universal human behavior — perhaps a trait that assisted the survival of our ancestors who evolved in small, tightly knit, competing tribes. Today it is elicited by the hail of opinionated marketing communications that besiege our thoughts.

Oops, my Fog Index just went up to 13. Here's how Ries and Trout put this same point in *Positioning*:

"The mind rejects new information that doesn't 'compute.' It accepts only that new information which matches its current state of mind. It filters out everything else."[2]

Indeed, the impetus behind positioning theory is provided by this very marketing communications conundrum. Just how do you get your customer to listen to a claim that conflicts with their beliefs? Of course, the best answer to this is to get there first, and as Ries and Trout point out, most market leaders did exactly that. They got into their customers' minds first, then made darned sure they never had good reason to think anything different.

To further paraphrase *Positioning*: Me-too brands come along later and run marketing and advertising programs as if their (first-in) competitors' positions don't exist. They advertise as if in a vacuum and are disappointed when their messages don't get through. You may know the feeling.

It has long been recognized by psychologists that persuasive communications are more successful at *creating* attitudes than *changing* attitudes. And change is doubly difficult when the attitudes are rooted in a person's self-worth or ego.[3] At your peril try to tell someone she's a bad mother because she's buying the wrong brand.

I'll talk shortly about specific techniques that may help you to get your facts across. At this stage the main thing is to recognize that the message-rejection phenomenon exists, and the risk you run if you ignore it. First I'd like to consider an equally weighty counterphenomenon that you may be able to employ to your advantage.

Me do it

If you've had any contact with small kids, especially aged between about two and five, you'll have come across "Me do it." (More accurately, fortissimo: "ME DO IT!!!") Together, you might be making a birthday card, putting on a pair of shoes, or merely ringing a doorbell. No matter how ineptly, the kid wants to do it.

I think this is because humans have an innate drive to learn via experimentation — a drive that is especially powerful in the very young. Indeed, so powerful that a determined toddler will head-butt you just for the right to insert a coin in a parking meter.

I also think it's very revealing in what it tells us about learning. There's an old Chinese proverb that goes something like this:

"I hear and I forget. I see and I remember. I do and I understand."

During the time I spent working in sales, much of my job involved the training of both new salespeople and sales trainers (having first been trained to do this myself). My final project before moving into marketing was to rewrite the company's sales-training manual. There was one particular model that was very effective.

We called it — unimaginatively — The Training Cycle. But that's what it was, and

Figure 63 Me do it. © Reproduced by kind permission of Warburtons Ltd.

that's just what it did. You could use it to impart even the tiniest technique or procedure.

Here's how it went:

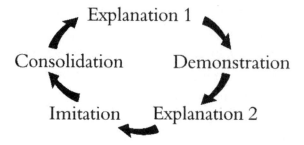

Explanation 1 was very short. You might say: "I'm going to show you how to calculate what share of shelf space we have got in this supermarket." Then you would do it: Demonstration.

Explanation 2 was a little longer. Perhaps: "Notice how I counted up the total number of facings for our packs, and then for competitors' packs, and then worked out a percentage. We have 25 percent of the space here, but 35 percent of the market sector nationally, so we need a plan to improve our representation."

Then, quick as poss, you'd hand over the clipboard and pen, and let your trainee have a go at the next section in the store. Imitation. In my experience, this was when the learning took place.

You could check this by questioning. Systematic questioning was a key tool for the sales trainer — after every call you went through a whole host of points (fundamentally so you knew where you were up to). Questioning proved to me that, without doubt, there was a strong correlation between *doing* and *learning*.

And by doing, the trainee gained a belief in the procedures. With belief came confidence. This was especially vital when it came to learn how to close a sale.

Not long ago I surreptitiously watched a training session in a large stationery store. A salesperson was briefing five members of staff who were clustered around a new photocopier. She spoke clearly, with economy and precision, and showed how various settings and papers produced different effects.

The trouble was, she was talking when I entered and still going strong when I left 10 minutes later. The staff were statuesque. Their minds were stationary.

They'd given up trying to take it in. No one even asked any questions (which is a sure sign of "lights on, no one home"). No doubt they'd resigned themselves to learning by trial and error as they were required to use the machine over the next few days.

The trainer was at least doing one thing right: demonstration. Unfortunately that's where it ended. In some circumstances demonstration alone is sufficient (recall the oven-cleaner salesmen I referred to in Step 4), but imitation can truly influence minds.

Academic research bears this out. Studies show that attitudes toward products based on direct experience are held with more confidence and strength than those based on advertising alone.[4] This has important implications for marketing communications.

Your customer can only want your product more if they learn more about it. In psychology, learning is a major area of study. Here's one definition:

> **"Learning: the process by which experience leads to changes in knowledge, attitudes and/or behaviour resulting from experience."[5]**

The two key components of learning are *rehearsal* and *elaboration*. Rehearsal, as you'd expect, concerns mental repetition, while elaboration means the act of comparing the new stimulus to existing knowledge. It means involvement. When a child battles to be the one who presses the buttons on the cash machine, he's not being self-centered, he's obeying his natural (and subconscious) drive to do what helps him to learn — and that means doing it.

Touch and go

The corollary for the marketer?

Let your customer do it. If at all possible, let them try your product. There's no more powerful way of building desire.

Paco Underhill writes at length about what he calls "the sensual shopper."[6] His thesis, founded on a career of practical observation, is that use of the senses — sight, touch, smell, taste, hearing — is a crucial part of the decision-making process. He proposes that 90 percent of new grocery products fail not because they were ill conceived, but because people never tried them.

It makes sense, so to speak. How can you know you really want a particular bath towel until you touch it? Underhill reports that towels are touched on average by six shoppers before they are purchased. In another study for a haircare brand, 23 percent of shoppers tore into the boxes to test the viscosity and scent of the products.

A girl I knew worked on a cosmetics counter. She once told me that if the store wanted to shift a slow-selling line (say a particular fragrance of hand cream), all they had to do was put out a sampler bottle, and remove the samplers of the other fragrances in the range. Most customers would only buy the variety they were able to try.

So "test driving" doesn't only apply to high-ticket items like cars and hi-fis. When Kleenex launched the first quilted bathroom tissue, we were called in to devise an in-store sampling solution because curious shoppers were breaking into the packs in their thousands. (The solution — you'll be relieved to know — was a simple shelf-edge leaflet containing a couple of sheets of the tissue, to allow the customer to feel the quilting and the softness.)

I'll repeat the statistics I quoted in Step 2 when I talked about the National Lottery: Studies have shown that free samples can create 40 percent more trial. And free-sample users tend to exhibit greater levels of repeat purchase (+12 percent), leading to almost 60 percent higher long-term penetration.

If you're lucky enough to be able to do it *cost-effectively* and in a *relevant* manner, sampling could be the most potent weapon in your marketing arsenal. (But beware the two italicized caveats in the preceding sentence. First, sampling has a high per-capita cost. If you can only afford to reach a tiny fraction of your customer base, you're probably wasting your time. Second, don't burn your budget sampling warm beer to housewives at 11am on a weekday.)

Charles Decker, writing about Procter & Gamble's introduction of Ariel detergent into Austria, reported the conclusion that sampling "wasn't the most *efficient* marketing programme, but it was the most *effective*." P&G ultimately sampled 100 percent of homes in the market. Ariel became the dominant brand.[7]

Remember my Leicas? I did eventually get a pair. I finally took the plunge, after saving up my small change for about three years.

There's a bunch of four of us who've been birdwatching together since we were teenagers. The first time I appeared with my shiny new Leicas my pals were queuing up for a look. They're as experienced users of optical equipment as you could find, yet to a man they were literally speechless. (Or rather, I can't print their reactions.)

When you look through a pair of Leicas you want to throw away your trusty old bins on the spot. Such is the clarity, you can recognize birds that you'd ordinarily use a telescope three times as powerful to observe. And the gearing of the focus mechanism means you can shift from near to far in a split second — you miss nothing.

The advertising copy I've just written in the preceding paragraph would have been no news to my pals. Like me, they'd been reading Leica ads for years. But it was the *doing* that communicated this *detail*. And doing builds desire. Suffice to say, that day I caused Leica sales to rise further.

The numskulls might try to block out your messages, but they can't resist the opportunity to meddle. Interrupt them with the chance of a no-obligation free trial and you might just get through. In the words of Claude Hopkins:

"A good article is its own best salesman."[8]

Figure 64 A repeat of the In Focus ad previously shown in Figure 23. This canny optical retailer consistently invests in taking its product to its customer. Reproduced by kind permission of In Focus.

Desire equals *knowledge*

"Knowledge is a major determinant of consumer behaviour."[9] I memorized this for one of my marketing exams. Like many truisms, it's easily overlooked.

In some marketing textbooks you'll find a model called the Innovation–Decision Process. This is based on the idea that members of a consumer population cumulatively adopt a new product, starting with the innovators, then the early adopters, next the early majority, followed by the late majority, and finally the laggards.[10] It's every product manager's dream to home in on the innovators and let the rest happen as if by magic.

But as Kotler puts it:

"No one has demonstrated the existence of a general personality trait called innovativeness."[11]

So rather than chase the Holy Grail of innovators, perhaps marketers would be better served to focus their efforts on building their customers' knowledge. What consumers buy, where they buy, and when they buy will depend on their knowledge relating to these decisions. Deal with knowledge, and you deal with desire.

Steps you can take

Know your onions

Cut an onion vertically in half and you get a nice set of concentric layers. You buy onions mainly by their external appearance, though the stuff you want to eat is out of sight, in the middle. There's a communication parallel here.

Newspapers — especially tabloids — are great exponents of what I would describe as "three-layered delivery." If you recall my observations in Step 1, I noted how the tabloids allow you to decide in seconds whether an article is something you want to devote precious minutes to. They know their onions.

For your own marketing communication, you may have many persuasive facts. Since you aren't selling face to face, you can't tell when the selling is complete. You don't know when your customer wants your product enough to go out and scale the hurdles that lie before them. And of course, some customers see more hurdles than others: Some want very little detail, others needs lots before they will buy.

Hence layered delivery.

Figure 65 *Layer 1. Note how, for the lead article, 95 percent of the upfront space is given over to a tiny fraction of the total message content. Reproduced by kind permission of News International.*

In Figure 65 I've repeated the front page from *The Sun* shown earlier. For the lead story, notice that almost 95 percent of the space is given over to just a tiny fraction of the total message content — two pictures and a four-word headline. That's layer 1. If the reader likes what they see, they can delve into layer 2: a succinct 66-word precis in the first and only column. If they want to digest still more... by now they've bought the paper. No need to waste valuable selling space on the front page — the rest of the article is tucked away in layer 3, on pages 8 and 9 deep inside the onion, where over 95 percent of the total message content can be found.

Direct marketers use a similar technique to deliver their messages. A good mailing works just like a newspaper. The layer 1 job is done by the message on the envelope, supported by the dominant headline and graphics on the letterhead.

For layer 2, the subheads above each paragraph summarize the main benefits, the action the customer should take, and why they should do it

Figure 66 Layer 2. How subheads can be used to tell the essential story.

now. In my view, the mark of a good sales letter is that you could take away all the letter text and still have a mailing capable of getting a response. (See Figure 66 for an excellent example, based on a real mailing.) John Watson goes so far as to say that body copy has no function for a customer who is highly interested — for them layers 1 and 2 will suffice.[12]

Finally, for layer 3, the letter text itself provides the chapter and verse that the interested-but-most-wavering customer needs to satisfy themselves that they should reach for their checkbook.

Long on copy, long on benefits

"The seductive love of narrative, when we ourselves are the heroes of the events which we tell, often disregards the attention due to the time and patience of the audience, and the best and wisest have yielded to its fascination." (Sir Walter Scott, *Rob Roy*, 1817)

The sad thing about being a marketer is that you can't even read a classic novel without looking for tips. The quotation above leapt off the page when I read *Rob Roy*. I think it makes a couple of enlightening points. First, it says talk about yourself and you'll bore your listener (remember two "you"s per "we"); second, it offers an insight into the length of copy.

Despite most marketers' first reaction being to turn up their noses at long copy, handbooks written by direct marketing practitioners unanimously espouse long copy. Who's right? Scott himself was no slouch with the pen: *Rob Roy* contains the best part of 200,000 words, with a pea-souper of a Fog Index hovering around the 20 mark.

David Ogilvy said that in his experience "long copy sells more than short." He wrote at length in its favor, citing one press ad containing 6,450 words that pulled 10,000 responses, without even a coupon.[13]

I think if Scott were an agency copywriter today, he'd say the same as he did in 1817: The key issues are the *time* and *patience* of the audience. There's nothing wrong with long copy, provided you don't abuse this privilege. As Drayton Bird puts it:

"Because one maxim is that long copy always outpulls short, bad writers often write far too much."[14]

In my opinion, there's no such thing as long copy, or short copy, only *enough* copy. Give your customer a stream of relevant, interesting facts and benefits, and they'll stay with you.

This view is supported by the findings of Starch, who concluded that:

"...people do read long ads and that, with the increase in text, readership decreases very slightly beyond the 75-word point. Length of text as such is a relatively minor factor. The most potent factor by far is the substance of the sales message and how it is presented. Vital content presented in appealing form, whether 100 or 500 words in length, will be seen and read by a substantial reader audience."[15]

Figure 67 *The sizzle versus the sausage. Two perfectly good ads from the same magazine, in the same product category. One boasts 32 words, the other 703 (or thereabouts). Copy is long enough when it completes the task in hand. Reproduced by kind permission of Pernod Ricard and Direct Wines.*

Use a chip-box

A useful tool in making copy easier to digest is what we named the "chip-box." I'm sure lots of people have independently invented this technique, but we laid our own claim to it. Basically it's what it says — a separate box containing a chunk of the text.

Figure 68 The chip-box: a simple device for untangling and juxtaposing the main strands of a message.

When I approve or edit copy, especially for ads and mailings, I often notice the writer is wrestling with two or more strands of the message. For instance, at its simplest, the writer will be telling the customer a) what to do and b) why they should do it.

A similar tangle can occur in an "informative" communication (i.e. one not requiring a response). Here the writer tells the recipient a) what to think about and b) why they should believe it.

I can empathize with the writer. The task is often to combine a navigation/ease message with an interest/desire message. Within a single letter text, it's not always straightforward to integrate these two components and maintain the flow of (the customer's) thinking.

The chip-box acts as a kind of pressure valve. If you look at Figure 68 you can see what I mean. Admittedly this is not a long-copy example, but notice at a glance how the chip-box pulls out (and emphasizes) a key section of information that otherwise would have cluttered the letter text. In this instance, the chip-box acts as a kind of visual aid, almost like a diagram or chart.

Thus the two main strands of thought that the letter is trying to communicate are kept apart, and so are easier to digest. You can use a chip-box (or several in a longer letter or ad) for sections of your message such as "How to apply" or "Reasons to buy" to equally good effect.

In one split-test we ran, a chip-box mailing outpulled a non-chip-box mailing by more than 300 percent, even though the content of the two letters was virtually identical.

Let the facts get in the way

It's long been known in direct marketing circles that factual propositions work best. For instance, here are two headlines, for an imaginary new dental anesthetic.

Headline A: "Dentists save time and money with new RapidoNumb."
Headline B: "How a dentist from Basildon increased his profits by £249 a week. New RapidoNumb — the tooth's ready to drill in 15 seconds."

While both headlines express similar benefits, my money would be on headline B, longer and more unwieldy though it is. Facts bring vague benefits to life. The introduction of a specific dentist, an exact cash sum, and a precise time converts a toothless platitude into a needle-sharp proposition.

All good direct marketers know this, but the principle is often ignored in other forms of communication. In two successive years we ran identical on-pack promotions on a leading tissue brand. The offer was: Buy four packs and send for a voucher for your next pack free. If everybody replied, four million free packs would have been despatched.

In year 1, the proposition stated: "Claim a free pack of tissues." The response was 4.7 percent.

In year 2, the proposition stated: "4 million free packs to be claimed." The response was 14.5 percent.

The first year's result of 4.7 percent was around about the industry norm for this kind of offer, and the outcome was viewed as satisfactory. Prior to the repeat promotion, I recommended to our client that we adopt the direct marketing technique of introducing a genuine, factual number into the proposition. The result: an extraordinary uplift in response. (Probably because — seeing that there were four million free packs — the customer believed the offer would be around long enough for them to collect and apply.)

Proof and testimonial

Facts prove benefits. Customers believe facts and convert them into sales. But in the absence of facts, customers turn to authority.

When Crest toothpaste was first launched in the US, despite its superior performance it was unable to break through in the market. Established competitive products were able to make similar promises about cavity prevention. However, after a full six years Crest finally secured endorsement of its claims from the American Dental Association. This enabled the customer to believe in the benefit. Sales tripled and Crest overtook Colgate as the leading brand.[16]

Authority comes in many forms. It can be as grand as the American Dental Association, or as undistinguished as your pal whom you ask in the

Figure 69 Facts sell. With hardly a superfluous word in sight, an extensive specification and a keen financial package do all the talking for Mitsubishi. Reproduced by kind permission of Mitsubishi Cars.

"In the last 20 years, only one thing has come between Bill and his birds."

During that time, Bill has become the UK's most recognised birdwatcher and has inspired a whole generation with his devotion to the study of birds and wildlife. So it is only natural that he would choose the best observation equipment - LEICA.

Bill's 20 year partnership with LEICA began when he asked some friends if he could try their LEICA Trinovid binoculars. Bill recalls, "they were smaller, lighter, had great eyecups and, best of all, the optics were brilliant!"

So brilliant, in fact, Bill hasn't looked back since!

LEICA binoculars carry a 30 year warranty and are available at your LEICA dealer.

 my point of view

Leica Camera Ltd, Davy Avenue, Knowlhill, Milton Keynes, MK5 8LB. Telephone: 01908 246300 for literature or 01908 666663 for general and service enquiries
www.leica-camera.com   LEICA is pleased to be a sponsor of Butterfly Conservation

Figure 70 Bill Oddie. A credible and endearing brand spokesman. Reproduced by kind permission of Leica Camera Ltd and Mr Bill Oddie.

pub because he knows about computers. Whichever, it's a fact that we all seek sources of authority when we're uncertain about making a purchase.

Leica has for many years employed Bill Oddie as brand spokesman for its binoculars; in my view, a well-considered endorsement. Not only is Bill Oddie a likeable, entertaining celebrity, but he also knows his birds (and his kit). Had comedian Peter Kay appeared in Leica ads, I may have read them out of curiosity, but I would have been doubtful about his ability to advise me on such an experience-based product.

Peter Kay as spokesman for John Smith's bitter, on the other hand – no problem. And not because it's easier to believe someone like him could be an expert on beer. Peter Kay's an expert on *Zeitgeist*, and that's what I would be buying into.

Certainly don't be fooled that for "celebrity" you can read "magic wand." A couple of years ago I remember being in a presentation by an advertising agency to a client for whom we were working on a separate project. The brand in question was beginning to flag and the advertising was getting the blame. Today was the "reveal" for a new strategy. The client services director gradually built up the suspense, finally to announce with great import: "The time has come to inject a little bit of fame into the brand." (I couldn't believe my ears. If fame's so good, why wait until now?)

In the next few months a small fortune (well, not even small) was spent in an exotic location filming a new commercial featuring a well-known rock group. It bore little resemblance to anything that had gone before for the brand, and the budget stretched to a single execution. It was ditched within the year; by then the brand team had all moved on.

What does the research say about this subject? In short it's this: The more credible the source, the more the persuasion. But the more deeply your customer needs to consider your product before purchase, the less likely it is that a "random" celebrity will have a persuasive effect.[17] (A problem overcome by choosing Bill Oddie to advertise binoculars, or David Beckham football boots. But you wouldn't do it the other way round.)

Some "celebrity" ads score very high levels of recall. But there is a caveat. Studies have shown that unless the product being advertised is perceived as relevant by the audience, viewers simply watch the ad for its executional values; i.e. as a form of entertainment. This sort of recall clearly has little value to a commercial enterprise concerned about sales. (It's a bit like sending your best salesperson round to all your customers, only for him to tell jokes for their enjoyment. It doesn't take much for showmanship to displace salesmanship.)

As I said above, authority need not come from a celebrity. Indeed, your customer is more likely to trust a "homophilous" person when they need information about a new product.[18] (Homophilous means someone who shares beliefs, education, and social status – hence the persuasive power of your homophilous pal in the pub.) So whatever the nature of your business, you should always be able to find credible sources to help back up your claims.

DRTV ads are packed with satisfied homophilous customers. And DRTV ads live or die by the responses they generate. Surely no coincidence?

In more traditional direct marketing parlance, this technique is known as the "testimonial." It is a staple of the industry and something every business can exploit. The key is to be credible: A blurred picture of "Mrs X from Ullapool" claiming she got whiter whites won't wash.

If you can't find real people to feature in your marketing, you might be able to exploit a more general angle instead. Copywriter Alastair Crompton calls it "testimonials from competitors."[19] The idea here is that you say something like this:

"The local garage that the directors of Toyota trust to service their limousines."

In Scotland, the best-selling single-malt whisky has long been Glenmorangie. In the rest of Britain it's Glenfiddich. I've always been surprised that more is not made of "The malt the Scots prefer."

Use the emotions to reach the intellect
If you start out by telling your customer they're wrong, the chances are they'll give you the cold shoulder. Their emotional reaction overrides their intellect. Roy H Williams puts it like this:

Successful Personal Investing

How to acquire the independent, unbiased, practical investing and money-management know-how you need, in one complete, no-nonsense package.

Here is just a small sample of the many, many enthusiastic responses to the SPI course:

"SPI is exactly what I have been looking for, for a long time." B.V. B., Crewe

"Don't change a thing ... As a result of SPI I now have a **large surplus at the bank** – tax savings – a small profit on shares." I. K., Walton-on-Thames

"...the first two lessons of SPI are absolutely fascinating..." B.B., Horley

"I couldn't stop reading SPI – I have read it three times." J. R., Porthcawl

"... SPI is a counter to the sort of waffle a stockbroker feeds one with. And so-called 'financial advisers' come to that!"
A. B., Ruislip

"£83,589.60. Not a bad return on my investment in SPI." Mr. F., Surrey

"This course should be taught in classes all over the country, so that the mystique surrounding investing can be removed." R.H., London

"Through your advice my investments have **increased more than £30,000** in the past 6 months. This course has been the best value for money that I have ever spent." G. H., West Bridgeford

"SPI is very clear and simple and has something for everyone including those who are starting out with not too much money, right to those who want to do their own wheeling and dealing." A. J., Kirkdale

"SPI has become my 'Money Bible'. I am also pleased that friends and colleagues now ask my advice."
S. W., Uxbridge

"Wish I had been introduced to Successful Personal Investing 10 years ago." C. S., Westhuntspill

"I would recommend it to all, including those who are already successful investors ... excellently presented in a forthright manner, **clearly guiding** one through all aspects of finance."
J. S., East Yorkshire

"Very brilliant course. **A passage to wealth** ..."
E. P., London

The full names and addresses of these SPI course participants are a matter of record and are withheld here solely in respect of their personal privacy.

Statement of Principles

1. IRS is an independent service offering unbiased education and information to assist you in making informed investing and money management decisions.

2. IRS is not affiliated with any stockbroker, unit trust or investment trust, agency or financial intermediary of any type. We make no financial offerings.

3. No salesman will call you – we have none. You may drop out of our course at any time and pay only for the materials you keep.

INDEPENDENT RESEARCH SERVICES,
5 – 7 Bridge Street, Abingdon, Oxon OX14 3HN
Tel. 01235 551727
IRS and Independent Research Services are trading names of Charterhouse Communications plc.
Reg. in England no. 3242649 Reg. Office Arnold House, 36-41 Holywell Lane, London EC2A 3SF

Figure 71 Classic use of the testimonial. Reproduced by kind permission of Charterhouse Communications plc.

"We usually do what we feel is right, then use intellectual logic to justify what our emotions have decided."[20]

Williams' view is that a marketing communication will be more powerful if it sets out first to engage the emotions, and to do so by reminding the customer of something they've always known or suspected. I wholeheartedly agree with this thesis: It gets right to the core of how a good salesperson would operate on a one-to-one basis. Here's an example translating the concept into advertising.

Not long after the merger that gave rise to the giant insurer Royal & SunAlliance (RSA), we worked on a project team to develop new advertising aimed at the company's 10,000 or so High Street brokers. RSA's marketing manager at the time, Steve Kingshott (one of the sadly rare breed I would describe as marketeer rather than marketer), was keen to blend NLP techniques with our own creative approach.

The structural upheavals in the insurance market in recent years have made life very difficult for the broker. Inevitably, service levels have fluctuated, as waves of new staff and new systems have rippled through the major insurers' organizations. Cynical and skeptical would best describe the attitude of the average broker.

A challenge. As a result of our project team's thinking, to appeal to the typical "auditory" broker (i.e. a person showing a preference for communication in words, rather than via pictures), I wrote the ad shown in Figure 72: "Announcing the launch of yet another household product that's *not quite right* for your customers."

Wow. "Not quite right." And Steve got it approved!

I wish I could tell you this was the most successful ad that RSA ever ran. Unfortunately, the scale of trade advertising just didn't justify the cost of sufficiently detailed research and measurement. However, anecdotally, it worked — certainly we were told it created considerable interest in the new product.

Here at last was advertising that the broker-liaison teams weren't embarrassed about. It was telling the truth. None of the usual platitudes about flexibility, support, and commitment.

Announcing the launch of yet another household product that's *not quite right* for your customers

(and seven reasons you should sell it)

ONE: *No one else can.* It's only available through Brokers like you.

TWO: *It's competitive.* You'll find it regularly among the Top 5 on your screen.

THREE: *It's easy.* With one of the shortest application forms around, it's a breeze for you and your customers.

FOUR: *And it's going to get even better!* That's where YOU come in.

FIVE: *Satisfy more customers.* Work with us to develop the products your customers want.

SIX: *And you'll see changes fast.* We are building a whole range of products in a flexible and adaptable way. Options will include Annual Worldwide Travel, Legal Expenses and Caravans.

SEVEN: *Choices One* is here from *November 1st.* The new base contract, it's perfect for customers with low claims histories, looking for low premiums to match.

So make a positive choice. Call your dedicated Business Team Manager now, or e-mail us directly on choices@royal-and-sunalliance.co.uk.
There are seven good reasons why you should.

www.royal-and-sunalliance.co.uk/broker

Figure 72 *Honesty equals credibility. Reproduced by kind permission of Royal & SunAlliance.*

213

I would have loved to have called on a customer and used the same script. "I'm here to talk with you about the launch of yet another household product that's not quite right for your customers. And I can give you seven good reasons why you should sell it." It's actually what a real salesperson would say.

The back-up story the RSA people related to brokers was like this: "Look, we know you need new products to compete with the direct insurers, and you need them fast. Rather than wait, we're bringing Choices One to market right now. We could tinker for years and still not get it right. Have the raw ammunition today and help us shape it to meet your customers' needs."

Intuitively, this type of approach makes absolute sense. Indeed, research supports the principle. Two-sided messages (those including pros and cons) have been shown to increase customer perceptions of advertiser truthfulness and believability, compared to one-sided messages (those presenting only pros).[21]

Maybe this is a technique you can use.

Not a million miles away from this approach is the broader issue of positioning. I've referred to this several times, and its popularization by Ries and Trout in their book of the same name. The theory goes that if you can't get into your customer's mind first, your best bet is to do it by reference to something they already understand and believe.

It certainly makes for quicker understanding. Think how quickly unleaded petrol caught on. Yet it took years for diesel cars to become popular. (Unless you studied organic chemistry you've probably got no idea what diesel really is.) Why didn't they just call it HMP — short for high-mileage petrol?

Often, positioning tactics have the simultaneous effect of repositioning the competition. The launch of *The Independent* surely forced many readers to re-evaluate the neutrality of their usual newspaper. Miller Lite, a runaway success in the US, raised calorie consciousness among millions of drinkers. And today's crop of organic line extensions are vexing brand managers, whose original offerings by definition must be unorganic.

The prize for the best positioning job in recent years must, however, surely go to a political party: New Labour. (And if at this point you're thinking, "Hey — NEW AIDA," you'd be right.)

Figure 73 *Positioning theory put into practice.*

Classical conditioning

If you didn't mess around in biology class you might remember Pavlov's dogs. Every time he fed them, he rang a bell. Eventually, just by ringing the bell, he could make the dogs salivate. It was the original classical conditioning experiment.

Psychologists who studied marketing in action realized that for many years marketers had been employing similar techniques, if inadvertently. (I mentioned in Step 4 the playing of Christmas carols in shops, and the questionable use of sex appeal.)

Here's how it's meant to work. The original Häagen-Dazs campaign is again a good example. The ads are designed to evoke pleasurable and warm emotions in the mind of the viewer. These emotions then become associated with the product. Later, the viewer, now a *shopper*, sees the product, recalls the emotions, likes the feeling, and buys the product.

In markets such as lager, cigarettes, and saloon cars, competing products are virtually the same. In these sectors, classical conditioning is heavily relied on to create a reason to buy. And brands that have been most successful are those that have captured key positions in the customer's mind: coolest, wittiest, sexiest, smartest, most daring.

My advice on classical conditioning? For the vast majority of businesses: Steer well clear. I say this not because it won't work, but because I see so many examples of it *not working*. (Please read on.)

The irrelevant simile

The irrelevant simile is a term I invented, so my apologies if there's a better version I've never heard of. A simile, as you may recall, is when "a thing is described by being likened to something."[22] Hence: drinks like a fish; fit as a fiddle; and reeks like a lumb (Scots for smokes like a chimney).

So, one thing being likened to another. I have no problem with this in an ad... except when the connection is irrelevant. Let me explain why I believe it's a mistake.

Imagine you're interviewing a candidate for a job. The job is for a relief position, so it requires versatility, filling in for anyone who might be absent. Thus you want to know if the candidate is a flexible sort.

"Oh yes," he replies. And he takes from his briefcase a picture of an international gymnast, bent over backwards in the crab position. He continues: "Here's a picture of a very flexible person. Because I'm holding it up beside me, it means I'm a very flexible person, too."

After you'd surreptitiously checked your escape route, you'd no doubt bring the interview to a close at the earliest opportunity.

Mad as it would be to attempt to sell yourself like this, you can pick up virtually any magazine or switch on the television and find big blue-chip companies doing just that. (Car manufacturers are among the worst culprits.) They think up the point they want to communicate, find an entirely unconnected example of the same concept, and hold it up beside themselves. Then they wonder why their ads don't work.

David Ogilvy politely advised against the use of what he called analogies. He wrote that Gallup found readers misunderstood them. Often, they thought it was the analogous item that was being advertised.[23]

I'll go a stage further and rudely advise against analogies. *It's dim to use them.* With so many other techniques available, why select an approach that is so patently nonsense?

And that's why I recommend you avoid classical conditioning. Nine times in every ten it comes out as an irrelevant simile.

Take the (disguised) ad shown in Figure 74. While the ad is for financial services, the image shows a jet airliner. The advertiser is trying to say they're both best when handled by ultra-professionals. True. And that this means the advertiser is ultra-professional. Not true. An irrelevant simile proves nothing.

What if the fictional interviewee had shown a picture of *himself* in the crab position? Still pretty irrelevant as far as the job is concerned, although at least you'd think he'd got a bit about him. But far better for him to have handed you a reference from a former employer, or described how in his previous job he was expected to cover any of seven different positions at short notice.

Killing them softly

If you deal in fragrances, fashions, or expensive watches and jewelry, you'd be excused for thinking I've neglected you. At first sight, many ads for these products seem to ignore most of the rules that lead to effective communication. No headlines, no benefits, sometimes not even a brand name. Just an extravagant piece of photography.

Some things are best in the hands of the ultra-professional

Pick up virtually any magazine or switch on the TV and you can find big blue-chip companies trying to persuade you with irrelevant similes. They think up the point they want to communicate, find an entirely unconnected example of the same concept, and hold it up beside themselves. But why on earth should you be convinced?

David Ogilvy politely advised against the use of what he called analogies. He wrote that Gallup found that readers misunderstood them. Often, they thought it was the analogous item that was being advertised.

Figure 74 An irrelevant simile proves nothing. That an aircraft needs a qualified pilot does not mean an unrelated financial services company has ultra-professional staff.

Yet you know you can't run ads with headlines like "Wear Armani and you'll look really cool." It doesn't work like that.

While in Step 4 I argued it was a fallacy that a picture is automatically worth 10,000 words, you might also recall I promised to show a vital and unique role for pictures. And here it is.

Because there is no way a customer can rationally justify spending £10,000 on a watch (or £1,000 or even £100), or splashing out on perfume that costs more per ounce than gold, or buying a new outfit that will be passé (if not past it) in three months... because of these intellectual barriers, you can only sell such products to your customers' emotions. And the good news is, when it comes to sales, the emotional outpulls the rational every time.

I'm not saying this can't be done with words. But it is the one area of marketing communication where visual techniques are in a class of their own. Like sensory language, pictures are a shortcut to the emotions.

The right picture can make your customer live your moment in their mind. It might be imagination, but they're "doing it" just the same. And doing builds desire.

Humans have sensitive antennae for picking up the tiniest of cues that impinge on emotional needs. And the eye is a vital conduit.

These needs include belonging, acceptance, status, sex appeal, and self-expression. They exert powerful influences over behavior. Together they make up the *self-image*.

Your self-image is how you perceive yourself and your relationship to the world around you.[24] And if you're like most people, you'll have a perceived gap between your *actual* self and your *ideal* self. Behavioral scientists have long established that a central human motive is to constantly enhance this view of self — and to strive to close the gap between actual and ideal.

Bring on shopping. The facts that appeal to the emotions — that I earlier called the soft facts — are every bit as real as hard facts like "washes whiter" or "kills moles" or "0–60 in 5.4 seconds." For instance, here's a soft fact put into words:

"Your pals won't take the mickey out of you if you wear Nike trainers."

Figure 75 Creating peer-group acceptance for a brand and its customers. Reproduced by kind permission of Nike.

This invented example might sound trivial, but peer-group rejection for wearing the wrong gear is just about every teenage boy's greatest fear. (In my day Doc Martens and Ben Sherman were badges that kept you in the gang.) Obviously Nike can't put this headline in an ad, but nor does it need to — subtle imagery does the job.

And soft facts can be just as important for mundane products. Take washing-up liquid. For what seemed like forever, Fairy Liquid was advertised on a dual hard-and-soft strategy. Hard-hitting ads showed how many more dishes it washed, while nice emotional vignettes of mum and daughter pulled at the heartstrings.

Soft hands, and lasts longer. Which is which? Actually, I think *soft hands* was the rational benefit, and *lasts longer* the emotional (because lasts longer translates into good housekeeping and thus boosts mum's self-image).

So if your communication objective involves an appeal to the emotions, then a visual appeal to your customer's self-image may be a powerful tool. If you're in the fragrance or fashion business, I think your biggest advertising challenge lies not in creating desire, but in making the most of the crucial steps that begin and end the buying process. A pictures-only approach imposes severe constraints on achieving both initial navigation and attention, and ultimate action — so that's where your efforts should focus.

I mentioned in Step 4 my 1,028-ad survey in which only 29 percent promised a benefit in their headline. For fashion ads, especially clothes and fragrance, we're talking low single figures. In fact, many of these had no headline at all. Yet when you're in a magazine like *Marie Claire*, competing with another 148 full-page ads (never mind 250 pages of editorial), your visual gets the briefest of scampers along the catwalk. At times like this, the marketer really should question a wordless execution.

In Figure 76 overleaf is an example of an ad for Sloggi that looks really good, and is enhanced by its headline. It promises two benefits, and demonstrates there is no need to leave to chance what the reader takes out of the message.

In Figure 77 is another really nice idea, this time for Lurpak. The image plus the packshot work together to reveal the answer to the conundrum. But note there's no headline.

Figure 76 *Resist the temptation... to drop the headline. Reproduced by kind permission of Triumph International Ltd.*

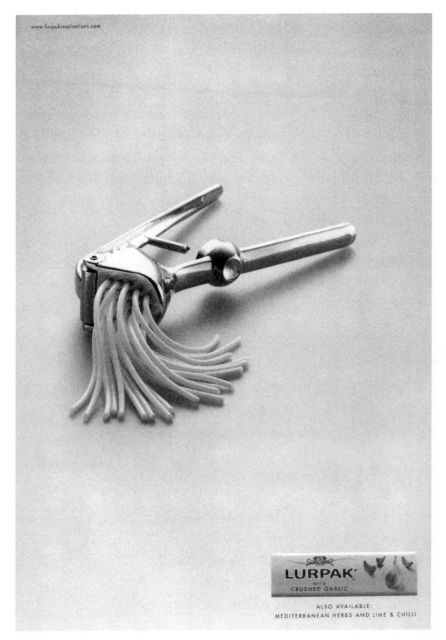

Figure 77 *"Delicious butter with fresh garlic already built in." Reproduced by kind permission of Arla Foods Plc and BMPDDB.*

The product benefit is "delicious butter containing freshly crushed garlic." That seems a pretty strong message to me, and not a light to hide under a bushel.

In the approval room this ad should be greeted by cheers. These should then be qualified by the sobering question: How will customer meet marketing? If it's by browsing at 1–2 seconds per page, I'd add a headline.

On the other hand, I have no doubt that if you can get your customer to work out the conundrum on their own, it's better than just telling them. The deeper involvement will have a greater impact on their learning. And knowledge determines behavior.

So yes, you can use your judgment... but you can also do some simple testing to understand a) how your customer mainly meets your marketing, and b) what they take out from it in different forms – for instance, with and without a headline.

DESIRE — SEVEN TOP TIPS

1 Start by telling your customer they're right.

2 Let your customer "do it."

3 Use imagery to reach their emotions.

4 Layer your message.

5 Use specifics.

6 Call on relevant authorities.

7 Avoid irrelevant similes.

KEY QUESTION
"Does my customer have all the facts?"

STEP 7 — ACTION

Help your customer to say *yes*

A t the end of my first week as a salesman — my first proper job — Bruce my sales trainer did a final review of my progress before we went our separate ways for the weekend. I thought I'd done quite well, and he largely echoed this sentiment, but as I drove home his last words were ringing in my ears: "I'm a bit worried about your clothes. We'll talk about it on Monday."

This came as a bolt from the blue. I'd borrowed money to make sure I had a decent new suit. (Sure, I was hoping no one would notice the cowboy boots until I got my first pay check, but I thought I'd gotten away with them.) That night I spent ages in front of the mirror, but was none the wiser.

Monday morning came and Bruce got into my car before we did the first call. "Right," he said, "Always remember that the buyer's natural instinct is to say no. He doesn't want to say no — he's a buyer, after all — but he can't help it. So our job is to make it easy for him to say yes. We call that the close."

Merde. He'd said close, not clothes. Like most new salespeople, I struggled with closing the sale.

After the call, in which Bruce had done the presentation to the buyer (remember *demonstration*), he asked me to evaluate *his* close. I replied, "What close?" I never saw it.

We'd located the buyer — the store manager — in his office. At first he'd muttered brusquely, "I don't need anything, do I?" Bruce proceeded to tell him about our marketing activity and special offers, and how many cases of each product he was proposing; plus the normal replacement order for lines not on promotion; how many cases that came to in total; that we'd deliver on Thursday as usual; and that there were a couple of lines missing from the shelves (but with stock in the warehouse) that we'd like to put on sale before we left. Then Bruce clicked shut his presenter and the buyer almost cheerily waved us off. What close?

Bruce's explanation went something like this: "What I did there, we call the 'assumed close.' You just keep going, and if you don't get any objections, well... you just keep going. I could have done what we call the 'straight close' — basically that means at the end I ask the question "Is that OK?" — but this guy seemed quite happy so I didn't see any point inviting him to pick holes in our order."

Gradually I began to appreciate the nuances of closing. It wasn't a con trick, but it certainly involved some psychology. And to Bruce's assertion that the buyer's initial reaction is always *no*, I added my own observation that at some indefinable tipping point in the interaction, the whole balance changes and it actually becomes distinctly uncomfortable for him to say no.

An informed opinion on closing comes from Derrick White:

"Teaching someone to close is very difficult. You'll hear the older salesman tell the novice, 'You should have closed him there.' Maybe. Closing is a very personal issue. If you simply do not feel right or you are just blindly following what someone else has advised, it can be very risky. Rather like someone else's chat-up line at a party. He gets away with it while you get your face slapped."[1]

The sales spell

Next time you get buttonholed by a *Big Issue* vendor or a shop assistant, think about how you react. My guess would be that you find saying "No thanks" or "Just looking, thanks" slightly uncomfortable. Since it doesn't take much to reach that mysterious tipping point, you're quick to take evasive action. You don't want to fall under the sales spell.

And I bet also — especially in a retail environment — that quite often after fending off a shop assistant, paradoxically you do feel a tinge of annoyance with yourself. Because you probably *do* need help, and you probably *are* quite interested in buying something.

Of course, the sales spell doesn't really exist. At least, there's no magic — it's inside your head... the customer's head. A good salesperson knows this and lets their customer's mind trip along to its own tipping point. The most effective close I was ever taught was the *silent* close.

The "no" reflex

(Here come the birds again.) Most mornings as I write I watch a robin in my garden defend "his" bird table from all-comers. There's usually more food there than he could eat in a week, but he fights beak and claw to stop the holidaying blackcaps grabbing even a tiny morsel. I'm sure it's instinctive behavior: Conservation of one's resources is a vital and universal trait for survival.

Indeed, my theory is that we share with the robin a kind of "no" reflex. Under sudden and unexpected pressure to yield resources, we invariably respond with a no. (Certainly, if I had a "yes" reflex, within a month I could sign away all my money to charity mailings alone.) Just like Bruce said, the buyer can't help it, even though he's paid to be an interested customer.

Cognitive dissonance

Cognitive dissonance might sound like gobbledegook, but it *is* worth understanding. It's one of the academic principles I'd bracket in the actually useful category. Why? Because I reckon cognitive dissonance — or, more specifically, fear of it — lies at the root of the "no" reflex.

Busting the jargon, cognitive means thinking and dissonance means unhappy. It translates into *doubt* and *regret*. "Did I make the right decision?" "Am I glad I bought it?"

Cognitive dissonance is a widely observed human emotion. It has been much studied in relation to buying behavior (when it is known as postpurchase dissonance). It's recognized as a transitory feeling, and it doesn't automatically lead to permanent dissatisfaction.[2]

It's quite natural when you think about it. We spend our lives gathering and protecting our resources. So it's no wonder we question our actions and wisdom when we give some of them up.

Faced with the pressure to buy, to exchange resources for an uncertain return, it's easier to say no. Preserve the status quo. Run away. (You can always buy another day.)

Indeed, even when your "no" reflex can't put you off completely, your underlying drive tries to make you buy the *cheapest*. (Paradoxically, this is just as likely to cause post-purchase dissonance, when later you begin to wish you'd paid a bit more for a slightly better model.)

Action equals *permission*

You're selling to an interested customer, who may really desire your product. It ought to be easy. But you should remind yourself that their subconscious programs may kick in at any moment. Their drive to avoid post-purchase dissonance means you can expect a reflex rejection — especially if you take them unawares with your message.

Traditionally (using old AIDA), the final emphasis is on telling the customer what to do. It's all about order forms, reply devices, and pre-paid envelopes.

NEW AIDA thinking, of course, removes these hurdles at the outset, through navigation and ease. (And in doing so, makes a massive contribution to your extraordinary response.)

And NEW AIDA therefore leaves you free to apply the skills of salesmanship to your interested customer's mind, which needs that last extra nudge to help them to buy. They want to buy but their defenses say no. Your challenge: Give them permission to say *yes*.

Steps you can take

Cultivate browsers

In some respects post-purchase dissonance is a misnomer, because your customer often gets it long before they buy. Indeed, they go out — sometimes for weeks in advance — and actively practice having it. We call it "shopping around."

Sure, shopping around is partly to check that you get a good deal. But that in itself is a key component of avoiding post-purchase dissonance. There's nothing worse than finding your new television on sale £100 cheaper the week after you bought it. Retailers know this, and try to remove your fear of dissonance by reassuring you that they'll refund the difference if you find the goods cheaper elsewhere. (Post-purchase *difference*, maybe?)

If you've ever been house-hunting, I'm sure you'll have experienced that dreadful sinking feeling when on viewing, things don't turn out as you'd hoped. Perhaps there's a cooling tower (just out of shot on the prospectus) casting its shadow across the lawn. Maybe the drum-and-bass you thought must be the teenage son in his bedroom turns out to be coming through the wall. Or you notice 17 cats peering out of the neighbors' grimy window, they've got geese out the back, and the greasy guy with the wrench leering over the fence looks like he was in *Deliverance*.

Do you recognize this disappointment? Actually it's worse than that. You feel in utter despair, such is the magnitude of the "mistake" you've made.

Remarkably, you go through with the viewing. You pick out little good points and build them up. You shrug off the damp patches and the uneven floors and the 1950s kitchen.

It's only later, perhaps when you're driving away (or downing a stiff drink in the local pub), that you realize *you don't have to buy it*. You'd got so excited about the particulars that your mind had leapt ahead of you.

Such is the relief, you feel like celebrating. Go ahead, have another drink. (You'll need one — you're just about to ride the same emotional roller coaster at the next property.)

Post-purchase dissonance is traditionally associated with high-ticket, high-commitment items like buying a new car, choosing a university, or the house-hunting example I've just described. But I believe it applies right across the spectrum of goods and services, consumer and business. And no doubt it varies by customer, according to their wealth and — in particular — the risk-averse nature of their personality.

So shopping around serves a potent purpose. It enables the customer to test out whether they're likely to suffer post-purchase dissonance, and to

Figure 78 *Tackling post-purchase dissonance ahead of the competition... and ahead of the sale. Reproduced by kind permission of MG Rover Group Ltd.*

assess how they feel about it. I think many retailers (indeed, marketers) fail to appreciate this. It's the source of many lost sales.

Recently I asked a couple of assistants in an electrical store what proportion of customers claimed they were just looking when approached. One said "more than half" and the other said "most." A straw poll, I agree, but I think it's reasonable to assume there's one heck of a lot of customers out there, every weekend, practicing dissonance.

Today, a browser. One day soon, a buyer. So why not tackle the dissonance while you can?

If the customer's in your store, that suggests it's convenient for them. A major reason for them to buy from you. All they need is permission.

You don't have to sell to them today. In fact, maybe don't even try. Instead, give them reasons to come back.

The lesson for the retailer? Basic staff training. Develop a means of dialog that recognizes that the customer is not trying to buy now — they're shopping around, which means they're seeking evidence that they won't suffer from post-purchase dissonance.

The dialog could be as simple as this:

Shop assistant: "Can I help you, Sir?"
Customer: "I'm just looking, thanks."
Shop assistant: "It's a good idea to check out a few stores for the right deal. Can I give you some back-up leaflets and prices to take away?"

I could run this on, but I hope it's obvious that it immediately opens a gateway to provide reinforcement without perceived selling pressure. If they're a genuine interested customer, they'll come with you. You might even make the sale there and then. (Always have a "today's offer" up your sleeve.)

Whatever the immediate outcome, the chances are you'll be the only retailer they've visited who's given them reasons to come back. You might have handed them a 10-day voucher giving an extra 10 percent off. You might have told them about your returns and exchanges service, or your in-home support. Or perhaps you'll have talked about future trade-ins to help them to get their head round the price in general.

Show your skill

In one study, entitled "The effects of salesman similarity and expertise on consumer purchasing behaviour," researchers varied the expertise of a music-store salesman, who tried to encourage customers to buy a deck-cleaning kit. When the salesman was seen as knowledgeable, 66 percent of customers bought the kit. However, when he admitted he was unfamiliar with the kit, only 20 percent purchased.[3]

When you hear evidence like this, you nod your head. Intuitively, it's so obvious. And it's such a simple card to play.

Clearly, a knowledgeable salesperson can help a customer deflect any sniping self-doubts. But I think it goes deeper than that. Knowledge encourages dialog between seller and buyer; during that process the customer's mind slips unnoticed past its tipping point; saying *no* becomes somehow undesirable.

Put your foot in the door

I talked in Step 6 about the power of touch in building desire. Contact can close sales too. Paco Underhill reports that in clothing stores, the shopper conversion rate increases by 50 percent if there is staff-initiated contact with the customer, and it jumps by 100 percent if the customer also uses the dressing room.[4] (And then how can you *not* buy when an attractive assistant tells you how great you look?)

Underhill bemoans the dowdy state of most stores' dressing rooms and the lack of subtle personal selling support, like suggesting matching accessories. He observes: "When the customer is in the dressing room, he or she is in total buying mode." Yet the moment is so often squandered.

More prosaically, Underhill reports a simple test in a fast-food restaurant. The counter staff were briefed to ask if the customer wanted to upgrade the size of their drink. They succeeded on 47 percent of occasions.

It's that tipping point again. Even a non-technical interaction between the customer and the marketing environment can make a real difference. Certainly, this is most powerful where personal selling (or at least *contact*) is possible, but there's a lesson for all parts of the communications mix.

Once more, I think it's to do with overcoming the customer's "no" reflex. And it can be further explained by an idea put forward by Freedman and Fraser called "Foot in the Door."[5]

In many tests it has been shown that more customers will agree to a big decision if they have first agreed to a small decision. The theory underlying this is quite fascinating, and (as usual) intuitively hits the spot. The idea goes that you can come to know your feelings about something by "observing" your own behavior. (This is called self-perception theory.) Foot in the Door enables a customer to enact a favorable experience toward a particular product area. They slide past the tipping point and suddenly (and statistically) they're more likely to buy big.

On lots of occasions I've watched sampling teams operate in supermarkets. They get a great strike rate, but a significant proportion of customers refuse free, no-obligation samples with very defensive body language. It's as if their "no" reflex knows all about Foot in the Door and acts to stop them having a positive experience before it's too late.

The practical lesson for the marketer must be to offer your customer a foot-in-the-door experience where it's feasible and appropriate. (Hence switched-on motor dealers focus a significant share of their marketing efforts on selling test-drives rather than cars.) For Reebok we developed a promotional mechanic that we called try-&-win. To enter a prize draw the customer simply had to try on a pair of trainers. Returns from stores consistently reported a 70 percent conversion rate from *try* to *buy*.

Advertise to your customers

Given the statistics I outlined in Step 5 (how a minority of your customers account for the majority of your sales), there's an immediate logic in advertising to your existing customers. But there's an important dissonance-reducing aspect to this, too. And that can be vital in securing purchase next time around.

Try as you might, for some of your customers you'll never eliminate post-purchase dissonance. Especially when decisions are hard to alter, like

Figure 79 "Try to Enter" — *a simple promotional mechanic that consistently reported a 70 percent trial-to-purchase conversion rate. Reproduced by kind permission of Reebok UK.*

In our view there's something even more important than the arrangement on the number plate. And that's the car itself. When you buy a used Mercedes E-Class from an authorised Mercedes-Benz retailer, you're buying a car that has undergone a comprehensive series of quality checks. Only when a car has passed this rigorous screening, do we deem it acceptable to sell. It's this professional integrity which takes the worry out of buying a used car. And prevents us getting too worked up about a number plate. For more information or to search for a vehicle visit www.mercedes-benz.co.uk/used or contact your local Mercedes-Benz retailer.

A used Mercedes is still a Mercedes.

Winner of over 70 industry awards in 7 years, so there's no need to worry about some perspex.

Figure 80 *A great deal of automobile marketing is designed with existing customers in mind. This Mercedes ad, ostensibly promoting the sale of used models, simultaneously sends a highly positive message to current owners. Reproduced by kind permission of Mercedes-Benz and CDDLondon.*

tiling a bathroom, having a severe haircut, and choosing a new home computer. So you need Plan B.

When customers suffer post-purchase dissonance, they seek reassurance that they made a wise decision. (Hence the question: "Does my bum look big in this?") Plan B is to talk to your customer like they just did (make a wise decision, that is).

People say you can't tell one car advert from the next. But I bet you most car owners can describe the ads for their brand. We've got whiskers like a wildcat's when it comes to detecting cues that reinforce our own egos.

The advantage of this tactic is that — if future dissonance is perceived to be high — you'll also reach the potential customer who at that very moment is "just looking." They're doing their homework, rehearsing what it will feel like to have taken the dreaded decision. When the time comes to buy, they'll behave like a satisfied customer. (I suppose the apocryphal "Nobody was ever sacked for buying IBM" comes into this category of message.)

At a more practical level — depending on your business — you can design simple communications to reassure your customers. If you're a tiler, call to ask if you can take a photo of the finished job to use in your publicity material. If you're a hairdresser, send a magazine clipping of a celeb wearing the same £100 cut you've just given to your client. If you install PCs in people's homes, mail out some notes of the basic, really useful procedures that your customer needs but didn't manage to write down when you did the demo.

When your customer feels good about their purchase, why would they risk changing brand or supplier next time around? They might even recommend you to a friend. You can close your next sale before the buying's even begun.

Bridge sentiment and sale

It has been shown in research that unrehearsed memories are typically lost in 30 seconds.[6] In Step 4 I mentioned an Epson ad that I particularly liked, but felt could have worked harder to close the sale. For me it missed the opportunity to build a tangible bridge between the customer's sentiments and the act of buying. After a great offer (of a free Xbox), the copy ended rather blandly with a general invitation to call or visit the website for more details. I'd have been inclined to try this:

> **"Phone, text or email** *now* **to claim one of 5,000 free Xbox vouchers. Hurry! The offer closes in 10 days."**

Even stronger would be an instant voucher tipped on to the page (although you would sacrifice the database of interested customers). Either way, how could an interested customer resist once they've got in their hand a promissory note that's worth an XBox?

The principle here is a simple one, and it's like the "no" reflex working in reverse. People find it hard to throw away items of value. Most of us would pick up a 20p coin, and by the same token a 20p coupon tends to get pinned next to the shopping list.

Couponing is much maligned but it really works. I've witnessed some fantastic (whoops, platitude) *30 percent-plus* responses for products as wide-ranging as cornflakes and whisky. We consistently reached 40–50 percent (and even 65 percent) for well-targeted trade promotions. For a consumer door-drop the "industry" says you can expect a 7.5 perccent response for a typical household product; using NEW AIDA principles we raised the bar to 15 percent.

Engel reported a major controlled study across four brands, in which coupons were shown to raise trial of new products from 7.4 to 15.1 percent of households. And although coupon-induced trialists were poorer "repeaters" (24.8 versus 31.4 percent), the significantly higher levels of initial trial still led to greater long-term penetration (3.7 versus 2.3 percent).[7] That's actually 60 percent more homes using your product.

The physical presence of a coupon builds that tangible bridge between sentiment and sale. In many respects it's a no-brainer. Indeed, in my experience, the key issues that should determine whether or not you use couponing are *misredemption* and *cost-effectiveness*.

For trade coupons, misredemption is quite easy to eliminate.[8] At a retail level it can be more problematic, since the grocery multiples are not averse

Figure 81 Simple but effective. A household couponing format that regularly doubled the industry-norm response. © Reproduced by kind permission of Warburtons Ltd.

Try the fresh-baked taste today

Experience the fresh-baked taste of the new Warburtons Bakery range.

Our traditional soft White and Wholemeal batch breads are just perfect for sandwiches or soup.

Try the delicious crunchy, nutty flavour of our Seeded batch loaf with smoked salmon, freshly-ground black peppercorns and a twist of lemon.

And enjoy the fabulous moist, warm flavour of our Carrot and Cinnamon loaf – on its own, or toasted and richly seeped in butter.

Because our loaves are baked with expert care and skill, using only the finest ingredients, we guarantee that each will taste like real bread should.

If you don't agree we'll give you your money back. Write and tell us why and we'll send you a cheque for the full amount paid, including postage.

So go on – you've got nothing to lose. Enjoy the fresh-baked taste of Warburtons today.

TESCO
Every little helps.

Warburtons
BAKERY

10p off coupon

to accepting their competitors' coupons, which I'm sure contributes to a general feeling among some shoppers that coupons equal cash. However, those with a foot in the couponing camp will tell you that most coupons are not misredeemed (consumer surveys indicate about 80 percent are used correctly), and I believe this to be true.[9]

Cost-effectiveness is easier to get a handle on, and mainly concerns the cost of delivery. Having worked as a marketing manager in a pure direct marketing environment, and having run hundreds of such campaigns for clients, one thing I can tell you categorically is that direct mail as a means of delivery is *not* cost-effective for most fmcg products. This is borne out by the fact that the majority of blue-chip firms who have properly evaluated their programs have subsequently withdrawn them.

We ran a direct program for Beck's for two years.[10] Because we were able to identify heavy users, the sums indicated that the activity was profitable. In this market there were ample households that bought around 600 bottles of premium beer per annum (that's a spend of about £500). But if your customer spends just £40 or £50 annually on your brand, you should consider the direct marketing vehicle a non-starter.

Make a real offer

Talking of vehicles, I used to own an MG, and although I eventually admitted my heart had ruled my head and I'd better switch to something more sensible, I nearly bought another one when I got the offer in Figure 82 overleaf.

It's not often a coupon for £1,000 lands on your doorstep. When an offer's this strong, you start to get cognitive dissonance about *not* using it! (Remarkably, one of the best bits of information — "The £1,000 is in addition to any negotiations between the dealer and the customer" — is hidden in 5-point type at the foot of the mailing.)

I am often asked: "Should we include an offer?" My answer is yes, if you can afford to make a real offer. (A real offer will commonly increase response by 500 percent.[11]) But if you can't, you're probably wasting your money.

Have you heard of the cardinal utility principle? It's quite thought provoking. For sales promotion, it goes roughly like this:

Which will you choose?

A   Take a guaranteed £250,000.

B   Spin a coin for £1 million.

Most people I've asked would choose A, the bird in the hand — even though, statistically, it's not the most profitable option. Indeed, it's surprising how low you have to reduce the guaranteed sum before they start opting for the gamble. (That, by the way, is why small guaranteed-free offers generally work much better than big chance-to-win offers.)

You can invent all sorts of combinations, and it gives a fascinating insight into how people balance risk and return. If you ignore the concept

Figure 82 *Real offers are hard to resist, especially when targeted at an interested customer. Reproduced by kind permission of MG Rover Group Ltd.*

when you design a promotional offer, you shouldn't be surprised if that offer doesn't work. It's basic, common-sense thinking: *Offer* does not automatically equal *effect*.

Recently I came across a fascinating case study in my local area, Edinburgh. A guy tried to raffle a house valued at £260,000 by selling tickets at £10 each. His idea was to sell a cap of 45,000 tickets, thus making a tidy profit (after advertising and publicity costs) and also funding a promised £9,000 charitable donation. I assume the idea of the cap was to make the odds of winning look attractive. There was a cash alternative of £220,000 and runners-up prizes of $1 \times £10,000$, $1 \times £5,000$ and $100 \times £100$.

Sadly, the scheme failed. Only 5,000 tickets were sold and the offer had to be withdrawn. So what went wrong?

One way of looking at it is to say that selling 5,000 tickets is actually quite a good achievement. This argument would depend on your assessment of the available audience. Judged solely on the number who might like or be able to move into the particular house, it's probably a very good response.

However, the presence of a cash alternative really takes the house (and related domestic dynamics) out of the equation. In reality this was a lottery in which you stood a 1 in 45,000 chance of winning £220,000, for a £10 investment. And it's the £10 investment that sets alarm bells ringing.

To most people, 1 in 45,000 means you probably won't win. (Statistically, you'd have to enter once a day for 123 years before you won at these odds.) So while you might throw £1 at this, £10 is too much. I think most people would rather play the lottery for 10 weeks instead, and have 10 goes at what they would perceive to be a similarly unlikely chance of winning – but at least with the prospect of becoming a multimillionaire.

It's easy with hindsight to make these sort of comments, and I admire the chap for having a go at it (I understand all of the tickets were either refunded or checks for them destroyed). But what it does illustrate is the fickle nature of the customer, and the difficulty in judging when an offer becomes a *real* offer. If you can test first on a small scale, that could be your surest way of finding a winner.

Crisp fivers

Here's a raffle-type offer that does work: the Walkers Crisps "moneybags" mechanic, which has been repeated on several occasions in various guises. Although it doesn't make you buy any more crisps upfront, it makes your kids eat them faster. (With a one in five chance to win, it's always worth opening another packet.) Soon you're back in Tesco's snacks aisle.

Figure 83 A real offer that targets an effective point of leverage. Your kids can always eat another bag of crisps. Reproduced by kind permission of Walkers Snacks Ltd.

This mechanic is known in the sales promotion business as "instant win." The offer and the mechanic have been carefully thought through and tested over the years. Together they target an effective point of leverage – the small act of opening another bag that the customer already owns.

And because it's a real offer in terms of the scale of rewards, it works. By this I mean the chances of winning are very high. It doesn't take long for the customer to get a reward – even if it's only a voucher for a free packet of crisps – which reinforces their belief in further winnings.

But as I said, the mere presence of an offer doesn't automatically guarantee success. Getting back to those loo blocks, recently I opened a pack advertising an instant-win offer: Win a trip to Italy. The small print said there was 1 holiday prize, plus 25 runners-up prizes of £40 leisure vouchers. 26 prizes... on *how many* packs?

Not only is this not a real offer (at that ratio of prizes to packs, why would I ever believe I might win?), neither is it targeting an effective point of leverage.

As Walkers knows, the instant-win mechanic works well on low-value products, where it is easy to consume another packet. Crisps are perfect. (Bottles of beer in the fridge are not bad.)

But how do I consume another loo block? It boasts on the pack it lasts for up to four months!

The chosen mechanic is not appropriate for the purchasing and usage dynamics of the product. The manufacturer must have spent a small fortune printing "sorry you lose" leaflets and inserting them into almost 100 percent of its production run. (Compare this to my suggestion of a reminder coupon in Step 5.)

As a general rule, the effectiveness of a promotional offer is directly proportional to the perceived value of the reward, with chance factored in: what the customer gets (or thinks they might get) in relation to what they give up. Spread your budget too thinly and it becomes invisible.

The offer of £1,000 to buy a new MGF is a real offer. Yet I have many times read national marketing briefs from blue-chip companies demanding *double-digit* volume increases from budgets that equate to *less than a penny* per sale. As the great generals say, you can't save your way to victory.

Action carrots

I talked in Step 2 about how "carrots" can be used to compensate your customer for their efforts, when you are asking them to leap extra hurdles for your benefit. This is not the same as closing the sale.

Ease carrots (if you get the meaning) have a practical role, while action carrots work on the customer's mind. If you think back to my Tesco–Sainsbury–Safeway conundrum, Safeway's 20p-off petrol offer (plus strong in-store BOGOFs) was, for me, an ease carrot. I always was going to buy the petrol, and I always was going to buy the essential groceries — it was just a question of *where*. Safeway's offer compensated me for going out of my way.

Sure, once I was in the store I might also have bumped into some action carrots: offers that swayed me to buy unplanned and arguably unnecessary items. And come to think of it, I did over a period of time buy from Safeway a new duvet and a portable radio for the spare bedroom — vague needs that had been in the back of my mind, in that category of stuff you could do with but feel it's a bit profligate to splash out on, until you bump into a special offer that's too good to miss. I'm sure we all carry with us a list of goods like this, things we're just looking for without even realizing it. Yet it simply takes an action carrot to give us permission to say *yes*.

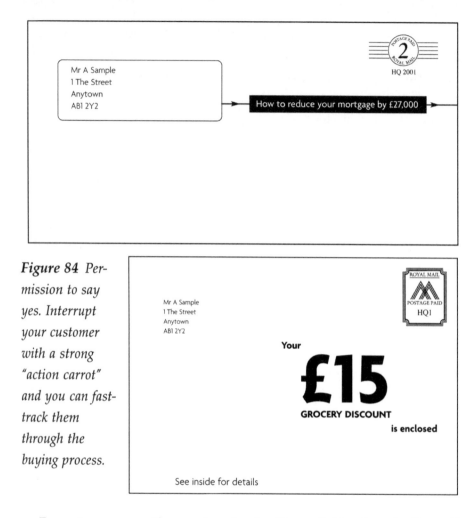

Figure 84 Permission to say yes. Interrupt your customer with a strong "action carrot" and you can fast-track them through the buying process.

Even at an apparently mundane level — like switching brand of loo rolls — shoppers are remarkably conservative. They perceive problems and risks that are easy for the marketer to overlook.

In 1984 I was appointed as product manager to work on the launch of what is now called Velvet bathroom tissue. It was made by a new thru-dried technology and was massively (no hyperbole) superior to anything else on the market at the time. It was preferred over the brand leader by 9:1 on softness (the most important discriminator) and 5:1 overall. It actually became market leader in multiples in the south of England, before machine problems hindered its growth and allowed competitors to catch up. However — marvelous though it was — many potential customers still would not switch brand. I remember sitting in on a hall-test (for new advertising, in case you're thinking the worst) and listening to one woman (an Andrex buyer) tell the researcher how much she preferred this new Velvet (there were samples available to touch). Toward the end of the interview, after viewing the ad, she was asked about her purchase intentions. How likely was she to buy it? Her answer: "Oh no — my husband wouldn't like this, it wouldn't be strong enough for him."

You might smile, but the fact is she'd anticipated a form of post-purchase dissonance: disapproval from her partner. Clearly, the best way to tackle a customer like this is to give them a free sample, or at least a deal that enables them to justify such "extravagance" with the household budget. (Our idea at the time was to buy a load of competitive product, break it up, and rewrap single rolls into twin-packs with a roll of Velvet. We'd only charge for our one roll. Sadly, production constraints... you know the story.)

For years I thought a friend of mine was a bit of a skinflint because he always had to get everything at a discount. (He once retiled his bathroom with the same pattern of tiles he'd stripped off, because they were on such a good offer at the local DIY shop!) But gradually I began to realize he was just a highly risk-averse type of person. Getting everything cheap was his personal strategy for dealing with cognitive dissonance.

So a real offer can play a major role as a catalyst for action. And a big part of that, once again, concerns post-purchase dissonance. If you can send your customer home shouting "Look how much I saved!" or "Look what I got free!" you'll close many more sales.

Set a deadline

This is a simple point, which is often overlooked. Get your customer to act while they're in buying mode. Since most of the time you can't be there with them, in lieu of a close it's a good idea to set a deadline.

Virtually every response graph I've ever seen has been forward-skewed. For mailings, you typically get half of your replies within a week of receiving the first one. The other half can take months to trickle in.

Mr A Sample
1 The Street
Anytown
AB1 2YZ

FREEPOST
York
YO26 6ZZ

Free Phone 0800 038 3333
Free Fax 0800 458 6448
www.postoptics.co.uk

Dear Mr Sample

As an existing Postoptics customer, I am writing to give you advance notice of a very significant price rise on Acuvue 1-Day contact lenses.

From next month Johnson & Johnson are increasing the trade price of these lenses by 50%. Whilst we are able to absorb some of this cost, the amount you pay will change and this table shows the alterations to our prices.

Quantity of lenses Purchased	Current price	Price from March 2002
3 Months (90 Pairs)	£79	£109
6 Months (180 Pairs)	£149	£209
1 Year (360 Pairs)	£279	£399

Any orders we receive before the end of February will of course be processed at the existing rates.

The most recent prescription we have on your record expired on 24 September 2000 and you will therefore need a new prescription before we can supply you with any further lenses. Our list of local opticians who will be happy to check your eyes and provide an updated prescription has changed considerably in the last few months. Please call us or check our web site to view this list or if we can assist you in any way.

Prices of other brands of daily disposable lenses are not being increased and these alternatives now offer savings of up to £200 per year over the Acuvue product. If you wish to consider changing to one of these lenses, please discuss this with your optician at your next appointment.

We appreciate your past business and look forward to helping you with your future contact lens requirements.

Yours sincerely

Trevor Rowley

Trevor Rowley BSc MCOptom

International
Tel: +44 1904 606600
Fax: +44 1904 606666

Postoptics Ltd is registered in England, No. 3912575
Registered Office: York Business Park, York, YO26 6RZ

Figure 85 *Impending price increase: one of the oldest shots in the direct marketer's locker, and a genuine reason to ask for a "reply-by." Reproduced by kind permission of Postoptics.*

So your customer is most likely to act while your benefits are fresh in their mind. David Ogilvy cited a survey showing that twice as many people tell themselves they'll "mail it later" but never get round to it as actually do respond.[12] That's a potential trebling of sales.

John Watson looks at it another way. He says (and I'm paraphrasing):

The time-close doesn't make any more people reply, it just stops those who would reply from filing your mailing for posterity on the mantlepiece.[13]

When clients ask me about setting a deadline, I usually explain that it can perform two different functions. The first is to create a sense of urgency, as I've described above, and the second is to close off the offer (nobody wants an indefinite liability). The trouble is, you can end up trying to do both jobs with a single date — and of course you fall between two stools. A possible solution to this is to have two dates: the first is *soon* (I'd go for just a week) and gives the customer an extra level of reward; the second is *longer* (say eight weeks) and closes both the main offer and the entire campaign.

Don't be shy to mop up

If you think back to what I said about how your customers prepare themselves for post-purchase dissonance — by going out and practicing — there's an interesting corollary for your marketing communications. What if your ad, or mailing, or brochure formed part of the practice? But that was early on... and now they're ready to buy.

The trouble is, you'd taken my advice and put a closing date on your offer. And now it's expired!

The answer, of course, is to approach the customer again. For a direct mail activity this is particularly easy, since you'll know they haven't responded. So don't be shy about extending the date: "mop-up" mailings will commonly achieve between 50 and 100 percent of the original response.[14]

PrecisionMarketing
THE WEEKLY MAGAZINE FOR DIRECT MARKETING

50 Poland Street, London, W1F 7AX
T 020 7292 3714
F 020 7970 4099
E pmciro@centaur.co.uk

LAST CHANCE TO SAVE OVER £130 PLUS CLAIM A FREE GIFT

Dear Mr Moore,
I wrote to you recently offering a risk-free subscription to *Precision Marketing* – the weekly magazine dedicated to direct marketing. The response has been overwhelming, which made me wonder why you had not yet responded.

As a marketing professional, I don't want you to miss out on the latest direct marketing news, developments and jobs. So, I've decided to extend the close date on this special offer.

To recap, this is what a subscription to *Precision Marketing* will bring you, every week:

- **FREE subscription to mad.co.uk Express:** a unique online news and jobs service, delivered direct to your desktop. At your request, we'll also send you daily email job alerts;
- **FREE entry into the DMShow:** an annual exhibition tailored to your needs;
- **SAVE 50%** off up to 3 Precision Marketing/Marketing Week conferences PLUS a £200 discount voucher for a colleague;*
- **The Agency Showcase:** find the best agencies to handle your accounts;
- **The Suppliers Showcase:** your overview of leading direct marketing suppliers;
- **Routes to Market:** 6 practical supplements looking at the key ways in which you can target potential clients;
- **The Response Awards Book of the Night:** featuring the winners and runners up from this year's awards;
- **Key Surveys:** 5 industry benchmark surveys including, Top 100 DM agencies, Top 60 list operators and the B2B Agency Survey
- **Access to** www.precisionmarketing.co.uk : our fully searchable archive contains over 7 year's worth of information on brands, companies, research and marketers themselves;
- **An extra copy:** we'll send this out to a named colleague at no extra charge.

Our package has never been so good... (continued overleaf...)

TO SUBSCRIBE TODAY - **Fax** 020 7970 4099 **Tel** 020 7292 3714 **Mail** Precision Marketing, Freepost WD1414/1B, London W1E 6JZ

STEP 1 CHOOSE

CHOOSE A SUBSCRIPTION TERM

★ Pay with order to get your privilege subscription offer ★

Pay now and save 15% on the subscription price

☐ 3 YEARS	☐ 2 YEARS	☐ 1 YEAR
(150 issues)	(100 issues)	(50 issues)
@ £184 PM12/PM33	@ £131 PM11/PM32	@ £81.50 PM02/PM31
☐ Please send my FREE gift	☐ Please send my FREE gift	

Normal Invoice price

☐ 3 YEARS	☐ 2 YEARS	☐ 1 YEAR
(150 issues)	(100 issues)	(50 issues)
@ £216 PM12/PM33	@ £154 PM11/PM32	@ £95.90 PM02/PM31
☐ Please send my FREE gift	☐ Please send my FREE gift	

Mr A Sample
1 The Street
Anytown
AB1 2Y2

STEP 2 NOMINATE

NOMINATE A COLLEAGUE

I would like to nominate one of my colleagues to receive their own copy of *Precision Marketing*

Title .... Job title – please tick

First Name ....

Surname ....

Telephone ....

Fax ....

E-mail ....

☐ Account Manager (ACMA)
☐ Marketing Manager (MAMA)
☐ Marketing Services Manager (MANA)
☐ Business Development Manager (BUDE)
☐ Brand Manager (BRMA)
☐ Direct Marketing Manager (DIMA)
☐ Campaign Manager (CAMP)
☐ New Product Development Manager (NPDM)
☐ Sales Promotion Manager (SPMA)
☐ Fundraising Manager (FUND)
☐ Other - please specify

STEP 3 PAYMENT

PAYMENT DETAILS

☐ I enclose a cheque made payable to *Precision Marketing* for £
☐ Please debit my ☐ Mastercard ☐ Amex ☐ Visa* for £
*Please enclose details of cardholder's name and address if different from above

Card No .... Expiry /

☐ Please invoice me ☐ my company (at normal invoice price)

Signature .... Date

We would like to keep you informed of Centaur's products and services including information about Precision Marketing. Please write to the Circulation Director if you do not want to receive this information. We may also from time to time make your details available to carefully screened companies who may be of interest to you. However if you specifically do not wish your details to be passed to third parties please tick here. ☐

Figure 86 Mopping up. A popular technique in the magazine business when selling to recently lapsed subscribers. Reproduced by kind permission of Precision Marketing.

Staff your website

So many websites are like shops where all the staff have gone to lunch and forgotten to lock up. The customer creeps in and pokes about, while the sales floor is left unattended. Later on, someone thinks to check and finds perhaps a few wet footprints, or some stock that's been deranged. Put it down to the cleaning lady.

But it wasn't the cleaning lady — it was an interested customer. They'd taken the trouble to type in your web address, or do a search on your product category and click on your link. They'd blundered about, not managed to find what they were looking for, and given up and left.

Go to Amazon as a first-time visitor and what happens? Up pops an unmissable window offering you £3 off your first order if you register now — because you're a new visitor. Bingo — they've noticed you. Placed upper center on the homepage is a prominent message labeled "First-time visitors," giving you the option to click on "How to order" and "Help Desk."

Recently I was interested in buying a motorbike, but it being some years since I last went anywhere near one, I felt rather apprehensive (did they still have kick-starts?). I certainly didn't fancy the idea of walking into a showroom and sounding like the greenhorn I had become. Of course, websites can now overcome this problem, but I was disappointed to find that few did. Yet all it would take is a pop-up — the most prominent single message on the screen — saying something like this:

New to bikes? Coming back to bikes? Not sure how things work these days? No worries. Just type in your full inquiry and we'll get back to you within 24 hours. Just ask — we don't expect you to be an expert or to have long hair (or even hair). We'll reply with a detailed answer in plain English, with suggestions for what might be right for you, and the name of a personal contact at your local dealership who'll also be briefed on your query. And nobody will contact you unless we get your say-so.[15]

You'd click on a link and there'd be a nice big box for you to type as much as you like. There'd be some prompts, you'd be able to look at other people's (anonymous) inquiries so you didn't feel like such a novice, and after that, some key fixed questions you could fill in at your leisure: customer profile, budget range, contact details... and permission to get in touch.

Placing an inquiry could even be incentivized, for instance with an instantly emailed free £10 discount voucher off a new helmet (funded, of course, by the makers in return for being featured so prominently on your site). Exactly the sort of technique to create a bond with the just-looking customer.

To do what I am suggesting doesn't need expert programming or super-smart software. It's simply making a selling virtue out of what on most websites is a passive "email us" facility. It's what you'd do if it were your shop.

Just sell it

If your product is capable of a digital existence (like music, news, insurance, or holidays), or even just direct delivery (like groceries or stationery or sofas), then it makes great sense to be developing the web as a strategic sales and distribution channel. (This is of course direct marketing.)

And with the approach of seriously clever mobile technology, I'd go a stage further and start thinking about how many more sales I could close. But I don't mean by mobile advertising. Quite the reverse, in fact.

Indeed, I don't believe the mobile will ever be a happy medium for unsolicited outbound marketing communication. (We don't want junk ads sent to our phones.) But as the mobile quickly evolves into a fully functioning, portable, multimedia PC-cum-TV, it will become a popular way to buy things.

I talked above about how direct mail sales could treble if only customers didn't file their mailings on the mantlepiece. I think one of the biggest causes of lost sales is that the customer was unable to buy when they *would have*. Yet the mobile of the not-too-distant future will empower your customer to act, there and then.

Already, when they leave the office feeling hungry, and it's late and they're too tired to shop, they can use their mobile to buy a curry as they drive home. If I ran a takeaway I'd go to great lengths to get my phone number into the memory of all my regular customers' mobiles. The trick is to "enable" your customer when they're in buying mode.

Soon, when their pals tell them about a great new music track while they're drinking in the pub, out will come the phone, down will come the track. When they're sitting on a train and notice a fellow traveler's magazine they like the look of, they'll be able to order it for delivery next morning. When they're out of change but need to park their car, all they'll need will be their mobile (the powers-that-be have already twigged to this one where I live).

If you can find this dynamic in your firm's marketplace, then start preparing for what must be the greatest sales opportunity since the internet took off.

ACTION – SEVEN TOP TIPS

1 Cultivate browsers.

2 Demonstrate your expertise.

3 Put your foot in the door.

4 Advertise to the contented.

5 Build a tangible bridge to the sale.

6 Make a real offer.

7 Set a deadline... and mop up later.

KEY QUESTION
"Have I helped my customer to say *yes*?"

SUMMARY

"So, will my marketing sell?"

I wanted to write a summary that you could actually use, so here it is, all on one page. After all, NEW AIDA is a simple tool that helps to produce more effective marketing. And as I wrote earlier, whether you're about to create or evaluate, it takes just a few moments to ask yourself the key questions:

☆ Step 1　Does my customer know what to do or think about?
　　　　　Navigation = understanding

☆ Step 2　Can my customer see that it's easy?
　　　　　Ease = convenience

☆ Step 3　Am I talking my customer's language?
　　　　　Wording = conversation

☆ Step 4　Will my customer meet my benefits?
　　　　　Attention = serendipity

☆ Step 5　Am I treating my customer as if they're already interested?
　　　　　Interest = persuadability

☆ Step 6　Does my customer have all the facts?
　　　　　Desire = knowledge

☆ Step 7　Have I helped my customer to say *yes*?
　　　　　Action = permission

In this book I have ranged across all kinds of marketing communications, from packaging and promotions, to personal interactions at a retail level, and the more conventional forms of marketing such as press and television advertising, direct mail, and websites. What I hope to have conveyed, however, is that in truth there is only one discipline: your customer's mind.

And through whatever means or media you approach it, your customer's mind responds best to good salesmanship. It's the magic yet common-sense ingredient that will make your marketing sell. Salesmanship always out-pulls showmanship.

APPENDIX

The origins of AIDA

H ere's an extract from a book published in 1922. I'd like you to make a guess at who wrote it:

"A FAULTY OUTLINE
A very commonly accepted outline, enumerating the steps in advertising and selling, is the following:

Favorable attention → Interest → Desire → Action → Permanent satisfaction

There is enough truth in this five-fold slogan to make it seem a very accurate statement of what are the essential steps in a successful advertisement or sales interview. It has done, however, as much harm to the development of a science of selling as it has done good."[1]

Any ideas? I'll cut to the chase. How about Edward Kellogg Strong, Professor of Psychology, Graduate School of Business, Stanford University.

Strong? What, *the* Strong? E K Strong? The guy who — according to all of the books on marketing — invented AIDA?

Yep. *Not only did Strong not invent AIDA, he neither promoted it as an acronym nor supported it as a model of buyer behavior.* Remarkable.

Kotler's *Marketing Management* (I imagine the world's bestselling marketing textbook) has attributed AIDA to Strong in its last 10 editions. In his reference to AIDA, Philip Kotler simply states: "E. K. Strong, *The Psychology of Selling*, 1925."[2]

Chris Fill, author of the excellent *Marketing Communications: Contexts, Strategies and Applications*, described as the "essential textbook for all Chartered Institute of Marketing Diploma students," begins his section on how advertising works with the words: "Developed by Strong (1925), the

Aida model was designed to represent the stages that a salesperson must take a prospect through in the personal selling process." Fill goes on to say: "An extension of the progressive staged approach advocated by Strong emerged in the early 1960s."[3]

Professor Michael J Baker consistently reports that Strong was responsible for AIDA. For instance, in his *Dictionary of Marketing and Advertising* he states: "AIDA. An acronym for Attention, Interest, Desire and Action, a hierarchy-of-effects model first proposed by Strong in 1924 [sic]."[4]

Kotler – wrong. Fill – wrong. Baker – wrong. Most authors – wrong. How could this be? (And how do I know about it?)

After thinking and writing about AIDA most days for over a year, to complete this final chapter I ventured into the National Library of Scotland. There, with little ado, were produced first editions of the books in which it all began. Or rather, in which it didn't.

The first immediate (though minor) revelation was that Strong's much-referred-to text *The Psychology of Selling* was actually entitled *The Psychology of Selling and Advertising*.[5] I liked that. (But why did nobody quote the title in full?)

The second was that, far from being "a roaming door-to-door salesman" as I have seen him and his peers described, Strong was, as you have already read, a professor of psychology at an eminent university. Respect.

Third – and here's the big one – no AIDA.

Most of Strong's efforts in *The Psychology of Selling and Advertising* are dedicated to the promulgation of his own rather curious "buying formula," which bears little resemblance to AIDA. At no point in the 468 pages of detailed text does the acronym AIDA appear.

St. Elmo's fire

Here's an excerpt from *The Psychology of Selling and Advertising* that gives an insight into AIDA's more distant origins:

> **"Many changes in selling procedure have of necessity been made in the past fifteen years. Among them is the growing recognition of the buyer's point of view.**

The development of the famous slogan — 'attention, interest, desire, action, satisfaction' — illustrates this. [Note that Strong considered it famous by 1925.] In 1898 E. St Elmo Lewis used the slogan, 'Attract attention, maintain interest, create desire,' in a course he was giving on advertising in Philadelphia. He writes he obtained the idea from reading the psychology of William James. Later on he added to the formula, 'get action.' [Stop right there! They didn't.] About 1907, A.F. Sheldon made the further addition of 'permanent satisfaction' as essential to the slogan."

So it would seem that if anyone can be credited with developing the AIDA model (though not the acronym), it is the wonderfully named E St. Elmo Lewis.[6] Strong himself refers to the version that includes the fifth element, satisfaction, as "this slogan of Lewis and Sheldon."

While striving to promote his own "buying formula," Strong did recognize the impact of the Lewis–Sheldon model. He wrote that it "has had a very profound effect upon the selling world" and that "the formula has caused order to come out of chaos." Writing in 1925, he acknowledged that the "majority of books and articles since 1907 have endorsed the slogan in one form or another."

Nevertheless, ending the section, he commented somewhat hopefully: "Judging from a perusal of recent literature, interest in this theory is dying out to some extent."

AIDA rules the waves

Today, it's no exaggeration to say that AIDA is probably the single most widely used model in the world of marketing, advertising, and selling. Marketing textbooks — academic or practical — that do not make significant reference to AIDA are few and far between. AIDA is right up there with the SWOT analysis, the 4Ps, the 80:20 principle, the PLC curve, the Boston Box, Maslow's hierarchy, Tom Peters' MBWA (management by walking about), and Rosser Reeves' USP (the unique selling point, which incidentally wasn't his either).[7]

AIDA is used by marketing professors and by the greenest of greenhorn sales representatives. It spans the highbrow and the vernacular. And it's a true brand name.

Modern writers who ignore AIDA are a scarce breed, and those who decry it positive rarities. Among these is Chris Fill, who comments:

> **"Through time, a variety of models have been presented, each of which attempts to describe how advertising works. Aida and sequential models, such as the hierarchy of effects approach, were for a long time the received wisdom in this area. Now they are regarded as quaint but out-of-date, for a number of hard hitting reasons."**

Fill goes on to suggest that the new view of advertising is that it should be regarded as a means of defending customers' purchase decisions and for protecting markets, not building them. This is the so-called "weak theory of advertising." I have some sympathy with this view, but only for a tiny minority of marketing communications (i.e. some television advertising campaigns, of the non-launch variety). This, of course, is not how most marketers spend most of their communication efforts.

Perhaps it's because I began my career in sales, and before that found myself selling pictures (and before that "windfall" apples and pears), that I can't avoid the conclusion that if you make the effort to do some "marketing" you should expect it to have some effect. Else why bother?

Marketing can work... does work. Likewise AIDA.

Indeed, the challenge facing the critics of AIDA (and I include myself here) is that attention → interest → desire → action is intuitively right and anyone in business can see that. Add to which AIDA is easy to remember, and therefore *it actually gets used.*

AIDA's antagonists claim that it is too simplistic, that it ignores a whole range of influences — psychological, cultural, environmental — and that the buying process is far too strung out and complex to be described by such a rudimentary model of behavior. But I think that's being ingenuous. No sensible marketer expects a customer to trip automatically through the steps of AIDA once their attention has been triggered. The marketer knows it's an unrelenting battle from beginning to end. AIDA just happens to be an elegantly effective weapon, whether for honing a simple piece of advertising copy, or for guiding a detailed analysis of a comprehensive long-term marketing communications program.

So my vote is to keep AIDA. For most marketing communications, AIDA *nearly* works. Use it in the fashion of NEW AIDA, with intuitive salesmanship, and it *really* works.

AIDA: What the writers wrote

Here is a selection of quotes about AIDA, many of which you can find in the business section of your local bookshop or library. Some, of course, are factually wrong and others — starting with Strong — rather disparaging. Nevertheless, they are all testament to AIDA's great staying power.

> "There is enough truth in this... slogan to make it seem a very accurate statement of what are the essential steps in a successful advertisement or sales interview. It has done, however, as much harm to the development of a science of selling as it has done good."
>
> E K Strong, The Psychology of Selling Life Insurance, *Harper and Brothers, 1922.*

> "Judging from a perusal of recent literature, interest in this theory is dying out to some extent."
>
> E K Strong, The Psychology of Selling and Advertising, *McGraw-Hill, 1925.*

> "Developed by Strong (1925), the AIDA model was designed to represent the stages that a salesperson must take a prospect through in the selling process. Now [it] is regarded as quaint but out of date."
>
> *Chris Fill*, Marketing Communications, *Prentice Hall Europe, 1999.*

"AIDA is probably the oldest acronym in marketing. It is the best and will never change."

Derrick White, Close More Sales, *Management Books 2000, 2001.*

"[AIDA] was found to be the most widely quoted [model] in a range of current British, American and French textbooks."

M J Baker, Marketing: Theory and Practice, *Macmillan Press, 1983.*

"Having defined the desired audience response, the communicator moves to developing an effective message. Ideally the message should get attention, hold interest, arouse desire, and obtain action (AIDA model). In practice, few messages take the consumer all the way from awareness through purchase, but the AIDA framework suggests the desirable qualities."

Philip Kotler, Marketing Management, *11th Edition, Prentice Hall, 2003.*

"Understanding the buying process is critical because it will lead to the possible routes to reach buyers. The buying process includes all the steps that a person takes leading to a purchase. It is called the adoption process and the problem-solving process by some academics. Some researchers call it a Learn/Feel/Do process. Others call it AIDA for Attention, Interest, Desire, Action."

Steven Silburger, The 10-Day MBA, *Piatkus, 2001.*

"Over the years many advertising writers have developed copy formulas for structuring ads, commercials, and sales letters. The best known of these formulas is AIDA – which stands for Attention, Interest, Desire, Action."

Robert W Bly, The Copywriter's Handbook, *Henry Holt, 1990.*

"Adoption as a process over time has been understood by marketing scholars for a long time. An early conceptualization of this process was called AIDA (Attention, Interest, Desire, Action). Alternative conceptualizations of this process use different terminology but are attempts to describe the same process."

> *J F Engel, R D Blackwell, and P W Miniard,* Consumer Behaviour, *Dryden Press, 1990.*

"The structure of an ad follows a proven outline. An effective... ad will get attention, build interest, create desire, motivate action, make sales. You will see this abbreviated more concisely as the AIDA formula."

> *Sarah White and John Woods,* Do-It-Yourself Advertising, *Adams Media, 1997.*

"This formula is variously known as AIDA or AIDCA. If you want to remember it, then recall the name of the opera by Verdi."

> *Drayton Bird,* Commonsense Direct Marketing, *Kogan Page, 2000.*

"The formula is derived from salesmen in America, at the turn of the century, who found they could achieve higher sales levels if they followed such a formula during their sales visits. It wasn't long before advertising copywriters picked up the formula and adopted it for their own purposes."

> *John Watson,* Successful Creativity in Direct Marketing, *Institute of Direct Marketing, 1993.*

"The acronym AIDCA stands for the key words Attention, Interest, Desire, Conviction and Action. These are the five stages that you should lead your prospective customer through in sequence to maximize the chances of a successful sale."

> *Robert Heller,* Selling Successfully, *Dorling Kindersley, 1999.*

"The... model has been traced back to Plato's elements of the human soul — reasonable, spiritive, appetitive... Marketers have developed a number of variants... of the... model... starting with Strong's AIDA (1924)[sic]."

> *M J Baker,* Marketing: An Introductory Text, *Macmillan Education, 1984.*

"At the turn of the last century, a roaming door-to-door salesman came up with the AIDA structure to maximise sales on his rounds.... AIDA is still relevant today for all direct marketers as a way of engaging our audience."

Daren Kay, The A to Z of Copywriting, *brandrepublic.com, 2003.*

"This well-used formula helps in the overall planning of an advertisement, and is particularly applicable to the hard-selling advertisement."

Frank Jefkins, Advertising, *Prentice Hall, 2000.*

"It is necessary to recognise that AIDA and its kin will remain the implicit conceptual underpinnings of present-day practice until marketing academics are able to produce a better model which practitioners can understand and are willing to use."

M J Baker, The Marketing Book, *Butterworth-Heinemann, 2003.*

"In 1898 E. St Elmo Lewis used the slogan, 'Attract attention, maintain interest, create desire,' in a course he was giving on advertising in Philadelphia. He writes he obtained the idea from reading the psychology of William James. Later on he added to the formula, 'get action.'"

E K Strong, The Psychology of Selling and Advertising, *McGraw-Hill, 1925.*

"Man is a credulous animal, and must believe in something; in the absence of good grounds for belief, he will be satisfied with bad ones."

Bertrand Russell, Unpopular Essays (1950), *Routledge, 1995.*

NOTES

Introduction

1   David Ogilvy, *Confessions of an Advertising Man*, Pan, 1987.

2   John Caples, *Tested Advertising Methods*, Prentice Hall, 1997.

3   A to Z, some of the brands I've worked with, either in a client or agency capacity: Allergan, Andrex, Appleton, Audi, Bank of Scotland, Baxters, Beck's, Bells, BMG, BMW, Bunnahabhain, Cadbury, Caledonian, Carex, Castaway, Chicago Town, Coors, Corning, Cussons, Deuchars, Direct Line, Disney, Famous Grouse, Edinburgh Marketing, Fosters, Glenmorangie, Goodyear, Halls, Heinz, Highland Park, Highland Spring, HMV, Huggies, Irn Bru, John Smith's, Johnnie Walker, Kellogg, Kestrel, Kleenex, Kotex, Kronenbourg, Lloyds Bank, Marion Merrell Dow, MBNA Bank, McEwan's, Mercedes, Merothol, Milk Tray, Miller Genuine Draft, Ministry of Sound, Morgan's Spiced, Mumm, Newcastle Brown Ale, Optrex, OVD Rum, Privilege, Pro-Sport, Pyrex, Reebok, Rockport, Roses, Rover, Royal & SunAlliance, Royal Bank of Scotland, Schwan's, Scottish Airports, Scottish Milk Marketing Board, ScottishPower, Seldane, Smiley, Sony, Supasnaps, Theakston, Toyota, Toys'R'Us, Unilever, Velvet, Virgin, Volkswagen, Warburtons, Warner Bros, Warner Lambert, Younger's, Zipfer.

4   The Blue-Chip Marketing Consultancy Ltd, of which I was a co-founder, sold its trading operations in 1999 to two separate management buyouts; at the time of writing they operate independently under the Blue-Chip Marketing name from their respective bases in Manchester and Edinburgh, with whom I work as consultant creative director.

5   There is no definitive source of "scientific" predictive data for response levels, since every marketing campaign is unique and subject to different environmental factors. However, as a general rule, the sales promotion and direct mail industries traditionally budget within a response spectrum of between 0 and 10 percent. A survey of 1859 direct mail campaigns by the Direct Mail Information Service in 2000 produced an average response rate of 6.5 percent, and 2.8 percent for door-drops (base 212 campaigns). Source: *The Marketing Pocket Book 2003*, World Advertising Research Center, 2002.

6   An activity to launch (then) Sun Alliance's "Feedback" communication campaign, targeted at High Street brokers and intermediaries.

7   An on-pack offer to support the UK launch of Newcastle Brown Ale in 330ml six-packs. This activity was the subject of a detailed feature in *Precision Marketing*, 31 March 1997.

8   The Reebok "Vector" program, a mailing campaign targeting independent sports retailers that ran during 1996–7. (See also 9 below.)

9   Blue-Chip's "Vector" campaign for Reebok is featured in *Marketing Communications* by Chris Fill (Prentice Hall, 1999); the Kleenex hay fever campaign is examined at length in *Sales Promotion* by Julian Cummings (Kogan Page, 1999); and a number of Blue-Chip campaigns form teaching case studies in *The Manual of Sales Promotion* by Dr John Williams (Innovation Licensing, 1996). In addition, Blue-Chip campaigns have been

featured in over 200 articles in publications such as the *Sunday Times*, *Marketing*, *Marketing Week*, *The Grocer*, *Precision Marketing*, and others.

10 Blue-Chip is the only Scottish agency to have won the prestigious ISP Grand Prix (see 12 below), along with 13 Gold Awards, which include copywriting, direct marketing, fast-moving consumer goods, and trade promotions.

11 After being speculatively briefed in December 1990 to suggest ways of selling more tissues in summer, I stopped off at my parents' on the way back to Scotland, and had the idea for the Hay Fever Survival Kit following a conversation with my dad, a life-long hay fever sufferer. I still have my original sketches in my notebook.

12 There were 803 entries for the 1991 Institute of Sales Promotion Awards. Blue-Chip won the Grand Prix, followed by British Airways in the silver position ("The World's Biggest Offer"). Other eminent entrants included Asda, Barclays, Brooke Bond, Cadbury, Citroën, Courage, Esso, Financial Times, Gillette, Heinz, NatWest, Nestlé, Rothmans, Safeway, Sainsbury, SKB, Sony, Toshiba, United Distillers, Virgin Atlantic and Weetabix.

13 The European Federation of Sales Promotion Awards.

14 See *Sales Promotion* by Julian Cummings (Kogan Page, 1999). Cummings writes that the Kleenex brand share "increased from 50% in 1990 to over 70% in 1996" and that the hay fever campaign "must take a major share of the credit." Reviewing the 2002 campaign, the January 2003 edition of *Incentive Business* described it as "The most amazing promotion ever."

15 The latest offer, currently in-store at the time of writing these footnotes, still follows the format first devised in 1991.

16 "[AIDA] was found to be the most widely quoted [model] in a range of current British, American and French textbooks." M J Baker (ed.), *Marketing Theory and Practice*, Macmillan Education, 1987.

17 For instance see Philip Kotler, *Marketing Management*, 11th Edition, Prentice Hall, 2003.

18 M J Baker, *The Marketing Book*, Butterworth-Heinemann, 2003.

19 G Smith and R Millington, "The Direct Marketing Roadshow," 1987.

20 "SWEARing" stood for See it, Want it, Easy, Action, Response.

21 Austria, Belgium, Denmark, France, Germany, Netherlands, Ireland, Italy, Norway, Portugal, Russia, Spain, Sweden, Switzerland, UK.

22 Malcolm Woods.

Step 1: Navigation

1 Prior to privatization, ScottishPower was known as SSEB.

2 *Money Observer*, Guardian Magazines.

3 From a non-national trading base, by August 2003 Warburtons had grown to become the eighth largest grocery brand, three places behind Hovis and one place behind Kingsmill. Source: IRI, *Marketing*, 28 August 2003, pp 23–31. In a study by Information Resources, published in *The Grocer*, 13 December 2003, Warburtons had overtaken Kingsmill to become the No. 2 bread brand.

4 Advertising Standards Authority.

5   The Advertising Association's *Advertising Statistics Yearbook 2002*. For 2001: Press expenditure £8514m, TV £4147m.

6   Charles Decker, *P&G99*, HarperCollinsBusiness, 1999, p 207.

7   See Step 3, Wording.

8   See Step 3, Wording.

9   Tell your "customer" they are interested in three subjects (e.g. watches, cameras, mobiles). Ask them to browse at normal speed – about two seconds per page – through a 30-page section of a magazine that contains the ad or ads you want to test. Then check their recall.

10   David Ogilvy, *Ogilvy on Advertising*, Multimedia Publications (UK), 1983, p 12.

11   Edward de Bono, *Why so Stupid?*, Blackhall, 2003.

12   *Director* magazine, February 2003.

13   I note IKEA supplies its customers with free disposable tape measures. Good idea, though with a hint of the stable door about it.

Step 2: Ease

1   This was for a leading brand of feminine protection.

2   This was for a leading brand of canned soup.

3   *Super Marketing*, 27 March 1987.

4   The chocolates contained within Cadbury's Biarritz were very similar to its declining predecessor, Bournville Selection; the novelty of Biarritz rested in its packaging and subsequent "gift values." Unfortunately, this was not a sufficiently enduring point of difference to displace Black Magic from its long-held position at the top of the dark assortments ladder, especially as there was also a well-established No. 2 in the market in the form of All Gold. Around this time the most significant entry into the market was made by Ferrero Rocher, which combined great gift appeal, a low price ticket, and lighter, nuttier chocolates that my research showed were the way forward for the increasingly calorie-conscious consumer.

5   J F Engel, R D Blackwell, and P W Miniard, *Consumer Behaviour*, Dryden Press, 1990.

6   In Spring 2003, the National Lottery introduced a series of low-level games that could be played online, and now the main draw can be entered online provided you set up an account. Of course, for many people internet access does not equal ease. In October 2003, the first "big-prize" instant (and simple) gamecard was introduced. This certainly seemed like a move in the right direction, following five years of declining sales.

7   Engel, Blackwell, and Miniard, *op. cit.*

8   Judith Donovan writing in *Direct Response* magazine, 24 August 1988.

9   Seth Godin, *Permission Marketing*, Simon & Schuster UK, 2002, p 145.

10   *Marketing*, 16 October 2003.

11   *Sunday Herald*, 29 December 2002. Survey by ICM.

12   a) *The Tipping Point*, Malcolm Gladwell, Abacus, 2002, p 98; b) Also, *Marketing Business*, March 2003, quotes a study by Leonhardt and Kerwi (1997) showing that children in the US, UK, and Australia see between 20,000 and 40,000 commercials a year.

13 Paco Underhill, *Why We Buy*, Texere, 2000, p 44.

14 I would recommend a) John Watson, *Successful Creativity in Direct Marketing*, Institute of Direct Marketing, 1993; and b) Drayton Bird, *Commonsense Direct Marketing*, Kogan Page, 2000.

15 F E Hahn and K G Mangun, *Do-it-Yourself Advertising and Promotion*, John Wiley and Sons, 1997, p 114.

16 At the time of writing, recently taken over by Morrisons.

17 *The Grocer*, 19 April 2003. Source ID Magasin.

18 Claude Hopkins, *My Life in Advertising*, 1927, reprinted by NTC Business Books, 1998, p 151.

19 BOGOF, an acronym for buy one get one free.

20 Drayton Bird, *Commonsense Direct Marketing*, Kogan Page, 2000, p 263.

Step 3: Wording

1 Joseph O'Connor, *NLP Workbook*, Thorsons, 2001.

2 I think most television ads need to be written with the lone viewer in mind. Cinema ads, on the other hand, are collectively consumed, and may be conceived with a view to exploiting an audience reaction and interaction — most likely shock or humor.

3 C F Edwards, *Teach Yourself Commercial Travelling*, English Universities Press, 1952, p 39.

4 The actual quotation is: "The reason why we have two ears and one mouth is so that we may listen the more and talk the less." Diogenes Laertius, *Lives of the Philosophers*, "Zeno," Ch. 7 (Zeno of Citium c.335–c.263BC). From *The Oxford Concise Dictionary of Quotations*, Oxford University Press, 2001.

5 Edwards, *op. cit.*

6 Drayton Bird writes that language expert Rudolph Flesch discovered a direct relationship between effective selling and the use of the word "you." *Commonsense Direct Marketing*, Kogan Page, 2000, p 275.

7 Ogilvy, *op. cit.*

8 The Burt Word Reading Test, 1974 revision.

9 Ogilvy, *op. cit.*

10 R L Trask, *Language: The Basics*, Routledge, 1999.

11 Bill Bryson, *Mother Tongue*, Penguin, 1991, p 51.

12 *Ibid.*, p 142.

13 Herschell Gordon Lewis, BDMA Conference, c.1989.

14 Trask, *op. cit.*

15 Steven Pinker, *The Language Instinct*, Penguin, 1995.

16 Bryson, *op. cit.*, p 128.

17 Alexander Pope in *Everyman's Dictionary of Quotations and Proverbs*, Chancellor Press, 1988.

18 Roy H Williams, *Secret Formulas of the Wizard of Ads*, Bard Press, 1999.

19 Pinker, *op. cit.*, p 312.

20 Trask, *op. cit.*, p 15.

21 *The Optician* magazine.

22 Survey by the Automobile Association, broadcast on Radio Five Live, 26 October 2002.

23 de Bono, *op. cit.*

24 *Chambers 21st Century Dictionary*, Chambers Harrap, 2000.

25 *Ibid.*

26 Julia Cresswell, *The Penguin Dictionary of Clichés*, Penguin, 2000.

27 Sam Goldwyn in *Oxford Dictionary of Phrase, Saying and Quotation*, Oxford University Press, 2002.

28 Roy H Williams, *Secret Formulas of the Wizard of Ads*, Bard Press, 1999, p 15.

29 Edward de Bono, *Serious Creativity*, HarperCollinsBusiness, 1996, p 177.

30 Herschell Gordon Lewis, BDMA Conference, c.1989.

31 Engel, Blackwell, and Miniard, *op. cit.*, p 378.

32 Decker, *op. cit.*, p 203.

33 O'Connor, *op. cit.*

34 Alexander J. Wearing, "The recall of sentences of varying length," *Australian Journal of Psychology*, 25, August 1973, pp 156–61.

35 George A. Miller, "The magical number seven, plus or minus two: Some limits on our capacity for processing information," *Psychological Review*, March 1956.

36 Trask, *op. cit.*, p 19.

37 Ogilvy, *op. cit.*, p 88.

38 Bird, *op. cit.*, p 272.

39 David Ogilvy, *Confessions of an Advertising Man*, Pan, 1987, p 144.

40 Ogilvy, *Ogilvy on Advertising*, p 97.

41 Red and blue together can work in some circumstances: I think the vibrant character of flags such as the Union Jack and the Stars and Stripes is due to this "clashing" phenomenon.

42 Ogilvy, *Ogilvy on Advertising*, p 139.

43 The traditional Johnson box was created on the old-fashioned typewriter, using a rectangular border of asterisks. It still works!

44 Ogilvy, *Confessions of an Advertising Man*, p 126.

45 Pinker, *op. cit.*, p 376.

46 John Caples, *Tested Advertising Methods*, Prentice Hall, 1997, p 30.

47 Hopkins, *op. cit.*, p 307.

48 Engel, Blackwell, and Miniard, *op. cit.*, p 422.

On reflection

1 John Stapleton, *Marketing*, Hodder and Stoughton, 1980, p 153.

Step 4: Attention

1 Engel, Blackwell, and Miniard, *op. cit.*, p 484.

2 Underhill, *op. cit.*, pp 18–19.

3   *Director* magazine, February 2003.
4   *Marketing Business*, March 2003.
5   Viacom Outdoor.
6   Caples, *op. cit.*, p 13.
7   *Marketing Business*, April 2003; research by London Business School indicating that a young, single woman spends 47 percent of her time on social interaction during commercial breaks.
8   Ogilvy, *Confessions of an Advertising Man*.
9   Ogilvy, *Ogilvy on Advertising*, p 160.
10 Caples, *op. cit.*, p 194.
11 *Ibid.*, p 226.
12 Hopkins, *op. cit.*, p 284.
13 Caples, *op. cit.*, p 194.
14 In an A/B split the two versions of your ad (i.e. version A and version B) appear in alternate copies of the publication. This means the two ads are spread equally among your customers, with no geographical or other bias. The same effect can be achieved by alternating versions of a mailing through a database, or for a door-drop by collating alternate versions of a leaflet prior to distribution.
15 Decker, *op. cit.*
16 The Direct Mail Information Service, Consumer Direct Mail Trends Survey.
17 Engel, Blackwell, and Miniard, *op. cit.*, p. 367.
18 Daniel Starch, "Measuring advertising readership and results," McGraw-Hill, 1966.
19 A Finn, "Print ad recognition readership scores: An information processing perspective," *Journal of Marketing Research*, 25, May 1988.
20 *Ibid.*
21 K Cox, "The effect of shelf space upon sales of branded products," *Journal of Marketing Research*, February 1970.
22 Starch, *op. cit.*
23 Finn, *op. cit.*
24 L Percy, "Ways in which the people, words and pictures in advertising influence its effectiveness," Financial Institutions Marketing Association, July 1984.
25 Bird, *op. cit.*
26 Starch, *op. cit.*
27 Smith and Millington, *op. cit.*
28 Decker, *op. cit.*
29 Engel, Blackwell, and Miniard, *op. cit.*, p 370.
30 Starch, *op. cit.*
31 Engel, Blackwell, and Miniard, p 373.
32 Bill Cather, personal reference.
33 Study by The Olympia Brewing Company, quoted in Engel, Blackwell, and Miniard, *op. cit.*, p 246.
34 Starch, *op. cit.*
35 As a compositional device the Golden Section or Mean avoids bilateral symmetry while preserving the semblance of harmonious order. Geometrically, there is a point (B) on

any line (A–C) at which the ratio AC:BC equals the ratio of BC:AB. I have calculated this by trial and error, and the answer AC:BC needs to be approximately 1.618 (at which point BC:AB equals approximately 1.618). To find the Golden Section in your ad, simply divide the length and the width respectively by 1.618, and draw lines across. Their intersection will be your point of visual focus. Another way of calculating this is to use the reciprocal of 1.618, which, neatly, is 0.618. The Golden Mean therefore lies 61.8 percent of the way up your page, and 61.8 percent of the way across. (Or in any of three other possible positions, although artists and photographers seem to favor the northeast quadrant.) Sources: *The Yale Dictionary of Art and Artists*, Yale University Press, 2000; *Penguin Dictionary of Art and Artists*, Penguin Books, 1997.

36 Engel, Blackwell, and Miniard, *op. cit.*, p 376.

37 *The Grocer*, 7 December 2002, p 52.

38 Frederick R Barnard, *Printers' Ink*, 10 March 1927.

39 Pinker, *op. cit.*

40 As a sales trainer, I consistently found that my "customer" (the trainee) could remember a point far better when they had provided the answer in the first instance. Though it's harder work upfront for the trainer to keep probing and asking "Why do you think we do X?" (rather than to tell "We do X because..."), it pays off in the longer run. Telling is a false economy.

41 Engel, Blackwell, and Miniard, *op. cit.*, p 246.

42 Ogilvy, *Ogilvy on Advertising*, p 71.

43 Decker, *op. cit.*, p 39.

44 "What really decides consumers to buy or not is the content of your advertising, not its form." Ogilvy, *Confessions of an Advertising Man*, p 111.

45 Williams, *op. cit.*, p 116.

46 OMD Snapshots survey, *Marketing*, 28 August 2003: 118 118 recall 82 percent, 11 88 88 recall 42 percent.

47 O'Connor, *op. cit.*

48 R L Klatzky, *Human Memory: Structures and Processes*, W H Freeman, 1975.

49 Hooper White, "Name change to Rusty Jones helps polish product's identity," *Advertising Age*, 18 February 1980.

50 Engel, Blackwell, and Miniard, *op. cit.*, p 368.

Step 5: Interest

1 Andrew White in Les Andrews (ed.), *The Royal Mail Direct Mail Handbook*, Exley Publications, 1988, p 185.

2 *Marketing Week*, 31 July 2003, p 5.

3 E G Longbottom in Andrews, *op. cit.*, p 17.

4 Engel, Blackwell, and Miniard, *op. cit.*, p 256.

5 Watson, *op. cit.*, p 23.

6 Rosser Reeves, *Reality in Advertising*, A A Knopf, 1961. The original quote appears in Claude C. Hopkins, Scientific Advertising, 1923: "That is one of the greatest advertising

faults. Ad-writers abandon their parts. They forget they are salesmen and try to be performers. Instead of sales, they seek applause." (Reprinted by NTC Business Books, 1998, p 223.

7   Alan Mitchell, *Marketing Week*, January 1995 (p 30), quoting a paper by Andrew Ehrenberg in the *Journal of Advertising Research*, a study analysing promotions for 25 products in the UK, US, Germany, and Japan.

8   Institute of Sales Promotion Awards nominations, Partnership Promotions, 1996.

9   K L Keller, "Memory factors in advertising: The effect of advertising retrieval cues on brand evaluations," *Journal of Consumer Research*, 14, December 1987; J O Eastlack, "How to get more bang for your television bucks," *Journal of Consumer Marketing*, 1, 1984.

10 Institute of Sales Promotion Awards 1996, Sponsorship (silver), Point of Sale (bronze), Retail (bronze).

11 Watson, *op. cit.*, p 156.

12 The 40 percent figure is from the Office for National Statistics, *Living in Britain 2001: General Household Survey*. The other figures were sourced from the *Marketing Pocket Book*, World Advertising Research Center, 2002.

13 Bird, *op. cit.*, p 315.

14 Watson, *op. cit.*, p 166.

15 Robert W Bly, *The Copywriter's Handbook*, Owl Books, 1990.

16 Bird, *op. cit.*, p 262.

17 Spam is junk (i.e. unsolicited) email.

18 *The Times*, 4 March 2003.

19 *Ibid*.

20 Hopkins, *My Life in Advertising*, p 102.

Step 6: Desire

1   W J McGuire, "The current status of cognitive consistency theories," in Joel B Cohen (ed.), *Behavioral Science Foundations of Consumer Behavior*, Free Press, 1972, pp 253–74.

2   Al Ries and Jack Trout, *Positioning: The Battle for Your Mind*, McGraw-Hill International, 1986.

3   C W Sherif, M Sherif and R E Nebergall, *Attitude and Attitude Change*, Yale University Press, 1961.

4   R H Fazio and M P Zanna, "On the predictive validity of attitudes: The roles of direct experience and confidence," *Journal of Personality*, 46, 1978, pp 228–24; L J Marks and M A Kamins, "The use of product sampling and advertising: Effects of sequence of exposure and degree of advertising claim exaggeration on consumers' belief strength, belief confidence and attitudes," *Journal of Marketing Research*, 25, August 1988, pp 266–328; R E Smith and W R Swinyard, "Attitude–behaviour consistency: The impact of product trial versus advertising," *Journal of Marketing Research*, 20, August 1983, pp 257–67.

5   Engel, Blackwell, and Miniard, *op. cit.*, p G-9.

6   Underhill, *op. cit.*

7   Decker, *op. cit.*, p 196.

8   Hopkins, *My Life in Advertising*, p 20.

9   Mita Sujan, "Consumer knowledge: Effects on evaluation strategies mediating consumer judgement," *Journal of Consumer Research*, 12, June 1985, pp 31–46.

10 Everett M Rogers, *The Diffusion of Innovations*, Free Press, 1962.

11 Philip Kotler, *Marketing Management: Analysis, Planning and Control*, Prentice-Hall International, 1984, p 348.

12 Watson, *op. cit.*, p 64.

13 Ogilvy, *Ogilvy on Advertising*, p 84.

14 Bird, *op. cit.*, p 262.

15 Starch, *op. cit.*

16 Decker, *op. cit.*, p 193.

17 Engel, Blackwell, and Miniard, *op. cit.*, p 437.

18 *Ibid.*, p 697.

19 Alastair Crompton, *The Craft of Copywriting*, Hutchinson Business, 1989.

20 Williams, *op. cit.*, p 83.

21 Engel, Blackwell, and Miniard, *op. cit.*, p 440.

22 *Chambers 21st Century Dictionary*, Chambers Harrap, 2000.

23 Ogilvy, *Ogilvy on Advertising*, p 82.

24 Engel, Blackwell, and Miniard, *op. cit.*, pp 254–5.

Step 7: Action

1   Derrick White, *Close More Sales*, Management Books 2000, 2001.

2   Engel, Blackwell, and Miniard, *op. cit.*, p 545.

3   A G Woodside and W Davenport, "The effect of salesman similarity and expertise on consumer purchasing behaviour," *Journal of Marketing Research*, 11, May 1974.

4   Underhill, *op. cit.*, p 171.

5   J L Freedman and S C Fraser, "Compliance without pressure: The foot-in-the-door technique," *Journal of Personality and Social Psychology*, 4, August 1966.

6   R M Shriffin and R C Atkinson, "Storage and retrieval processes in long-term memory," *Psychological Review*, 76, March 1969.

7   *Insights*, NPD Research, 1979–1982.

8   The normal situation is where independent retailers redeem coupons through their wholesalers. To avoid misredemption: 1) laser the retailer's name on the coupon and indicate that it must be clearly signed by both parties; 2) do not use a national clearing house – have the wholesaler return the coupons direct to you (or your handling house); 3) cross-reference the response against a direct offer, i.e. where retailers have replied directly to you and have supplied copy receipts as proof of purchase. You can also conduct store checks to confirm stocking. In my experience, when the process is tightly managed and closely monitored, misredemption of trade coupons is minimal.

9   In March 2004 the Institute of Sales Promotion expressed concern that misredemption of consumer coupons was in some cases reaching 50 percent, a practice encouraged by the policies of retailers. *Incentive Today*, March 2004, p 10.

10 This was called Beck's ClubX. Over 43,000 consumers were recruited through off-the-page ads in men's style press. Members built up a bank of points by redeeming Beck's tops in specially supplied polythene envelopes. Points were exchanged for a variety of cool gear supplied by third-party partners. ClubX members accounted for 5.2 percent of the brand's annual volume. The campaign won awards in three categories: alcoholic drinks, direct marketing, and loyalty building.

11 Watson, *op. cit.*, p 156.

12 Ogilvy, *Ogilvy on Advertising*, p 146.

13 Watson, *op. cit.*, p 78.

14 *Ibid.*, p 202.

15 In passing, an observation on wording: this text has the equivalent of 15 "you"s and 4 "we"s.

Appendix: The origins of AIDA

1   E K Strong, *The Psychology of Selling Life Insurance*, Harper and Brothers, 1922.

2   Kotler, *op. cit.*

3   Chris Fill, *Marketing Communications: Contexts, Strategies and Applications*, Prentice Hall, 2002.

4   M J Baker, *Macmillan Dictionary of Marketing and Advertising*, Macmillan Business, 1998.

5   E K Strong, *The Psychology of Selling and Advertising*, McGraw-Hill, 1925.

6   Despite much searching I can find few references to E St. Elmo Lewis. Robert East (*Consumer Behaviour*, Prentice Hall, 1997) fleetingly credits him with inventing AIDA, as does Charles Doyle (*Collins Dictionary of Marketing*, HarperCollins, 2003). Lewis wrote *Getting the Most out of Business* (Ronald Press, 1915), but there is no mention of AIDA.

7   Note that Rosser Reeves does not himself claim to have invented the concept of the USP. In his book *Reality in Advertising* he says that the theory of the USP "originated at Ted Bates & Co in the 1940s."

INDEX

101 Dalmatians 165–6
80:20 principle 158, 164, 174

A

A/B split 127
action 4, 6, 38, 39, 224, 225–51, 252
active attention 153, 181
ad seekers 32
adaptation 141, 155
advertising
  off-the-page 52
  press 16, 133, 252
  television 15, 100, 128, 155, 172, 252
  trade 98, 237–8
AIDA 4–7, 11, 25, 38, 114, 155–6, 160, 190, 228
  origins of 253–60
Amazon 24, 61, 249
American Dental Association 206
analogies 217
Andrex 165–6, 245
Ariel 180, 197
Arnold Clark 173
association 95
attention 4, 6, 16, 35, 72, 78, 113–56, 161, 168, 221, 252
  active 153, 181
  profitable 115, 128, 129, 141, 160
  random 128, 141, 156
  relevant 145–6
authority 206–10, 224

B

Bacardi 139
bar, local 49–50
Barnard, F R 144
BBC Radio Five Live 61–2
Beck's 239
Beckham, David 209
Ben Sherman 221
benefits 22, 78, 113–56, 172, 190, 201, 202–3, 206, 217, 221–3, 224, 247
Biarritz 42–4
Big Issue, The 115–16, 179, 226
Bird, Drayton 72, 130, 181, 202–3
Birds 56
Black Magic 176
blocked-fixture display 114
Blue-Chip Marketing Consultancy 7, 12, 36–8, 49, 116, 144, 157, 204
Bly, Robert W 183
Bob the Painter 170–71, 174
body copy 96, 120, 145, 202, 205
BOGOFs 71
bolt-on offers 165, 168, 169
bound-in coupons 52
Bounty 177
Bournville Selection 42
brainstorming 95
brand awareness 170, 172
British Airways 3, 137, 158
Bryson, Bill 82
Burton 165

C

Cadbury Schweppes 2, 42–4, 113, 171, 174
Caledonian Brewery 63–4
Cancer Research UK 25–7, 28–9, 67
Caples, John 1, 108, 124–5, 142, 145, 149
cardinal utility principle 239
Carlsberg-Tetley 62
carrots
    action 243–5
    promotional 71–2, 169
Carson, Frank 152
case
    lower 105
    upper 105
Castrol GTX 154
Cather, Bill 133, 136
celebrity 130, 138–9, 209–10
center, dominant focal 131, 138
Centre Circle 185–6, 188
chip-box 204–5
Cif/Jif 83
Clarke-Hooper 2–3, 9
clichés 90, 93–5, 97, 124, 142
closing 225–6, 245
cognitive
    consistency 191–2
    dissonance 227–8, 239, 245
    miser 149
    resources 164
Colgate 206
color 130, 132, 181
conditioning 130, 139–41, 215–16
Connor, Ted 113–14
consistency, cognitive 191–2
consolidation 194
contact 232
content 152, 181, 187–8, 190, 203
contrast 130, 132, 134
convenience 36–72, 141, 151–2, 156, 252
conversation 73–110, 252
copy
    body 96, 120, 145, 202, 205
    long 119, 202–3
cost-effectiveness of coupons 237–8
countlines 113
coupons 237–8
    bound-in 52
    cost-effectiveness of 237–8
    misredemption of 237–8
    reply 52–6
    tip-on 52
crazytivity 18, 22
Crest 206
Crompton, Alastair 210
Crunchie 113
curiosity 141, 145, 147–9
customer relationship management (CRM) 175
customer retention 157–8, 159
customer
    not telling what to think about 20
    telling what to think about 23
customer-service programs 49–50

D

de Bono, Edward 18, 22, 88, 95
deadlines 245–8, 251
Decker, Charles 132, 197
deduping 158, 160
demonstration 194–5, 225
demotic language 81, 110
designeritis 90, 104–5, 107
desire 4, 6, 16, 138, 145, 189–224, 228, 232, 252
desired customer reaction (DCR) 25–7, 35
detail 190–91
Deuchars IPA 63–4
direct mail 16, 66–72, 106, 128, 180, 184, 238, 247–8, 250, 252
direct marketing 5, 13, 66–72, 127, 130, 158, 162, 168–9, 181, 182, 190, 201, 205–6, 210, 238, 239, 246, 250
Direct Wines 203

directionality 130, 133, 135–6
direct-response ads 16, 51–6, 117, 210
Disney 92, 165–6
dissonance
    cognitive 227–8, 239, 245
    post-purchase 227–31, 233, 236, 245, 247
distress purchases 169–72, 188
Doc Martens 221

E

ease 16, 36–72, 112, 129, 156, 168, 205, 228, 252
Edinburgh Zoo 91–2
elaboration 195
elephant.co.uk 51–2, 118
emails 183–4
emotions 210, 212, 216, 219, 221, 224
empathy 2
Engel, James F 108, 128, 149, 160, 237
envelopes 66, 180–81, 182, 201, 228
Epson 143, 236–7
Esso 154
experimentation 193–5, 224
exploded-diagram technique 22

F

F&C 54–5
facts 189–224
    hard 190, 219
    soft 190, 219, 221
Fairy Liquid 221
fast-moving consumer goods (fmcg) 164–5, 238
faxback 36–8, 39, 65, 70, 78, 127
Financial Tactics 32–3
first mental image 153
first-time customers 33–4, 176–80, 188, 249
Flake 113

flow, go with the 61, 70–71, 72
Fog Index 103–4, 192, 202
foot in the door 233, 251
form 152, 181, 187–8, 190, 203
format 16, 66–70, 169
Fraser, S C 233
Freedman, J L 233

G

Garmin 145–6
General Motors 49
Giggs, Ryan 166–8
glance, at a 21, 22, 28
Glemnorangie 210
Glenfiddich 210
go with the flow 61, 70–71, 72
Godin, Seth 60
Golden Section or Mean 131, 138
Goldwyn, Sam 93
Google 117
GQ 168
grammar 82–3, 90, 110
granny test 78–9
guardian salesman 6–7, 87, 127
gutter 54

H

Häagen-Dazs 141, 216
habitual shopping 116
Hahn, Fred E 68
hard facts 190, 219
Harley Medical Group 121
Harris, Rolf 144
headlines 22, 85, 96, 120–21, 124–5, 129, 142, 143, 145, 147, 156, 169, 181, 201, 205–6, 217, 219, 221–3
Heinz Tomato Ketchup 176
homophilous people 210
Hoover 169

Hopkins, Claude 2, 71, 108, 126, 164, 185, 197
hype 91–3
hyperbole 90, 91–3, 95, 97, 142, 183
hyphens 85

I

I can't believe it's not butter 109
IBM 236
images
    imitation 194–5
    impact 4
    right-facing 135
    single 131
Imperial Leather 44
In Focus 56–60, 198
Independent Research Services 211
Independent, The 214
innovation–decision process 199
instant win 242
Institute of Direct Marketing 152
intellect 210, 219
intensity 130, 132
interest 4, 6, 16, 116, 157–88, 205, 228, 249, 252
    groups 164–9, 171, 188
    latent 162–3
Iowa, farmer in 78
irrelevant similes 216–18, 224
isolation 130, 131, 136–8

J

Jack Daniel's
Jacob's Creek 203
jargon 81
JJB Sports 166–7
John Smith's 209
Johnson box 106
Johnson, Samuel 84

Jones Bootmaker 140
just looking 161–2, 163, 231, 236, 250

K

Kay, Peter 209
Kellogg 46
Kenwood 147–8
key question
    action 251
    attention 156
    desire 224
    ease 72
    interest 188
    navigation 35
    wording 110
Kimberly-Clark 2, 113–14
kitchen sink brief 27
Kleenex 3, 45, 96, 169, 196
knowledge 199, 232, 252
Kotler, Philip 199

L

language
    demotic 81, 110
    sensory 141, 152–5, 156, 219
    speak that of your customers 73
latent interest 162–3
Latin words 80
learning 193–5
Leica 197, 208–9
Leicester Co-op 177–8
Lever 83, 121
Leverhulme, Lord 1
Lewis, Herschell Gordon 81, 99
listening 77–8, 84, 110
Lloyds TSB 2
location 113–56
    ten ways to improve 129–39
lower case 105

Lurpak 221, 223

M

M&G Financial Services 119
magic margin 161–2
mailback 36–8, 70, 127
Marie Claire 221
marketing engineering 45
marketing proposition 169
matching 73–4, 110
McDonald's 97
"me do it" 193
mechanic, promotional 39–41, 234, 242
memory gaps 175–6
Mercedes-Benz 235
merchandising 114
merging and purging 158
messages
    one-sided 214
    personalizing 75–7, 110
    two-sided 214
metaphors 153–5
metaprogram 133
MG Rover 230, 239–40, 243
Milk Tray 42, 171, 175–6
Miller Genuine Draft 24
Miller Lite 214
Miller, George A 104
Mingles 40
Mirror, The 18
misredemption of coupons 237–8
Mitsubishi 207
mobile phones, as promotional entry
    device 61–5
mobile technology 250–51
Money Observer 159
money-back guarantee 39–41
mopping up 247–8, 251
Morgan's Spiced 49
Mortgage Advice Network 33–4
motor dealers 172–3, 233, 235

movement 130, 136
moving away 136
moving toward 133, 136
Mr A 76–7, 110

N

National Lottery 47–9, 196
navigation 8, 9–35, 38, 112, 124, 126, 129,
    143, 145, 147, 156, 168, 181, 183, 184,
    188, 205, 221, 228, 252
    implied 30–31
    leading design 28–30, 35, 52
    of forearmed customer 30–31
    point 27–8, 35
needs 160, 161
negative-reinforcement products 108–9
negatives 108–9
NEW AIDA approach 7–8, 13, 111–2,
    155–6, 160, 215, 228, 237, 252
New Labour 215
Newcastle Brown Ale 3, 46
news 141, 149–51, 156, 184–8
News of the World 120
newsletters 184–8
Next 180
Nicotinell 109
Nike 139, 219–21
Nikon UK 23
NLP 73, 133, 135, 212
"no" reflex 225, 227–8, 233, 237
Norfolk Ornithologists' Association 187
novelty 130, 138

O

Oddie, Bill 208–9
offers
    bolt-on 165, 168, 169
    on-pack 45–6, 62–5, 206
    real 239–41, 242–3, 245, 251

off-the-page advertising 52
Ogilvy, David 2, 72, 78–9, 108, 109, 120,
    147, 149, 190, 202, 217, 247
Ogilvy, Francis 22
one-sided messages 214
on-pack offers 45–6, 62–5, 206
Opticron 56–60
OVD Rum 96

P

packaging 44–6
Pavlov's dogs 215
pens, free with mailings 67
perception 2
permission 228, 231, 243–4, 252
personalizing your messages 75–7, 110
persuadability 112, 161, 163–4, 252
pictures 87–8, 141, 144–6, 147, 156, 219,
    221, 224
Pinker, Steven 82, 108, 144
platitudes 90, 95–8, 122–3, 142, 182, 212
playing to the world 74–5, 162, 164, 172,
    180, 188
plays on words 90, 97–100
plumbers 170, 172, 174–5
Pope, Alexander 83
positioning 192, 214, 215
positive rewards 108
Postoptics 246
post-purchase dissonance 227–31, 233,
    236, 245, 247
Precision Marketing 248
press advertising 16, 133, 252
pressure selling 115–16, 162
price cutting 164
Pringles 97
Procter & Gamble (P&G) 17, 44, 100, 132,
    150, 197
profitable attention 115, 128, 129, 141, 160
    seven ways to stimulate 141
promotion, sales 132, 164–5

promotional mechanic 234, 242
proposition 127, 169, 181
Pro-Sport 96

R

racing tips, online service 8, 69–70
Radio Five Live, BBC 61–2
random attention 128, 141, 156
random input technique 95
Reader's Digest 72
reading age of supermarket shoppers 78–9
real offers 239–41, 242–3, 245, 251
Reebok 3, 166–8, 233, 234
rehearsal 195
relevant attention 145–6
reply card, tear-off 9–11, 14–15, 38, 69
reply device 68–70, 72
reply, making easy 45–6
retention of customers 157–8, 159
riddles 90, 100–102, 147
Ries, Al 192, 214
right-facing images 135
Rob Roy 202
Roper Starch Worldwide 128
Roses 42
Royal & SunAlliance 3, 185–6, 188,
    212–14
Royal National Institute for the Blind
    (RNIB) 100, 102
Royal Society for the Protection of Birds
    (RSPB) 30–31, 56
Russell, Bertrand 144
Rusty Jones 153
Ryvita 154–5

S

Safeway 70–71, 243
Sainsbury's 70–71, 113, 243
sales environment 114, 118, 232
sales promotion 132, 164–5
sales promotion mechanics 39–41

sales spell 226–7

salesmanship 1–8, 13, 17, 22, 25, 27, 111, 155–6, 210, 228, 252

sampling 47, 196–7, 233, 245

sans-serif typefaces 105

Saxon words 80, 103

Scotsman, The 134

Scott, Sir Walter 202

Scottish & Newcastle 83

Scottish National Party 191

Scottish Widows 12

ScottishPower 9–11, 14

selective targeting 164

self-image 219, 221

self-interest 124–5, 142, 149

self-perception theory 233

sensory language 141, 152–5, 156, 219

sensual shopper 196

sentiment 236–7

serendipity 128–9, 252

serif typefaces 105, 106

Seriously Strong Cheddar 141

seven top tips

    action 251

    attention 156

    desire 224

    ease 72

    interest 188

    navigation 35

    wording 110

seven wordly sins 90–105

sex appeal 139–41

shopping around 228–31, 251

showmanship 1, 17, 22, 65, 88, 92, 155–6, 210, 252

sight, poor 86–7

similes, irrelevant 216–18, 224

size 130

Sloggi 221–2

Smith, George 70, 132, 182

soft facts 190, 219, 221

Sony 139

spam 183–4

split-test mailing 181–2, 205

Stapleton, John 111

Starch Readership Service 120, 127, 129–39, 203

steps you can take

    action 228–51

    attention 129–56

    desire 199–224

    ease 66–72

    interest 164–88

    navigation 25–34

    wording 90–109

stickiness 129

storytelling 17, 100, 102

straplines 95–6

Strong, E K 4, 124, 253–5

structural style of writing 103

Stuff 18, 21, 22, 142, 147

subheads 201–2

subway 118

Sun, The 17, 60, 200–201

Sunsilk 121

Surf 40–41

S-W-E-A-R 7

systematic questioning 194

T

tabloid newspapers 17–18, 97, 100, 103, 199–202

Taper, Bernard 93

targeting 180

    selective 164

tear-off reply card 9–11, 14–15, 38, 69

tear-strips 42–4

television advertising 15, 100, 128, 155, 172, 252

Terry's 133

Tesco 70–71, 243

testimonials 210, 211

testing 37, 125, 156, 224, 241

text 'n' win 63–4

think "one customer" 75–7
think tabloid 17–18, 68
Thixo-Tex 153
three-layered delivery 199–202
Tide 150
TIME 131, 138
tip-on coupons 52
tipping point 39, 65, 68, 72, 226–7, 232, 233
touch 196, 232
Toyota 210
tracking 54
trade advertising 98, 237–8
trade press 16, 74–5, 88, 122, 181
traffic-building mailings 70–71
training cycle 193–4
Trask, R L 82
Trout, Jack 192, 214
try-me-free 39–41, 65
Twining's 44
Twirl 113
two-second test of understanding 12, 35
two-sided messages 214
type size 48, 86–7
typefaces
   sans-serif 105
   serif 105, 106
typographical tips 105–6

V

Velvet 181, 244–5
visual cues 87–8, 133
visual humor 89

W

Walkers Crisps 242
Warburtons 14–15, 44, 69, 193, 238
Watson, John 66, 161–2, 168–9, 202, 247
websites 22, 24, 60–61, 116–18, 184, 188, 249–50, 252
Which? 13–14
White, Derrick 226
Who's Mailing What 183
Wilde, Oscar 104
Williams, Roy Hollister 152–3, 210, 212
wording 73–110, 112, 156, 168, 252
words
   choice of 79–84
   Latin 80
   plays on 90, 97–100
   Saxon 80, 103
world, playing to the 74–5, 162, 164, 172, 180, 188
write what you would say 83–4, 90, 110

U

Underhill, Paco 65, 87, 114, 196, 232
understanding 9–35, 252
   two-second test of 12, 35
uniform resource locator (url) 117–18
Unilever 115
unplanned purchases 113
upper case 105

X

Xbox 143, 237

Y

Yellow Pages 16, 32–3, 132, 151, 174–5
yes 225–51
York Fruits 133
you and we 78, 90, 151, 202

ACKNOWLEDGMENTS

I would like to thank my publisher Nick Brealey — not least for publishing this book, but also for his foresight in recognizing that amid the box of jumbled jigsaw pieces I first presented lay a coherent picture, and for his dogged insistence that it would eventually materialize! I hope you agree that it has.

Also many thanks to my literary agent Judith Chilcote, without whose initial words of inspiration this would not have been possible, and for all her patience and hard work during the publication process.

I am also indebted to the expert panel of marketers and authors who acted as readers and critics: Roz Cuschieri, Marketing Director, Warburtons Ltd; Ted Garratt, Managing Director, Target Resources; Kyle Hardie, Associate Director, Blue-Chip Marketing; Peter Muscutt, Marketing Manager, ChevronTexaco; Dr Michael Riley, Senior Lecturer in Education, Bath Spa University College; Ken Scott MBA, Managing Director, Develop Solutions.

My thanks to Lisa, Stuart, and the guys at Zero Design, and likewise the team at Blue-Chip Marketing, in particular Kevin Carter for all his work on permissions, and to Managing Director Fiona Laurie for her overall support in this project.

Finally, I would like to express my gratitude to the advertisers and promoters whose visuals are featured in this book, the various companies and organizations who supplied information and statistics, and the many authors and publications whose works I have quoted. I have endeavored to credit all sources — either in the figure captions or the footnotes — but my apologies if at any point this is incomplete.